DESERT

MAGNOLIA

DESERT

MAGNOLIA

A Southern Belle
and
A Jordanian Tribal Prince ...

Their Lifetime Love

Donna J. Habib

This is the true story of my family, taken from my mother's journals and my own memories, written to the best of my abilities. If I have erred in any details, please know that it was not intentional.

Donna J. Habib

Cover design by: Nurtan Murad
Painting of Jordan River on cover by: Nurtan Murad

ISBN 13: **978 1097969333**

Published in the United States of America

By

G

G J Publishing
515 Cimarron Circle
Loudon TN 37774
www.neilans.com

DEDICATION

BETTY JEAN CLARK EL GAZZAWI
AND
SAEED EL GAZZAWI

My father and mother taught us what true love was. As far back as I can remember, our home was blessed with loving memories. Granted, they also showed me what it was like to lose the love of your life to an unforeseen power, but the important fact remains: they taught me how to truly love another, how to never judge but to accept, and how to learn from our differences.

Donna J. Habib

PROLOGUE

If I close my eyes, I can see my mother, diligently writing in her diaries at different times of the day. I recall her telling my sister and me that one day she would write her life story. She wanted to tell the world about her experiences and the many changes that overwhelmed and transformed her, creating new habits, tastes, and thoughts. Later on, her words gradually changed from, "I will write my story," to "You girls will write my story; the diaries are for you." At some point, and only she knew when, she had realized that she would never be able to fulfill her dream of writing this book.

And so, at this late time in my life, and much later than her world ended, I have written her story. I strove to be satisfied with every line I wrote, to be pleased with the telling of each detail of my parents' lives, and to be contented with the final result.

The symbol of this story is the delicate magnolia uprooted in 1954 from her original moist soil in the Tennessee Valley and replanted in the foreign, dry soil of the Jordan Valley in the Middle East. This is the tale of how that flower grew into a strong tree that not only survived but took hold with sturdy roots and flourished. Yes, this wonderful tree reached tremendous heights, blooming with beautiful blossoms whose scent carried for miles. This tree touched all who beheld it, affected all who inhaled its captivating perfume, and changed the landscape of the desert forever.

Donna Jean Habib

CHAPTER 1

AL-GAZZAWI TRIBE

On a cold February night in 1930, the Amir of the Gazzawi tribe stood at the edge of the huge tent he called home. He looked out at the vastness stretching to total blackness, engulfing everything; a point where sky and earth met without ever touching. He took a deep breath that filled his nostrils with the aromas of the night: the coffee brewing nearby, the musky scent of the tent, and the horses secured behind it. He could even smell the sheep at a distance and hear them nestling together for warmth. Standing tall at the helm of the tent, erected to face the highest mountain south of the valley, he took another deep breath. The smell of the many fires swelled to match the dark cloud in his heart.

The Amir hugged his *abaya* closer to him; he felt an inner wind that was going to change his life. His tribe had been in the Jordan Valley, known as the *Ghor*, for five hundred years. He was now their leader, and he did not know who would take the reins after he was gone. He sought warmth from the giant wrap that covered his body. Dressed in the traditional Bedouin manner, under his abaya he wore a dark blue *gambaz* resembling a nightshirt topped with another light blue cotton wrap around garment, which tied at the side with strips of cotton. Belted, this clothing held the Amir's silver dagger. He put his hand on his checkered black and white *kufiya*, a square cotton cloth folded in the middle and wrapped around the head, and pulled on the *agal* which held it in place. The Amir's agal was made of camel wool and was richly decorated with metallic threads. He tugged his kufiya closer around his neck. He glanced back and watched his men speaking in low tones. They didn't wish to disturb him. How important his tribe was to him! It was his whole existence. Divided on both sides of the Jordan River between trans-Jordan and Palestine, the tribe proudly claimed descent from Khalif Omar Iben Al-Khattab, the second Caliph ruling the Muslim Empire. Although they had no documents to support such a claim, everyone believed and protected that birthright.

The Amir looked down at his sandals as he slowly walked away; with each step, different sounds filled his head. Sounds of the night creatures replaced men's voices until they completely took over. As he neared the river, he could hear the frogs croaking, and at some point they drowned out all other sounds. For a moment he welcomed this, wishing to disengage his thoughts from his feelings. Taking the weight off his feet, he rested on a boulder whose inviting shape beckoned. He cupped his face in broad hands and smelled the lingering musk. He closed his eyes for a brief second and removed his kufiya before his long fingers proceeded to part his thick, wavy hair and then came to rest on his neck.

His thoughts were on his first wife, Hamda, who was in labor at that moment. He knew she wanted to give him a son and an heir. He tilted his head back as he looked at the stars and also wished for a son.

The Amir breathed heavily as his head rested on his chest. He closed his eyes and willingly traveled to a life long ago; to another time and a much younger self when he was on one of his trips to the north of the tribe's territory alongside Syria's border. There had been skirmishes between two other tribes in this region. Bedouins had their own tribal laws. When there was a dispute, the heads of the tribes would meet to discuss it and vote on a solution. Everyone present respected what the council agreed upon, and there was no turning back.

By noon the group reached a well nestled between the river and the surrounding mountains. The Amir gazed at this river that had given their tribe its power and prosperity. He got off his black Arabian horse, Anter, and led him to the well as his men followed his lead. Anter was larger than average to accommodate his rider who was six feet three inches tall with broad shoulders and a massive chest. But the Amir's size wasn't the only thing that commanded respect. His political authority depended upon his wealth and fair personality. He had eyes that reminded one of moonless desert nights and a hooked nose like the beaks of the majestic eagles that crowned themselves kings of the sky. His jet-black hair curled at the ends from the sweat slipping from his scalp. His ruddy flesh contrasted beautifully with the rest of his features. He was a man women looked at from under their lashes, a trick they had learned early on, for it wasn't proper for a female to openly eye a man.

Scanning his surroundings, he walked to the north side of the well and sat under a cluster of trees where his men had laid a hand-embroidered quilt.

A group of women were filling their water jugs to take back to a nearby town. This was a good well used by the nearby tribes. The women hurried to leave before the men came to fetch water for their Amir. The woman leading the procession turned her head slightly to take another look at the Amir. Their eyes locked for a mere second before she quickly looked away.

The men came back with water for their Amir, who had taken his abaya and kufiya off. He wore a white cotton gambaz. He gave thanks to God as he washed his hands, face, and hair with the water Abed poured over a basin on the ground. The water cooled him further; he heaved a sigh as he leaned his back against the trunk of a tree.

"To which tribe do these women belong?" The Amir asked aloud to everyone and to no one in particular.

"They're from the Abadi tribe, Amir," ventured Saad, as the women departed, carrying their pottery squarely on their heads.

Saad was average height, with dark eyes. He had dark olive skin, dry and wrinkled from the harsh sun's rays and dry weather. His lips formed a thin slit on his face.

3

"Hmm, you know who that girl is, the one with the green eyes?" inquired the Amir.

"Hamda! Yes Amir, she is the niece of their Sheikh (elder)," he said, as he started a fire from coals he carried to make coffee.

Hamda was well known because of her rare dark green eyes. Most women of the tribe had dark or light brown eyes. Blue, green, and hazel were far less common. Accentuating her eyes were her long black hair and dark olive skin.

Within days, the Amir asked for Hamda's hand in marriage and the two were married within the month. For three days and nights, the tribes' men and women rejoiced as the newlyweds stayed in their wedding tent away from prying eyes and ears.

Life returned to normal and Hamda proudly took her place as the head of the Amir's tribe. Before their first anniversary, she became the proud mother of a first-born son. The Amir named him Saleh, in honor of his late father. The tribe celebrated for days the arrival of an heir and everyone prayed for many more to come. But fate had different plans and although Hamda had three more births in the next five years, none survived. Each new baby either died at childbirth or in his or her first year.

Hamda knew the inevitable would happen; her husband would take another wife. Although she braced herself for this, his words, when uttered aloud, caused her much pain. She tried to appear unaffected as he informed her of his plans to ride to a neighboring tribe to ask for a woman's hand in marriage.

"I understand," Hamda nodded, as if he had merely informed her of a hunting trip. "I will make things ready for your return." She looked away, fearing he would see her misting eyes. She knew he had to take another woman. She ventured to ask, "Have you seen her before?"

"Yes, I saw her when we asked for her sister's hand in marriage to my brother Abid El-Gadir," the Amir answered reluctantly. He knew his wife wished he would marry a strong woman to bear his children, not a woman he admired. He opened his arms and Hamda involuntarily ran into his embrace and began to sob. The Amir had no words at first, but after her shudders softened, he said, "You know I need to have another wife; she will never diminish your status or my love."

4

Hamda held him in her dark green eyes as she spoke her heart, "I knew this day would come, but I always prayed against fate and wished it wouldn't." She lowered her eyes as she clung to him. He tightened his grip and sighed,

"Oh Hamda, I will always be your husband and you will always be the mother of Saleh."

The week before the actual wedding was hard to endure. Hamda had to oversee many of the details. As the wife of the Amir, this was part of her duties. She tried to ignore the men erecting the bridal tent on the other side of the main one.

Finally, the day came when he rode off to bring back another to share his bed, and she tried to busy herself with preparation of the feast that would await the wedding party, and felt grateful for this distraction.

The Amir ordered food to feed one hundred men, and in the tradition of the Bedouin life, *Mansaf* was the only chosen dish. Bedouins rely on sheep to give prestige to their tribes, and the Gazzawiya were proud to own thousands. Mansaf was primarily lamb cooked in *jameed* (yogurt) and served heaped over rice.

Hamda stood and watched over the many open fires cooking the lambs. Finally, she made sure the women placed the coveted heads of the lambs squarely in the middle of every huge tray. Bedouins enjoyed eating almost all parts of the lamb, considering it a delicacy to be savored by important guests. The men marched in rows, four strong men carrying each tray. Shouts of congratulations mixed with the piercing sounds of gunshots as the tribe's men honored their leader.

Hamda saw little of the celebrations. She knew her husband had another wife. She consoled her heart with thoughts of her first born. "I am the mother of Saleh, future Amir of the tribe." Hamda's pain came from sharing a man she truly loved. Whenever the Amir spent the night with his new wife, Hamda lay sleepless. She was a good woman who had much compassion, wisdom, and fortitude. These were traits that made the Amir love her, but these wonderful qualities didn't stop him from wishing to be with his younger wife who would, hopefully, bring him more sons.

Hamda was always gracious to the other wife and gave her respect. However, the new bride's life was brief. When the young wife was in the tent delivering her first baby, Hamda was there to help her. She looked into the woman's glazed eyes as she urged, "Push child, push ... push ..."

The young woman clung to Hamda as her nails dug deeper into her hands. "I can't push anymore." Her breathing became shallow and her eyes began to close. Hamda held her by the shoulders and shouted, "Push, child. Don't give up. Your baby is almost out."

The young woman opened her eyes and looked into the distance above Hamda, as if she could no longer see her. She heaved one last push and fell back. Hamda looked at the midwife sweating profusely as she held up the lifeless infant boy. The young bride died in Hamda's arms as she stroked her face and wept for the girl who never became a mother. She wept for the shared harsh reality that they all endured. She wanted another son for her husband, and wished for another brother for her Saleh. She knew how important the Amir's brothers were to him. He depended on their loyalty to strengthen his position and carry out his commands.

Sadness swept over the Amir for the loss of his young wife and most of all for his son. He buried his wife and son together and wept for them as well as for himself.

Saleh, who was six years old, stood at his father's side, mourning the loss of another brother and wishing, for his father's sake, that a miracle would happen. "Don't be sad, Yubba. I will marry many wives and give you many grandsons."

****

Less than six months later, the head of a tribe in Syria visited the Amir to trade wheat and conduct other business. During the three days of negotiations, the Amir agreed to marry the man's first born daughter. He told Hamda he was planning to marry a woman from another country; new blood was needed to dispel the bad luck. The Amir never mentioned what he had heard of this woman's beauty.

Zuhriya was a tall beautiful girl with flaming red hair, sapphire blue eyes, and a porcelain complexion. She also had child-bearing hips

6

the Amir appreciated; he felt sure this woman would bear him many sons and daughters.

God gave Zuhriya looks women envied and men wished to possess, but soon after they wed, the Amir discovered his young wife had an affliction that caused her to scream hysterically, mostly at night. The Amir finally banished her to a tent of her own. He would visit only to satisfy his needs and then return to Hamda's tent to sleep.

Within the first year of marriage, Zuhriya gave birth to her first daughter, Fayga, named in honor of the Amir's mother. The Amir was proud of his daughter, and he loved her. Zuhriya gave birth to three more daughters, all endowed with beauty. Although this gave the Amir joy, he openly wished for a brother to Saleh. Hamda helped raise the daughters and doted on them all, especially Fayga, for she was the first-born daughter to the Amir and also had many of his features.

Nine years passed and although the Amir sat in his *majless* surrounded by his tribesmen, he felt all alone. He sighed and turned to look into his brother's eyes as he said, "*Ya-khou*, how am I going to break the news to Hamda?"

Abid-El Gader said nothing; he wished he had an answer. They both knew there was no other way; the Amir had to do as the soothsayer had said. He wanted a son. Memories of the day he lost his first born son, Saleh, aged his face in seconds.

The Amir had gotten up early that day to mediate a dispute between two neighboring tribes, one of many conflicts to which he had to attend. He wanted to take Saleh, who was then fifteen years old, with him, but Saleh was overseeing the construction of their first stone house. The young man was excited about their new home, which was going to be a tribute to the strength of the tribe and its importance, and didn't wish to leave. He smiled and his whole face lit up. The Amir marveled at his son's ability to capture all with such a simple gesture. Saleh looked back at many of his tribesmen who wished to be with his father and continued in his jovial way, "I'm sure you men wish to stay here and see what we will be able to accomplish in a day. Right?" The Amir rode on as the sound of his tribesmen's laughter echoed on in his ear.

7

Saleh had a glowing personality and people loved him. He had his father's physique and dark eyes and hair. Although he lacked his father's commanding air, he possessed a rare gift of willing people to please him. Did they sense deep within their beings that he was not going to be among them for long?

Saleh stood until his father rode out of sight before he turned his attention to the house. The central room was the majless where the Amir discussed the tribe's daily affairs and met with visitors. Rectangular dwelling units were organized around this inner room, each with a private balcony. High ceilings allowed for cool interiors; floors and walls were bare, with little work done to them other than some designs to add color.

That day as Saleh helped with pouring concrete on the roof, he fell and broke his neck.

Darkness descended upon the tribe; the wailing and weeping of women could be heard far away, echoing into the desert and beyond. The Amir heard the wailing long before the news reached him. He heard the sounds of mourning which everyone dreaded - the noises women emitted deep within their throats. His horse could not gallop fast enough to learn the reason; his heart beat as one with his mighty Anter. Time stood still as he stumbled upon the scene. The Amir saw Hamda wailing, her arms flung in the air; her hair uncovered as she hugged a body. He fell off his Anter and ran toward her; he felt his blood pumping into his head as he lurched upon his beloved Saleh in her arms. He remembered holding and kissing his son, willing him to wake up. He had little recollection of that night; he had been numb with the pain. The proud Amir openly shed tears he didn't notice. His wounded heart lay open for all to witness. He showed more emotions in that one day than he had in his entire lifetime.

****

The Amir jolted back to the present; he shuddered as he wiped the sweat from his forehead. He rubbed his eyes and for a moment stared at the wetness on his hands. Two years had gone by and still the memory was so fresh.

"God have mercy on me, have mercy on Hamda. Have mercy on us, merciful one."

He sat with his legs crossed as he greeted several men and took the offered coffee mug. He sipped it slowly, enjoying for a moment the strong hot brew and the cool evening air. There were only a few men sitting in the room, and the atmosphere was subdued. They sensed the mood of their leader and guessed his thoughts. The Amir and his men gathered in the council room, the majless; construction on the house had stopped the day Saleh passed away. He refused to complete the big house that the whole tribe had so anticipated. They stayed in the spacious tent that had taken two hundred men to erect.

The tent was called *Bayt El Char* and was crafted from strips of cloth woven from goatskin, the most valued kind because during rain, the weave contracts and doesn't let water in. In the middle of the tent, a small fire sent warmth and bright reflections. The tent was divided into many different quarters that housed the majless, guest areas, and sleeping areas for the Amir, his wives, and children. Storage rooms, rooms for the help, as well as a place to prepare and eat food lay at the other end of the tent.

Ya'goob, the coffee man, rose as soon as he saw the Amir. He had several tiny cups stacked on top of one another. After he served the Amir, he commenced to serve, clockwise, the other men in the majless. He poured for two or three men in a row, then went back to retrieve the cups from the men he served. The Amir held his cup straight and did not tip it from side to side, indicating he would like a refill. Ya'goob poured a generous second helping. Satisfied that all had been served, he went back to his station and began washing the cups.

Lost in his memories, the Amir watched the sun set as he drifted off to the day he went to visit Abu-Imad, the soothsayer.

It had been a little over a year since Saleh's death. Hamda had come to tell him that she was pregnant. She had waited until she started to show; she always dreaded, yet welcomed, her pregnancies. She never ceased to have faith in God, the all merciful, the all giving. The Amir felt the glimmer of a wish he nursed inside his heart. He knew he needed to go see the renowned soothsayer, who lived a day's journey away.

Early the next morning, the Amir took off with his Ya-khou and other members of the tribe. They rode hard and fast, his faithful Anter always delivering what his beloved master wished, as if the steed could sense his mood. The horse galloped with all his might. The rider's mind teemed with questions and apprehensions. The Amir was dressed as usual, with his kufiya wrapped around his face to shelter him from the desert climate. The horses' hooves barely touched one piece of ground before simultaneously claiming another. They stirred the sand, surrounding the riders with a dusty cloud. Engulfed in a sandstorm, their abayas flew along like winged avengers rushing to their fate. Finally, at sunset they reached the soothsayer's house.

The Amir had known the soothsayer for years and had sought his council more than once. They were as opposite as any two could be. One was tall while the other was short; one was light while the other was dark; and one frowned while the other smiled. Abu-Imad always wore a smile that bespoke of inner tranquility and contentment.

"Greetings Amir, I pray that your journey was not tiring." Abu-Imad smiled broadly as he said these words and rushed to greet his important visitor with a hug.

"Greetings to you; it is good to see you," The Amir towered over the soothsayer as they embraced. "The trip was easy and we arrived by God's will."

Abu-Imad ushered his friend and his traveling entourage into a good-sized room. Mattresses topped with colorful cushions for arm rests lined the walls; woolen carpet covered the floor, and the walls were devoid of any hangings except for a large crucifix in the middle of one wall. On the opposite wall, a statue of the Virgin Mary cradling the infant Jesus rested inside an alcove. The men took their shoes off before stepping onto the carpets, as was the tradition.

Fruits and coffee were served and the travelers drank and praised God and their host for the refreshments. The Amir's companions knew that he wished to discuss a personal matter with the soothsayer, and at an opportune time, they made their excuses and withdrew. Finally, the Amir and Abu-Imad were alone in the room, and the conversation shifted from the common to the intimate.

The Amir disclosed his reason, pouring out his anguish and fear to the wise man. The soothsayer looked at him with compassion and listened respectfully until all had been said. The Amir heaved a sigh from his heart, felt great fear, and clutched the soothsayer's hands. He looked into the soothsayer's eyes and said, "I need God's help and yours. I want a son, and I want him from Hamda!"

Abu-Imad got up and paced the room twice; he was deep in thought. He closed his eyes and looked as though he was praying silently and with all his might. He continued in silence as the Amir looked on without really seeing. Finally, after what seemed like an eternity, the soothsayer opened his eyes, stared openly at the Amir, and spoke.

"Amir, your wife is pregnant, she will give birth to her second and last son." He paused for a second and went on. "You will name him Saeed." Another quiet moment passed; the soothsayer knew Saeed was not Saleh - the name that the Amir wished for his heir. He also knew Saeed was used by more Christians than Muslims.

"Saeed?" repeated the Amir, realizing the implication, yet not wanting to voice it for fear of insulting the wise man.

"After his mother is through nursing him, you must put him in the care of a priest until he is seven years of age." The soothsayer knew that his words shocked the Amir of the Gazzawiya tribe; he said the last words more quietly, although they seemed to reverberate in the small room.

"Otherwise, he will not live."

****

The midwife's voice blared joyously, jolting the Amir out of his memory as she ran through the majless to place the infant under the Amir's loving gaze.

"A son, you have a son, Amir! A fine boy! May he live to become the best Amir."

The Amir rose as soon as he heard the women's *zaghareet*, the traditional ululating cry of Bedouin women when they are rejoicing and celebrating important events. He felt the multitude of men kissing him

11

on the shoulders and hands; they congratulated him; they were happy for their Amir.

"Long life to Saleh; may he live to be 100 years; may he flourish in your wealth." On and on men were wishing him and his son, Saleh, the best as the sound of gunshots reverberated in the night air in celebration.

The Amir's voice rang out, clear, loud, and nonnegotiable. "Saeed. I will name my son Saeed."

The Amir entered into the quarters where Hamda lay nursing her son.

"Congratulations!" he said as he kissed her on the head.

She felt her being come to life and she pushed back her hair and gazed on her beloved, "Congratulations to you!" She rubbed her son's head as she said, "He looks strong and the birth was easy. Two good signs, God willing!"

"God willing," the Amir said as he sat crossed legged and leaned against one of the many tent poles. He took off his headdress, rubbed his face, and watched as Hamda covered and laid the sleeping baby beside her. "I never told you about a trip I made when I first heard of your pregnancy."

Hamda's reaction turned from amusement, at first, to disbelief. Her mind went numb as the Amir related the details of his visit to Abu-Imad. She picked up the sleeping baby and clutched him closer to her bosom as she heard him whimper. She wanted to shout and scream, she wanted to wail out her heartache, but all she did was look down on her son and pray silently for God the merciful to take pity on her, to make fate intervene on her behalf.

The Amir watched her actions and lived her anguish. "We have to be strong for our son, Hamda. You will have others, a daughter as strong and as beautiful as her mother. You would like that, wouldn't you?" Abu-Imad had said that Saeed would be her last son, not her last child.

"Yes, a daughter would be a great gift, Amir." She did not wish to cry on this joyous day.

Fayga came into the enclosure and asked, "You need anything Yumma?" she asked, as she considered Hamda her second mother. She came closer and looked at Saeed. "He is beautiful and his breathing is strong. God willing he will live a long life."

She exited after kissing the Amir's and Hamda's hands and giving Saeed a hug. Fayga loved the boy the moment she saw him.

The implications of this deed were grave for everyone in the tribe. Few knew in the beginning, but it was hard to keep a secret this weighty. Once people knew, they began to wonder where their Amir was going to send Saeed. Discussing the matter privately, they marveled at his will to send his heir to live with a Christian priest, when they were one of the biggest Muslim tribes in the country.

This situation was paramount in the Amir's mind throughout the first two years of his son's life. He tried to hold and play with him, a habit that he had never engaged in with previous children, always having left the rearing of children to the women. This time things were different. Hamda and the Amir spent more time with this child than with any other.

Saeed ran into the Amir's embrace as soon as he saw his Yubba. Hamda watched and began to laugh out loud when Saeed pulled on the Amir's headdress. The Amir heard her laugh and joined in as he allowed his son to take his headdress off and run away with it. This became a daily game and many heard the Amir roar with laughter as he chased, caught, and hugged his son.

Many times Saeed would run outside the tent, where his sisters, especially Fayga, would run after him. Saeed loved this game and squealed with pleasure when he was finally caught by one of his sisters or his many uncles, aunts, or cousins.

The Amir's mind continually mulled over the thought: *my son will be raised by a priest. Will that change who he will become?* In the end, he succumbed to the inevitable and began researching where to place his son for those first important years of his life.

At last, he decided on the village of Taiba. It was small, not too far away, and had Muslim and Christian inhabitants alike. Now he needed to tell Hamda. He walked into their quarters and carried Saeed, who had jumped into his arms. Hamda looked quizzically at him.

"We will ride to see Saeed's home in Taiba tomorrow." He kissed his son, put him down, and quickly left the tent.

13

Hamda sat down, covered her face and began to sob.

The ride was short and Saeed slept most of the way. Hamda got off her horse slowly after the Amir took the child from her arms. The priest's mother, Om Easa, hugged Hamda and kissed Saeed's head. Both the Amir and Hamda liked her and knew she would love and care for Saeed.

Hamda watched this woman as she held her son, and was comforted by the unspoken promises in Om Easa's eyes. Hamda knew she would take care of her baby.

Om Easa never forgot this first meeting with Hamda, and never forgot the silent promise she made to her.

For the next short months, Hamda's days were centered on her son; she would gaze at Saeed and sing to him for hours. She felt she lived on borrowed time, but time does pass, and the day came when her son neared his second birthday. Bedouin women nursed their babies at least two years.

Weeping began as soon as the Amir and his men rode off into the sunlight toward what would become Saeed's new home for the next five years. Happy to be riding with his father, the little boy did not shed a tear as he trotted off, clasped in his father's embrace.

Hamda comforted her sorrow with thoughts of her son growing to become a great Amir like his father, the leader of the Gazzawiya. She had fulfilled her destiny despite the fact that her husband had taken other wives: Saeed was his only son. Hamda knew she was again with child, and that brought some comfort to her heart. She hung to her faith, clinging for survival and clutching the glimmer of hope that time would pass quickly. She would see her Saeed again, and she would give birth to another son.

In the evening, the Amir came back looking much older. Hamda waited for him and watched as he dismounted. "Your son is fine; he will get used to his new home." He patted her on the shoulder as he continued. "In no time, he will be back in your arms. Have faith!"

Meanwhile Saeed kept trying to find his mother as he cried out for her, "Yumma, Yumma!" He didn't understand why he couldn't find her. She was always with him. Why did his father leave without him?

He didn't know who this woman was, or who these boys were. He wanted to go home.

Om Easa tried to console the little boy. She rocked his shaking body as she softly sang to him, but she knew only time would erase the memory of his mother. Only then would his heart heal and his weeping cease.

He cried for almost two weeks before he accepted his new Yumma and could willingly go to her without crying or cringing. This wrenching experience at such a tender age taught him to fear losing those he loved, and so he clung to Om Easa, the priest's mother. She couldn't leave him for a second without seeing panic on his face. Saeed, firmly attached to Om Easa's waist, soon became a common sight in the small village at the edge of one of the many *wadis*, seasonal watercourses. Saeed's memories of the musky smell of the tent were now replaced with the aroma of incense and candle wax.

Hamda's health was not good in this pregnancy. She lost her vigor and easily tired. Different healers prescribed various herbs and medications, but nothing worked. Hamda reached the point where she couldn't even rise from her bed for extended periods of time.

The Amir thought of bringing Saeed back, but he was uncertain of how or when to do it. He had visited his son one month after leaving him. It was very painful to see blankness in those eyes that used to welcome him, but Saeed happily sat in his lap and ate the candy the Amir gave him. The Amir wished Hamda could be with him, but she had been unable to get out of bed that morning. He consoled his heart with the thought that the next time she would be able to make the trip with him. He hoped that after the birth of her child, she would regain her health.

Saeed's new home was larger than average since it shared the same courtyard with the village's only church. It was a small, domed, one-room, mud brick dwelling. Inside, the walls were painted with murals depicting the Virgin Mary and Child. Three rows of wooden benches and an altar, consisting of a rectangular table covered with a white tablecloth, were the only furnishings.

Om Easa had married the man she loved as soon as she was old enough to love, and remained happily married until he had fallen ill eight years earlier. He never recovered. She grieved for her husband, but her sons comforted her. Her eldest, Easa, was the town's loved and respected priest. Priests made little money, and their income came from what few coins the people could spare.

Saeed started calling Om Easa "Yumma," as the memory of his own mother faded into a forgotten past.

"He's not crying any more, Yumma!" Omar said, with glee in his voice. He loved having a younger brother. "Can I hold him, Yumma?" he asked for the hundredth time.

"Let us see if he will let you hold him. Put your arms out to him," Om Easa instructed her son, who seemed much older since Saeed had become a part of their family.

Omar put his arms out and smiled. "Come brother. Come on."

Saeed laughed as he threw himself into his new brother's arms.

Hamda never reclaimed her health. Everyone feared for her; she remained pale and tired. She went early into labor, and was gone when her baby arrived. To everyone's sorrow, it was a girl. The midwives tried everything they knew to stop the bleeding, but at the end, there was nothing more they could do. Hamda bled profusely, and they lost her.

The Amir was sitting in his majless with his men, and this time he hardly heard his wife scream. He heard a baby's cry and realized that it must be a girl, for there was silence instead of the zaghareet. *Abu-Imad was right*, he thought, and before he took another breath, he heard the dreaded wailing of the women. His heart stopped for a second, his face void of color as he raced through the tent, ripping the dividing cloths to get to his wife. The women all scrambled back, stumbling on one another when they saw their Amir charging into the birthing room. He knelt and held Hamda in his arms.

Eyes closed, she looked peaceful, sweat still glistening on her skin even after she had let go of life. He looked down and saw the blood – so much blood, and he knew she was gone. He hugged her as he shed unseen tears. He laid her head back on the moistened pillows. The Amir heard the baby crying, and he shouted at the women,

"Take her away; I don't want to see her!"

16

And so the poor baby, labeled as bad luck, was called *Shamma*, a derivative of the word "curse." Shunned by her father and at the mercy of all, she realized early on that she was a second-class citizen in her father's home. Shamma grew into a maiden with little grace or beauty. Instead of inheriting her mother's beautiful green eyes, Shamma had small, lifeless, brown ones. She could have been blessed with her father's height or light complexion, but instead she was average in height with a dark complexion. She had nicely shaped thin lips that hardly ever smiled, forever pursed in a disdainful pucker.

If Hamda had lived, she would have given her daughter the gift of laughter. The power of a smile on her features would have been like the rays of sunshine on dewy morning flowers, revealing their beauty.

الأمير محمد الصالح الغزاوي

The Amir Of the Al-Gazzawi Tribe

Chapter 2

The Clarks

White clouds resembling cotton candy flew in a bright blue sky. Ernest Jr. strolled to the general store to buy tobacco. He pulled the door open and as he stepped in, his eyes fell on Lolli. She looked pretty indeed. She had ringlets in her blond hair, fair complexion, and the palest blue eyes, like a perfect summer sky.

She and her friends were buying ice cream. Ernest Jr. couldn't keep his eyes off her. He was smitten and stared until she finally looked back at him and smiled.

"Hi, my name is Ernest," he stammered, while extending his hand.

"I'm Lolli," she replied. She touched his hand briefly, then withdrew her hand and looked up into his eyes.

"Where are you from?" she asked. She had never seen him before.

"I moved down from Sevierville a couple of months ago. I work at Fulton," he said, as he tried to think of more things to say. He didn't want to stop talking to her and continued, "Pa used to work in the mines, in Hazard, Kentucky?"

"Oh, I've heard of other folks who moved from Kentucky," she said as she flashed a smile his way. "So what made you leave the mine?"

"It's a long story and I don't wanna bore you," He looked down at his shoes as he tried to think of something interesting to say. He finally asked if he could call on her, and she gave him directions to her house.

This soon became his evening ritual, a walk to her house and a walk back to the store where they both got ice cream. The walk back was always slower as they talked and laughed at nothing in particular.

"What was it like living in a camp?" Lolli asked one evening as they rocked in the chairs on the porch and sipped iced tea.

"It was really nice; we were given one of the houses on the hills behind the lower part of the camp. We liked it because it was close to the Commissary store, movie theater, Union Hall, the poolroom with snack bar, churches, schools, doctor's office and even a barbershop."

Lolli's mouth was open wide as she stared laughingly at him, "You're not kidding me, are you? A movie theater and a poolroom! That must have been really nice. Why did you ever leave?"

Ernest looked up at the sunset for a second before he looked back at Lolli and said, "Well, it was the year nineteen twenty eight and it sure was a cold winter. I was helping ma pump water from the drinking hydrant outside our front door when we heard a loud, thudding noise coming from the mineshaft," he paused for a second and took a sip from his ice tea before he continued, "Well, everyone was running toward the hilltop. I was one of the first to get there, and I was scared. I remember seeing Pa lying motionless on a stretcher and I thought he was gone."

Lolli moved closer to him and held his hand, "That must have been so hard," She felt like hugging him but knew better than that.

Ernest felt his whole body shudder from her touch and it took him a couple of seconds to resume his composure and finish his story, "Pa was okay, but he hurt his back and couldn't work at the mines anymore. That's when we decided to come to Sevierville where our kin lived. It's good farming land, but I didn't wanna stay there. I wanted to come to Knoxville, to a big town. Anyways, Pa and Ma moved down here after I did and so we are all together again." He smiled broadly at her.

"Well, my real Pa passed on when I was a little girl and I have no memory of him. Mama married Thomas and he was the only daddy we ever knew. I was the youngest and he always doted on me. My mama's family love to play music and I love to sing and dance." Lolli said as she got up and twirled for her young admirer who appreciated every movement.

Ernest Jr. loved his mama and never thought much about what kind of woman he would marry. In fact, he never thought he would feel so strongly about anyone until he saw Lolli. She looked the very opposite of his mother, who was quiet with dark hair and eyes to match.

It didn't take Ernest long to propose to the woman he loved and she accepted with happy tears. Ernest Jr. never worked so hard in his life; he wanted to make Lolli happy. His pa had given him a plot of land to build a house. He began working on their home the minute Lolli agreed to marry him. Everyone helped, but it still took longer than they both wished. They finally got married that spring. Lolli, who was accomplished with the needle, sewed her own wedding dress. She had flowers embroidered all around the neck and hemline. She even had a matching headpiece.

Before their first anniversary, Lolli was pregnant and excited about becoming a mother. One spring evening after checking on the evening meal, she went into the living room to tidy up. She emptied the ashtrays, fluffed the cushions on the sofa, and then headed back to the kitchen to set the table. She wiped the plates before she laid them on the table and was about to place the glasses when a sharp pain pierced her abdomen. She stood still for a second, willing the pain to go away, as she calmed her racing thoughts with, *Surely not? It's too early!*

Moments later, the pain faded as her senses relaxed. She put her hand over her belly and rubbed it slowly. All returned to calm. *It's probably just gas.* She slowly proceeded to set the table as birds whistled in the background.

Just as Ernest walked in the door, she had another contraction. One look at her face told him they needed to call the doctor.

Half an hour later, Ernest felt great relief when he saw the headlights of Doctor Hawkin's blue and gray Plymouth through the curtains. Ernest rushed to open the door and almost collided with the man. "It sure is nice to see you, doctor."

Although the doctor told Lolli that her labor pains were normal for a first time mother, she would have definitely disagreed had she been given the opportunity. Doctor Hawkins's calmness and steady hands relaxed her as she continued to have contraction after contraction, breathing heavier with each passing spasm.

Minutes later, Ernest heard his baby cry. He beamed with pride as he gazed on his first child, "She sure is pretty, Darling, just like her mama." He kissed the top of the baby's head and turned around.

"What you gonna name her, Lolli?"

"Betty Jean. I'm naming her Betty Jean Clark."

Betty Jean was a healthy, happy baby and had the good fortune to have doting parents and grandparents. They wanted the best for their child, and Ernest worked hard to achieve what he wished for his family. He added a new bedroom to their home and finished the basement before Betty's first birthday.

Lolli was busy making Betty a special dress to wear on her first birthday. A talented seamstress, she knew how to sew the prettiest dresses and was equally as good with dainty frilly ballet costumes with their multiple layers of chiffon and satin leotards with fancy ribbons and brass buttons. She made Betty a pink, ruffled dress with green bows around the hem. She also sewed a matching green-and-pink ribbon to put in her hair. She loved to dress her doll up and do her hair. She would roll the soft tresses around her finger and hold them with pins until they dried. In the morning, Betty would have beautiful ringlets framing her pretty little face.

She baked a pretty cake and made her famous hamburgers that everyone loved. She would always say that the finely chopped onions made them so juicy. Betty was the belle of her party, and she loved every second of attention she received.

Junior was born two and half years later. Betty replaced her dolls with a new brother. She loved taking care of Junior. She bathed and dressed him as many time as Lolli would let her.

"I hardly feel I have two kids. Betty is always looking after her brother; she acts more like his mama than I do. I swear she does," Lolli would tell Skeet, her closest friend and sister-in-law who lived next door.

"I know. Betty is such a young lady. I wish Leroy would take such care of Patsy. But you know, boys are just different from girls," Skeet said, as she shuffled through some of Lolli's patterns. She was looking for a dress and knew Lolli would have pretty ones to pick from.

They heard the children running down to the garage, where Ernest was working on a car. He enjoyed it, and made a little money doing it, too. He, also, heard the kids, and hid behind some tires in the back of the garage. Leroy entered the garage first and looked for his uncle. Close behind him, Betty stopped suddenly and Patsy and Junior bumped into her. Just as they were about to exit the garage, Ernest jumped out from his hiding place and hollered, "Boo!" All four kids began screaming.

Seconds later, Leroy, Patsy, and Junior started laughing. Betty didn't like that and said, "I don't like to get scared, Daddy. It gets me all shaking."

That evening, he expressed his worries to Lolli who assured him that Betty was just a sensitive child, and not to fret about it.

Ernest and Lolli Clark

CHAPTER 3

SAEED

Every morning, Yumma gave me a coin to put in my *uja*, a clay piggy bank securely placed at the back of a shelf. I loved the part of the morning when I dropped the coin through the little slit and waited a second before I heard it *clink*. I was about four years old.

I walked to school with my brother, Omar. We both had on our white *dishdashas* and worn-out sandals. My hair was longer than Omar's and it always got into my brown eyes. I remember that I was shorter than other four year olds. My ten-year-old brother always watched over me and was constantly by my side.

I enjoyed school where we learned to read and write the *Engeel*. I especially liked the singing part:

> *You attained what no one could,*
> *O Mother of the Mercy,*
> *and you became filled with grace.*
> *To the Divine you became*
> *a veil for the Word,*
> *and greatly marveled were you*
> *among the scholars.*

"Very well, now let us open to page five." Father Easa read the passage and commenced to explain it to his young students.

"When are you going to tell us a story?" I asked, as Omar gently nudged me to be quiet.

Father Easa nodded his head, "Just give me a second, and I will tell you the best story yet."

I always loved Father Easa's stories and many a night fell asleep to Yumma reciting one of my favorites.

Yubba, or the Amir as I knew him first, was a special visitor who came laden with food and goodies. I loved the way this man smelled, and felt so important when he would hug me and let me sit on his lap. He would give me candy and I always took more for Omar. I wished he would visit every day! I treasured the times when he took me for rides on his magnificent horse.

One summer day I was playing in the field with my brother, throwing marbles into a carefully dug hole in the ground.

"Use your black marble, little brother." Omar advised.

I nodded, dug deep down in the pouch Yumma had sewn for me, and pulled out the black one. I carefully placed it squarely in the middle of my hand, moved my thumb behind it, and then gave it a precise flip that sent it rolling into the hole, taking my brother's marble along with it.

"I got it!" I shouted jubilantly, jumping up and down.

"Good shot, little brother." Omar patted me on the back as I ran around him. We both turned as we heard riders coming up the hill.

"It's the Amir!" we shouted as we ran toward our home.

I was the first to run into the courtyard where I saw Yumma motioning for me to come inside.

"But Yumma, the Amir is coming. I want to go see him," I said, impatiently.

"You will see him later; I just want to tell you something."

I looked at my brother for help, but Omar ran back out into the courtyard. Puzzled, I went to Yumma who sat cross-legged on one of the mattresses piled in the corner of the room and she guided me to her lap. She told me the truth as I stared in disbelief; my mind couldn't fully comprehend what she was telling me.

"What are you saying, Yumma?" My lips quivered, and my eyes brimmed with tears. "I don't understand." The information shocked me,

26

but the look on her face and the tears running down her cheeks confirmed her words and made them true.

"The Amir is your Yubba, and he is going to take you to your real home."

We heard the commotion outside, and the excited shouts reached our ears. I looked for comfort from the only mother I knew, but her swollen eyes made me reach out and hug her. I didn't wish to leave her arms and I began to cry. Yumma patted my back and kissed my head before she wiped my eyes with her scarf, "Come, my darling, I will walk with you to your Yubba. Be brave and remember you are his heir. Always remember that."

We came out of the house and walked straight to the Amir. Yumma let go of my hand and gently pushed me forward into the open arms of my Yubba. Everyone was laughing and hugging me. I felt important and no longer wished to cry, but then I thought of something. "Wait, I forgot my uja. I have a lot of money in it, and I want to take it with me!" I ran inside and came out with it, held it high above my head, and threw it to the ground. It shattered into pieces of clay. To my great disappointment, there was not a multitude of coins among the shards. Instead, a lone coin gleamed amid the rubble of the former uja. I searched Yumma's face, hurt and perplexed.

"Where is all the money I put in it?" All my pent up emotions suddenly surfaced for all to see and I began to cry. *All my money is gone and I too will be gone.*

Yumma looked stunned. She had never thought about the uja and the likelihood of my remembering it. The poor priest's family could not afford a daily allowance. Every night, Yumma had been retrieving the coin to give it back to me the next morning. Now I knew why she never let me shake the clay container.

I can still see Yubba rushing to hug me in his arms. He dug out all the coins from his pockets and gave them to me, saying, "Don't cry, son."

I felt comforted by this man whom I had known all my life but only now realized was a part of me. I wiped my tears and tried, without success, to carry all the coins at the same time. One of the men pulled out a worn, leather wallet and handed it to me. I admired it for a moment, and then proudly put all my coins inside.

I looked up and saw Yumma. "Yumma! I don't care about the money. I want you to have it," I ran after her and hugged her. She turned around and our misted faces touched for a moment before we separated.

I felt Yubba's hand on my shoulder as he guided me to his horse. My excitement at being on top of the horse subsided as my predicament became clear. I was going and not coming back; I turned my head and saw Yumma going into our house.

Yubba saw what transpired and sensed my fear. He knew I was fighting the urge to cry. He cuddled me and said softly, "Son of my heart, don't be sad. We will race the wind, and I will take you to a big tent full of people waiting to see you."

The Amir wished his son had a mother to go to. He tightened his arms around the seven year old son he had given up, in order not to lose him..

"Yubba, we are going so fast! Anter is the fastest horse. I want a horse just like him!" I shouted to be heard over the horse's hooves.

Yubba cocked his head toward me saying, "There is a great mare waiting for you, Son. She is as light as the wind and as gentle as a hare."

Amazing scenery softened the rough ride. The Jordan Valley nestled between two majestic mountains that housed ridges, and ravines flowed down in a multitude of reds, browns, and beiges. Fields of wheat glimmered like gold under the steady rays of the sun.

The Amir and his riders pushed their horses on, eager to get to their tribe. They knew everyone awaited their honored guest.

I will never forget the first time I saw my new home. It was like a giant spider. "Yubba, I can't see the end of it. It doesn't end!"

The Amir's laughter softened his face as he ruffled my hair, "Our *Bet El Char* is the largest in the land, son. It takes two hundred men to set it up."

As the horses' hooves stirred up dust all around them, people started to emerge from the tent. I heard gunshots and cringed into

Yubba who tightened his grip on me. "Our tribesmen carry guns, Son, and now they are welcoming you home."

I must have been kissed a hundred times before Yubba took me inside the majless. Stepping inside the tent, cool and dark in contrast to the heat and glare of the sun, instantly soothed me. Sun rays filtered through the fabric like gleaming stars at night. I watched and mimicked Yubba who took off his shoes before he stepped on the lush carpet. He motioned for me to sit on his right side and I did. Three boys ran toward us as soon as we sat down. I watched as each of them kissed the back of Yubba's hand. "Come greet your eldest brother and welcome him to his home."

I couldn't believe I was suddenly the eldest; I had been the youngest in the priest's household.

"Hala, Ya-khou," the tallest said, as he hugged my shoulders, followed by the others.

I wanted to ask their names but I didn't know how to be an older brother. They seemed so much older than I was, and so much more commanding. I didn't know what to say or how to act; I looked up at Yubba and saw him watching me.

"I am Mamdouh," the tall one said. He had a low gentle voice, and he smiled as he pointed to the other two boys. "These are Abid-El-Kareem and Talal."

Mamdouh had blue eyes, a light complexion, and fine hair – a sharp contrast with Abid-El-Kareem, who was much darker with mischievous brown eyes. Talal was the best looking one. His curly, jet-black hair framed a round, porcelain face.

"We have been waiting for you for years," Mamdouh said shyly. "Every time Yubba went to see you, I wanted to go, but he never took any of us."

"Why not?" I asked, puzzled, but Mamdouh seemed equally as baffled.

"I would never ask Yubba that; maybe you can." Mamdouh said.

I watched as an elegantly dressed woman crossed the carpet toward Yubba. Her long dress was heavily embroidered with red and pink colors. I saw her headdress and admired the golden peacock pinned to it. She kissed and hugged me as she smiled, showing one dimple on her right cheek. Her scent reached me and lingered as I saw her scooping one of the younger boys lovingly in her arms.

"Are you our mother?" I asked excitedly.

Silence fell as swiftly as death descends on its prey. I quickly turned to Yubba, now by my side.

"Son, your Yumma died when you were an infant. But yes, Arifa will now be your Yumma."

I wished she was my real mother, this elegantly dressed woman. But I wanted to cry and run back to my Yumma, whom I had left with tears on her face.

Mamdouh came and sat beside me, "Ya-khou, you also have five sisters who are much older than you. You will like them all."

"Five sisters? You mean I have three brothers and five sisters?"

Mamdouh laughed out loud. "You have four brothers. Yumma Arifa gave birth to another son a few moons ago. His name is Gazi."

I recall wondering why Mamdouh referred to Arifa as Yumma Arifa and not just Yumma. "Is Yumma Arifa your mother?" I asked, confused.

"No," Mamdouh lowered his head "Yumma Arifa is Talal and Gazi's mother. My Yumma gave birth to all our sisters, as well as Abid-El-Kareem," Mamdouh said with pride in his voice.

"My Yumma only gave birth to me?" I sensed reluctance in my new brother, who shuffled his feet and averted his eyes.

"Shamma is your sister."

"I want to see Shamma; where is she?" I stood up and ran to Yubba.

"What's the matter, son?" The Amir looked concerned.

"Yubba, I want to see Shamma!"

"Son, your backbones are your brothers. Shamma is inside with the other girls."

Yubba waved his hands in the air in a subtle gesture and I felt he dismissed the whole incident. I wanted to see Shamma, but instead, I went back to Mamdouh who tried to change the subject. "Are you hungry, Ya-khou?"

"Yes, are you?" I answered with the same question to which Mamdouh nodded with a big grin.

30

I watched as men brought pitchers into the majless and everyone washed their hands, including us. When the food was brought in, my eyes lit up. I had never seen such huge trays or so much meat. They even had the head of a lamb in the middle. I ate until I could eat no more. After we washed our hands once more, we went outside and played marbles with my brothers and many cousins.

"Saeed!" Over and over everyone called my name. I had never felt so important but at the same time did not like all this attention. Later on, we ate cheese and bread and drank sweetened, warm milk.

"Goodnight, Ya-khou, I will see you tomorrow." I saw Mamdouh and Abid-El-Kareem go off to a nearby tent to sleep with their Yumma Zuhriya. I didn't understand why they were not staying in the big tent.

"Talal, come and go to bed." Fathiya, another one of my sisters, called out. She gave me a hug. "You, eldest son, will sleep with Fayga, first born daughter."

I had no idea what she meant, but I had seen Fayga earlier that day. She was striking, tall with fiery red hair and captivating green eyes. She had kissed me multiple times and I liked her.

"You are my favorite brother. I loved your Yumma Hamda and I always took care of you before they took you away."

Her words comforted me and encouraged me to ask, "Fayga, where is Shamma?"

"Shamma? She is somewhere. You want to see her?" she asked me as she sweetly looked into my nodding face.

"Futha!" Fayga's voice rang out loud, "Go find Shamma! Saeed wishes to see her."

In no time Futha came back dragging a girl with straggly, unkempt hair that covered half of her oblong face. I saw fear in her eyes before she looked down at her bare feet. She appeared frightened and unhappy and I hardly heard her when she said, "I know you."

I didn't know what to say and felt so sorry for her. We stood and stared at each other until Fayga gave Shamma some candy, and she flitted away.

I felt very uncomfortable sleeping beside my sister; I didn't know her but thought the mattress and covers were soft and had a nice flowery smell. I felt restless. I finally slept and in the middle of the

31

night, I woke up. At first I had no idea where I was and then I remembered and I wanted Yubba. I ran through the curtained sectionals in the huge tent as I screamed out his name, "Yubba! Yubba! Where are you?"

I recall Fayga trying to catch me and that made me run faster; I had no idea where I was running but I kept on running until I crashed into Yubba's body.

"In God the Merciful's name, son, what is the matter?"

"I want Yumma, I want Yumma!"

For a second I was afraid he was going to be mad at me. He was so big and looked so strange without his headdress and abaya. I thought of running away from him when he tightened his grip on me as he carried me in his arms, "Don't cry son. Yubba is here and Yubba will always be near."

I felt like really crying then but I controlled myself and just lay in his arms. He carried me deeper inside this big place and wiped the tears from my face. "You can sleep with your new Yumma and your Yubba for as long as you wish, son," he said as he placed me on the mattress beside Arifa.

******

Miles away, at this same moment, Om Easa awoke with a pang and a loss in her heart. She arose from her bed and said a prayer to the Virgin Mary, beseeching her to take care of Saeed, to quell her loss, and to ease her worry. She cried for the child she had lost. Easa woke up and saw his mother on her knees. He went to her and hugged her as they both prayed.

******

The next morning Yubba told me to follow him as he headed out of the tent and up the small hill into another tent. I could hear the horses neighing and swishing their tails as we walked on the straw ... and there she was. Soda was grey and displayed the beautiful characteristics that set the Arabian apart from other breeds. Her head had a dished profile with prominent eyes that held gentleness, large nostrils that could take in all the air she needed when racing, and a small, teacup muzzle. She had a large forehead, a high tail carriage, and an arched neck. She was perfect. I fell in love with her immediately and gladly spent all the time I could in order to learn how to ride her and take proper care of her.

****

"Ya-khou, I hear that Saeed is sleeping with you every night." Abid El Gader couldn't ignore this new trend; he smiled as he rolled his cigarette.

"The heart and the way it rules, Ya-khou, my own feelings stun me. He is the soul of my heart. I know I am not fair, but I can't help how I feel. Only fate is the culprit." The Amir took the cigarette his brother offered and inhaled deeply as he looked up into a cloudless sky.

"How does Arifa feel about this?"

"I don't think she likes it, but it is how it will be." The Amir's tone indicated that there will be no more discussions on this matter.

Abid El Gader turned his attention to his cigarette.

Arifa was a woman deeply in love. Along with love, other emotions surfaced that controlled her heart and diminished the power of her reason. She possessed a strong will and never wished to be the second wife to anyone.

"I love Saeed, but you never show Talal any love or bestow on him any attention. It is always toward Saeed," Arifa would say when the Amir questioned her love for his eldest.

"He had a tough childhood, and he is my heir." The Amir quickly defended his actions. "Talal has you to dote on him. Who dotes on Saeed?"

"Everyone treats him with love; he lacks nothing."

These conversations with Arifa troubled the Amir. He began to think of an alternative life for Saeed. A boarding school seemed to be the best solution.

****

I was on one of my many rides on Soda where I felt free and away from all the happenings in the tribe. I would find a spot and just stare at the sunset and think of the different lives my brothers led. How different their lives, depending on their mothers. I often wished my mother was

33

alive. I remember thinking of how Yumma Arifa prayed in contrast to how Yumma prayed. I asked and was told that we are Muslims and Yumma Om Easa was Christian. I didn't understand, so they sat me with the Sheikh who taught me how to read the Qur'an. I was confused about why they were so different; many of the stories were so similar.

"Saeed, Saeed!"

I heard my name and was told Yubba wanted to see me. I jumped on Soda, and was greeted and kissed by a stranger the minute I stepped into the majless.

"Hala, young Amir. What a fine young man you are." He looked at Yubba and then back at me, "Your father loves you dearly and wants you to go to the best school around; you are a lucky boy."

The man kept on talking about his school and its great building and teachers and I felt heartbroken. Yubba didn't want me to stay with him. I must have done something wrong.

"Yubba, I don't want to leave you. I want to stay with my brothers and sisters. Did I do something wrong?" I remember holding him by the sleeves, as I wanted answers.

"Son of my heart, don't say such things." He cupped my face and looked into my tearing eyes. "This is for your own good. I am sending you to a great school where you will learn how to speak the tongue of the foreign man. This will help you become a great leader. This hurts me more than you can imagine, but a good leader has to sacrifice for his people."

"I want to be a good leader, Yubba, but why can't I learn here like my brothers and sisters?"

"You are not like your brothers and sisters. When I am gone, you will become the Amir."

"What about Soda, Yubba? Who will take care of her?"

"Soda will join you, son." Yubba's answer gave me pleasure as he hugged me closer, but I still wished to stay.

I wanted to become a Bedouin but I wasn't comfortable in these new clothes Yubba had bought me. On my last night, Mamdouh wanted to stay the night with me. I knew he enjoyed being with me and more importantly, being with Yubba.

34

"Of course you can stay with me! We will stay up all night talking."

I was awakened to Fayga calling me, "Saeed, Saeed, your Yumma Om Easa is here to see you! Hurry, put your clothes on."

I saw Yumma and Omar the minute I walked out of the tent, and I couldn't run fast enough into her open arms. I missed her so much and had only seen her a handful of times since I left her almost four months ago. I nestled in her arms for a minute before I turned to Omar and hugged him as I blurted out. "I am going to a big school to study!"

"I know little brother. The Amir had sent us news of your departure, and we have come to see you off with the rest of your tribe. You grow bigger and taller each time I see you."

"Do you like my suit, Yumma? Yubba bought it for me. He said I will wear the *dishdasha* no more." I twirled around, showing off my new clothes.

"You look really nice; you look so different in them." Omar said, as he caressed the buttons on the suit.

"Do you want to try the jacket on?" I asked, and Omar readily nodded.

Yumma looked happy as she watched and said that the Amir was making a wise decision. I wanted to say that I was only seven and didn't want to go, but decided not to. I was afraid she would become sad.

My life transformed from one of living in a tent, to living in a building that had floors, stairs, dining areas, library, and, indoor plumbing. Adjusting to so many new things required much coaching. Eating with spoons and forks, and using a knife instead of my hands to cut meat was taxing in the beginning, but with time, the life I once lived seemed far away.

At the school, students came from different Arabic countries and many from prominent families. I was different; I was the only boy in the whole school to belong to a real Bedouin tribe. Many of the boys and even the teachers listened intently when I talked about my life in the huge tent. I didn't like to talk much and preferred to listen, but when I was pointed out, I would speak. Teachers were amazed and once asked Yubba to validate my stories. Remembering Yubba's displeased face and words on that occasion always brought a smile to my face. He sternly said, "Whatever Saeed says is always the truth; we don't raise our sons to lie, for their word is our honor, and we don't take our honor lightly."

Our morning routine was the same each day. We woke up early, took our showers, and dressed in identical clothing: khaki shorts, white half-sleeve shirts, and a tie and cap. I enjoyed school and loved my teachers. I wanted to learn and be the best I could. I wanted Yubba to be proud of me. I made many friends, and some I stayed in touch with for the rest of my life. I looked forward to the weekends, when I visited Soda. Yubba had found family tribe members who camped near the school who pledged to take care of her. I would brush and clean her before and after we rode. I would ride in different directions and learned the land in that way. Those were the moments when I thought and did my most learning. Soda, nature and me!

Summertime arrived quickly, and I was eager to go back to the tribe and live in our *Bet El Char*; I missed my brothers, sisters, and stepmother, Arifa. I also couldn't wait to go visit Yumma Om Easa. After half a day of traveling, I was there and again it seemed so different, but adjusting seemed to take less time each year.

Bedouins do not lead a routine or predictable life, it changes as the weather and the events of the day unfold. On my second day I heard shouts that men were approaching. I quickly ran to the majless and stood to the right of Yubba as he watched the horizon. A few seconds later one of the tribesmen shouted out, "Sheikh El Elyan!" Yubba smiled as he recognized the head of the tribe who lived close to ours.

The two men embraced in the traditional Bedouin way, and the newcomer kissed the Amir on his right cheek. A procession of hugs and handshakes ensued between everyone in the party and everyone in the majless. The Amir's man Ya'goob came quickly to serve his perfectly brewed coffee. He poured for the guest first, and then his Amir, followed by whomever was sitting at the right-hand side, until all were satisfied.

I lived for these moments when I was able to witness and learn more about proper conduct in the tribe. There were so many untold and unwritten rules that were essential to follow, lest tempers flare. I

36

gathered that there was a dispute over a piece of land that adjoined the Elyan's land to that of their neighbors to the North. Yubba listened and interjected with a few questions now and then until he was satisfied that he had all the information he needed to make up his mind for a just solution.

"Yakhu, I see your point. I think it is valid, and the land should be yours. I will ride with you now, and we will settle this thing before its size gets bigger."

Mamdouh and I rode along with the tribesmen, and I was able to hear and see firsthand mediation between strong-willed desert men. The talks started after coffee and pleasantries were exchanged, and then just like a well-organized courtroom, everyone had the chance to state his cause and plead for his point. Sometimes, everyone was talking at the same time, voices rising, tinged with excitement.

I learned that day that someone has to admit wrongdoing and then the two parties will have to forgive and forget. The laws of the Bedouin decreed that there should be no hard feelings, no grudges; everyone had to be satisfied with the verdict. Resentment in any fashion or form was dangerous to all.

The next ten years were pretty much the same. I spent my winters learning city life and my summers learning Bedouin life, when yet another change came in 1947. This time the change rocked all the country. I remember being in the library watching the rain and my gaze rested on a bird trying to hide its little head from the droplets of water. Loud voices around me drowned the sound of the rain and alerted me that something was not right. I recall everyone talking at the same time; so many questions and little answers.

The United Nations had passed the Partition Plan which stated that Haifa was within the area allocated to become a Jewish state. Haifa's population of 146,000 was pretty much evenly split between Arabs and Jews, but with the news of a new Jewish state being formed, many non-Jewish Arabs left the city.

We all were looking forward to our last two years of school at Haifa and moving was not a part of our plans. That evening I rode Soda to the bay as we often did and talked to her as she so patiently listened. "I don't want to go, Soda, and more importantly, where will I go now?

Will Yubba send me to the school my brothers are going to or will I go farther away from Yubba and you?" I stroked her neck as she nudged mine and I felt confused. I loved this port city that had become my home. Haifa was a unique, beautiful city known for its tolerant inhabitants. I loved that the most; being tolerant meant being a loving human and not trying to force your beliefs on others. The city was divided into Muslims, Christians, and Jews who all lived together harmoniously.

I felt great relief when school did not close and I was able to finish that year with my friends. Sadly, things started to change and due to riots and skirmishes, the school closed the following year while I still had one more year to graduate.

****

Yubba looked pensive as he said, "Maybe it is your destiny to go to Aley, son. You will love Lebanon"

"But I wanted to be around to see how the building of our house goes." My disappointment clouded my face. It had taken years of convincing before Yubba agreed to start rebuilding our stone home. I heard about my brother Saleh and wished that I had been more like him. They said he was tall, a great horseman and a great hunter. I often wondered why I wasn't called Saleh, but Yubba never answered that question. I remember asking Mamdouh once and he too said that he also wondered at that. Mamdouh stayed with Yubba while Talal and Abid went to a boarding school in Amman.

"Son, you are not going that far. You will still be able to visit your home," Yubba said as he patted my shoulders.

I had heard of Beirut, the capital of Lebanon, from some friends who had visited there and loved it. I really wished I could tell Yubba that I didn't want to go. But I knew better and so I resigned myself to going to Aley.

I was dressed in a light beige suit, which complemented my bronzed olive skin. A white shirt and a dark brown tie completed my look. My thick black hair was combed back and I had the beginnings of a mustache. I was of medium height and had come to accept the fact that I would never be as tall as Yubba or Mamdouh. I loved the school nestled in the mountains when I first saw it, but I hated Yubba leaving and not having Soda with me. I felt this would be a long year.

A few months passed before I began to feel comfortable in my new surroundings. Most of my friends were with me from Haifa, and we pretty much stuck together. Fou'ad, who was also Jordanian, and I became much closer. He had jet-black hair and matching eyes that seemed to twinkle and laugh constantly. His light complexion and dimples completed his suave appearance. Taller than average, he had a lean muscular body that enhanced his looks. We explored the city together and by the end of the year, we were in love with it. Many firsts occurred for us; our first time in a bar, first time watching a belly dancer, and the first time experiencing alcohol.

"I feel like I'm living two separate lives," I confided to Muneer, one of the many boys who transferred with me. "I can't imagine what Yubba would think if he saw me drinking and smoking."

"We all feel somewhat like you do, Saeed. We are a new generation. That's all there is to it."

We were in the twelfth grade and planning for higher education. The education in Lebanon was delivered in French, and so, naturally, many students were interested in the Sorbonne, located in the center of the famous Latin Quarter of Paris.

"Wouldn't your father love to know that you want to go to France to study how to speak Français?" Fou'ad said, as he tilted his head backward and let out a loud laugh.

"Yes, and I am sure your father would be equally happy," I answered, laughing as I shook my head at him and thought of Yubba's words, *We need to have an agricultural engineer in order to take care of our lands and our people. The government keeps sending these foreigners to tell us what to grow and how to grow it.*

Someone advised us to go talk to counselors at the embassies if we were serious about going abroad. I felt happy that Fou'ad's father agreed to let him study abroad. I realized Fou'ad spoke the truth; most parents didn't wish their boys to go away, and many opted for closer capitals. I thought that London was a lot closer, and I was already used to the British accent. America seemed so far, but it had great agricultural education.

39

The next day, I took a cab to the Embassy and met with Mr. Dennis. I explained to him that I was a Jordanian from the Al-Gazzawiya tribe, and that we owned land in the northern Jordan Valley. I told him that I wished to become an agricultural engineer. After several visits, he told me that he would recommend me to one or two great universities. The University of California or the University of Tennessee! After all was said and done, I decided to let fate pick my destination. I reached into my pocket and produced a coin, which I casually, yet pointedly flipped. Fate decided on the University of Tennessee in Knoxville.

Graduation day came, and Yubba and many of our tribesmen were present for this important event in the life of the Al-Gazzawiyas. I was the first to graduate from a certified school and the first to be educated in English. Bedouins valued education, but because of a lack of resources, they usually had access to only basic reading and writing skills. I had made a point of requesting the presence of Shamma, whose life had changed when I asked Fayga to take her under her wing years ago. *No one would bother her if they had to answer to Fayga.* I was right; Shamma had begun to grow in a world that had become kinder since her birth. I saw a difference in my sister's demeanor, and it filled my heart with satisfaction, yet I did see her look of fear the minute Yubba was nearby. I wished he would be kinder to her, but I knew not to say anything to him. He wasn't unkind, he just didn't see her.

I enjoyed my summer, knowing that I would not be a part of this familiar world again for a long time. I rode Soda every chance I could and she would nicker the minute she saw me walking her way. Many times I rode off to see Yumma Om Easa; I loved telling her my latest tales, and she always laughed. I always brought food: fruits and nuts.

"Yumma, I will be leaving for America."

"Where is that, son? I never heard of it."

"I will be gone for four years this time, and I pray I will see you healthy when I return." I kissed Yumma's hands as she showered kisses on my head, forehead, and cheeks. Goodbyes never became any easier. On the contrary, I thought they became harder to deal with. Every new experience brought the realization that time would have to pass before I could forget the pain of parting; still more time was needed before I would become acquainted with a new place. Although excited about my next adventure, I felt nervous about how far I was going.

Saeed

CHAPTER 4

BETTY JEAN

I will always remember the first time I climbed up the steps of the big yellow bus; I looked back and waved at Mama and everyone. Little Jimmy shouted out something, and I giggled as I walked down the aisle in search of a seat. I instantly forgot Mama and the rest of my family as they headed back home. I picked a back seat beside the window as I touched the pink ribbon Mama had pinned in my hair. I straightened the pink dress Mama made me; I didn't want it to wrinkle, not after all the ironing she had done. It had tiny flowers sprinkled all over it and eight buttons down the front. When I looked up, I was gazing into the eyes of a neighbor, Pearl, who lived down the road,

"Hello Pearl. Do you want to sit next to me?"

"Yes," Pearl said, as she slipped into the seat.

She was much taller than I, with short, curly, light brown hair and hazel eyes. She was a pretty girl. I looked out the window and thought of Mama home without me. I wondered if she was propped on her stool in the kitchen smoking a cigarette. It had been a hectic day.

"Do you have sisters and brothers?" Pearl asked,

"I have two brothers. Junior wanted to come to school with me. I hated leaving him. I know he's going to miss me. Do you have sisters or brothers?"

"No, I don't, I think that would be fun!" She looked out the window and we both watched as other kids got on the bus.

I was glad Mama, Junior, and little Jimmy had walked me to the bus stop. Daddy was asleep; he worked the late shift and didn't come home till eleven o'clock. We had to be careful to not wake him up. Lord have mercy on us if he woke up with one of those headaches. Mama never knew what caused them or how long they were going to last, but they sent Daddy plum crazy, as Mama always said.

I felt a little guilty about being happy that I was not going to be doing chores today. There was always something to be done in our home. We all had to share and do our part to help with cooking, cleaning, and of course, the laundry. I chased those thoughts away as the bus stopped in front of the big school. I had seen it before because many of my cousins had gone there. I walked behind Pearl and stepped down off the bus.

We strode side by side following the older kids until we heard a somewhat loud female voice say: "Good morning children! My name is Miss Nickels, and I am going to be the teacher for our new first graders." She lifted her hand in a sort of wave as she continued, "If you are new at Mount Olive, please stand in line in front of me."

Pearl and I walked quickly toward the woman as other children joined us. We both looked up cheerfully at her, and she looked sweetly down on us. She was about average height, with short dark brown hair that came below her ears. Her light blue eyes reminded me of Mama's eyes, and an image of laughing eyes and a round sparkling face framed with golden curls flashed into my mind. For a split second, I missed Mama and longed for the familiarity of home. Those thoughts soon disappeared, and when I resumed my scrutiny I saw that the blue eyes hovering behind round glasses gave our new teacher a serious look. I noticed her clothes and planned to tell Mama all about her; even her pretty, shiny, black shoes. I looked down at my own new shoes. I was so proud of them; Daddy had bought them for me the week before so I could wear them on my first day of school.

"Children! follow me into the classroom," her voice rang out, and we all followed. The room was fairly large with desks placed neatly side by side, with a big blackboard covering most of the facing wall. In front of the board sat the teacher's large desk and chair.

"You can sit wherever you wish. Please, no running; walk to your desks." Miss Nickels looked at the boys even as she addressed the whole classroom.

I sat down next to Pearl and as I looked around I noticed another girl looking at us.

"Hello, my name is Betty Jean, what's your name?"

"My name is Betty too," she answered with a grateful smile,

"Do you want to sit next to us?" I offered, as Pearl smiled.

The three of us quickly became the best of friends and were inseparable throughout our years at Mount Olive.

The recess bell sounded, and immediately everyone jumped up and ran outside. It was as though someone had turned on a faucet containing boys and girls who spilled right down the hallway and out into the back yard. The grounds surrounded the school in a semicircle and were neatly arranged with three swing sets and a slide in the left corner. A patch of concrete pavement in the middle provided us a place to jump rope, enjoy hopscotch games, and hold our daily competitions.

****

I was now in the fourth grade, and I sure loved school, just as I loved Bible study and going to church. I loved reading and learning and I liked all my teachers and most of the students. I even liked the principal, Mrs. Gassett. Many of my friends didn't like her and said she looked scary. "Just because she's an elderly woman with dark hair and dark eyes and always dressed in black does not mean she's scary," I would say. I always smiled and greeted her in the hallways and she always smiled back.

The children were all outside and it seemed that everyone ran around in circles while laughing at the same time. Watching them was like watching a merry-go-round, but instead of horses, they were children. They ran around and around and around, laughing, giggling, falling, and getting up instantly. I loved play time and I was the hardest to catch. I would run as hard as I could; I didn't want to get caught.

"Miss Walters, did God make the same number of men as he did women?" I asked the one person that must know everything.

My teacher looked down on me and said, "You know Betty, I have thought about that question a time or two myself. I don't know the right answer to that, but I suppose that it would make sense to have the same number of females as males." She came and patted my head and I felt happy when she said that I asked good questions. I remember asking the same question of Mr. Hank, our Bible study teacher, and he said that God created the same number of males as he did females, just like he created Adam and Eve. Later that day we had a quiz and I didn't miss one question. I was very happy; I always just hated not getting an A in any of my classes.

****

Mama belonged to the Church of Christ; pretty much the entire Mount Olive community belonged to it. Daddy was a Baptist, but not a strict one; he wasn't one to attend weekly sermons. Although he occasionally joined us, he never made it on a regular basis. Daddy's parents were good people but not necessarily frequent churchgoers; they believed in the church and in God, but they didn't go every week. I loved Grandma Clark, but was always closer to Grandma Riley; going to church was one thing that bonded us. I would stay many nights at her place and she would tell me stories about miracles that God gave his beloved prophets.

In Sixth grade, Betty Shepard's parents bought a house down the road from us. It was fun having her live nearby and she liked Mama and Daddy; they were popular parents with all my friends. They allowed me a lot of liberties that Betty didn't get to enjoy because her parents were much older and more conservative. We always had a great time together. Once we both competed in a Bible study competition, and wouldn't you know it, we both won and got to go to summer camp for free. I couldn't believe it happened; I had always wanted to go to summer camp, but knew we couldn't afford it. It was so much fun being with girls and boys my own age; it was then I realized that being the oldest child is a lot of work and not so much play.

I wanted to throw a Halloween party in seventh grade. I asked Mama, knowing in my heart that she would say yes. It wasn't the first time I'd had a party; I had given two other birthday parties that the whole class remembered.

"A Halloween party? Oh, please, Mama," Junior chimed in, as he jumped up and down.

"A Halloween party … now let me see!" Mama exclaimed, as she gave us an astonished look that quickly turned into a big grin. "Why would you want to have a Halloween party, Sweetie?"

"Well, Pearl and I were talking about how much fun it is to dress up and go around the neighborhood, but it always ends too soon. We want to dress up and dance and have a *long* good time, Mama, not just a little time."

****

Betty Shepard, Pearl, and I sat around the kitchen table excitedly discussing the party.

"We can line jack-o'-lanterns along the walkway to the house. What do you think?" I asked my friends.

"That would look really nice. We also need to complete the decorations by adding a ghost. Now how are we going to make a ghost?" Betty Shepard asked.

"I know how to do that!" Pearl joined in eagerly.

"You do?" my enthusiasm for this project was building.

Just then, Mama walked in and heard the girls. "How about making paper decorations, girls? The boys will help with those."

At ages ten, eight, and seven, Junior, Jimmy, and Bobby helped us prepare for the party. Everyone began coloring paper, cutting out circles, and drawing pictures of witches, cats, and pumpkins. At the end of the afternoon, we had scary silhouettes and cuttings hanging on the windows and walls of the living room and kitchen. Finally, we put out candles, dishes of alcohol, and salt all around to keep the bad ghosts away.

I loved the costume Mama made for me. *She is such an artist*, I thought as I put it on. It was a dark blue satin dress with plush sleeves, a tapered waist, and a billowing skirt. Gold thread stitched the sleeves, waist, and hemline. I pinned a blue and gold ribbon around my ponytail. I looked at myself in the mirror, twirled twice and wished to live a life where I could dress up and go to parties with my Prince Charming.

I invited all my class along with a few friends from the neighborhood. Almost thirty kids were at our house. There were ghosts, cowboys, Indians, clowns, Snow Whites, and Cinderellas, as well as a Tom and Jerry and Winky Dink. I blushed when Danny told me I looked "real pretty." We had a great time playing our favorite games, such as the Postman, and one that was especially for Halloween where the winner had to spell thirty-five words of two or more letters by using only the letters in the word 'witches.'

I enjoyed the attention I got the next day in school when kids thanked me and bragged about the party. I was on cloud nine the whole week; I loved throwing parties and wished we had enough money to throw a party every week.

More than anything, I loved to dance. I wanted to take ballet and baton lessons, but Mama said it would cost too much; so I started to babysit and soon made enough money to pay for ballet and tap lessons.

I loved reading as much as I loved dancing; thankfully, it was a cheaper hobby and I got to do more of it. Reading books allowed me to escape to different worlds and live other lives. I loved to imagine myself in whatever novel I was reading. I would sit curled up with a book and dream my afternoons away; that is, whenever Mama didn't need me. All this daydreaming made me want to be in front of a crowd and show off my talents. *Elmer* was the big production in eighth grade. Betty Shepard and I auditioned with many others for the parts of the fourteen-year-old twins, Jeanie and Janie Collier. Miss Casey picked us for the roles and we were ecstatic.

Mama, Daddy, Junior, Jim, Bobby, and baby Bill all came and watched me on stage both evenings. Tears rolled down Mama's cheeks and she told me I had so much talent!

I thought I would like to be an actress; it was so easy for me to portray other personalities. I couldn't imagine how some kids were having trouble playing their parts. My talents on the stage also helped me when I was named the class speaker of our eighth grade and got to speak on the podium in front of the whole school. I wanted this moment to last forever.

****

High school was so different; I will always remember how nervous I felt that first day. I walked the half mile to the bus stop with Pearl and Betty Shepard. We wore the dresses we had decided on the day before. I had on a pale blue, one-piece sundress with a square, blue-and-white front neckline. Pearl had on a white-flowered sundress, and Betty Shepard wore a light-green dress with dark-green buttons adorning the length of the front. All three dresses had flared skirts.

A chaotic and disorganized scene greeted us, with no teachers to watch as we departed the bus. The parking lot was lined with buses as well as cars crammed with boys and girls. We walked up the front stairs of the school and into a big hall. Long tables and teachers lined the far wall, which displayed school banners and various team pictures. We three friends tried to stay in touch, but being in different classes made it harder and harder. As the year went by, we saw less and less of one another at lunch, but we still rode the bus together and would sometimes visit each other.

After the Christmas break, Miss Scout, the principal's secretary, asked me if I would like to work in the front office, and I liked that. I also worked in the library. I couldn't believe how many books they had and I wanted to read every one.

****

Junior year was a blast; I made many new friends and felt a sense of belonging. Working at the front desk made me more visible, especially to the guys who often needed help with one thing or another. I had always watched what I wore, but now I became even pickier and always made sure I had a light color on my lips.

"Hello, Betty. I was wondering if you'd like to go see a movie with me this Saturday night." David asked after I had helped him with some paper work for his coach.

"A movie? I'd love that, David." I didn't want to seem too willing, but I sure felt good about it. David was one of the nicest boys I'd met, and he had been in one of my classes last year but never seemed to notice me. This year was different; he always talked whenever we chanced to meet. He had blond hair, which he always combed neatly, hazel eyes, a straight nose, and full lips. I also liked that he was the captain of the basketball team and that girls liked him. I told Mama all about him and that he was planning to go to the University of Tennessee when he graduated, to become an engineer. Mama liked everything I said about him and sewed me a new dress to wear to the movies. We had a great time and began to spend more time together. At the end of the year, we were going steady.

One day as Mama ironed Daddy's shirts, she asked, "Sweetie, why don't you sign up for the Autumn Beauty Queen? I'm sure you'd win."

"Oh, Mama, do you really think I should?" I asked as my mind raced to the thought of entering and, just maybe, winning. Held every fall, the contest celebrated the autumn beauty of the Great Smoky Mountains.

That night, I drifted off to sleep with visions of winning. Wouldn't that be wonderful? David would be so proud of me if I won!

The next day, I signed up for the pageant and considered what dress I should wear. Mama and I were discussing different colors and designs when I yelled.

"I got it, Mama! I got the best idea ever, and it will be a sure winner." I smiled broadly.

"What, Sweetie, what?" Mama smiled even before she knew what I was thinking.

"Oh, Mama, only you can make it happen!" I ran across the living room and hugged her as I continued. "I want a dress made out of the letters." Mama didn't know what I was talking about. I slowed down and said, "When I was signing up for the pageant today, Miss Simmons helped me, and she said that the Knoxville Tourist Bureau had received

50

a whole lot of letters of requests about this year's pageant. I can ask Miss Simmons if she can help me get some of the letters, and then *you*, Mama, can make them into a dress for me!" By now, I had Mama's hands in mine, looking pleadingly into her eyes.

Mama thought and talked at the same time. "I reckon I can do that. I can make a background from cotton and attach the letters onto it and . . ."

"You're the best Mama in the whole world!"

After school the next day, Miss Simmons drove me down to the Tourist Bureau. We were met by a kindly lady who welcomed us with a smile. She thought our idea of a dress made out of the request letters was simply ingenious, and gave us a sack full of letters they had received. Later, Miss Simmons insisted on driving me home and I couldn't thank her enough for all she had done for me.

"Mama, I'm home, and guess what I've got!"

After sorting through all the letters and envelopes we had, we thought carefully about how to arrange them.

"I think we should use the ones with a drawing in them on the front Mama, and maybe the different colors would look nice at the bottom." I talked as I tried to arrange the letters while Mama listened as she contemplated what would really work best.

"Well, Sweetie, you can pick what letters you want in front. I think that if we arrange them at an angle, they will cascade down nicely."

Mama was good at what she did, and she always put her whole heart into her work, especially when making something for me, and this was exciting.

I prayed real hard the night before the pageant; I asked the Lord to be with me and to make Mama proud. I knew he loved us and I felt really good the next morning. Mama helped me into my dress of letters; it was beautiful and so different. I loved it! Mama had arranged envelopes for the shoulder pieces in a V-shaped plunge. The dress was cinched at the waist, and the skirt displayed all the letters, arranged by color and design, as best as mother and daughter could plan. A red elastic band held back my curled hair. I left one strand of curls loose, which fell to the side of my forehead. Red, red lipstick completed my outfit.

I sensed my face blush as I walked, twirled, and smiled at the judges. I could tell they loved my dress and it surely attracted attention. But when I heard my name announced as the winner of this year's Autumn Beauty Queen, I about fainted from excitement. I felt tears running down my cheeks even as I unsuccessfully tried to stop them. I felt like a princess and my heart pounded as I met David's prideful smile.

"My picture's in the newspaper!" I shouted out the next morning. My popularity took a different turn that year; the attention I received gave me a new and exhilarating recognition among my schoolmates.

****

Months had passed since I had won the beauty pageant, and life returned to normal. One night when Daddy came home, Bobby and I heard our parents talking downstairs, and then we could hear Mama laughing as their bedroom door closed.

We didn't like the noises we heard later, and the sounds scared Billy. "Betty, are you awake?"

"Yes I am," I knew right away what was happening, and I scooted to the far end of the bed so he could sleep next to me.

"I just feel that Mama's hurting."

"I told you she's *not* hurting." I wished they would be quieter. I vowed to myself to never make such noises where my kids can hear.

Summer came and went and I was now a senior. One day I was out fabric shopping with Pearl, something we often did since both our mothers were accomplished seamstresses. On this day, we both had prom night in mind as we sampled the many fabrics and colors.

"I think I'm going to buy my prom dress. Mama said they had beautiful dresses at Nellie's Place," said Pearl.

"Oh, they do have the most beautiful dresses there, but there's no way I can make that much money babysitting. I barely make enough to take the ballet and tap lessons."

Pearl tried to convince me that my family could surely afford to purchase one of those dresses. I knew Pearl's parents had more money and they only had one child to take care of.

"Well, Mama works all the time trying to get us one thing or another. Junior and Jimmy are pitching in more now that they're doing yard work." I felt like I had to defend Mama and shrugged my shoulders as I shifted my legs.

Pearl tried to change the subject. "I wish Betty Shepard was with us. She has changed a lot, hasn't she?"

"Well, I think that happened when she joined the Penguins. They think they're better than everyone else. Just because you have a car does *not* mean you're better." I made a face at Pearl, who laughed and agreed.

We later stopped and had ice cream. "David really likes you, Betty; a lotta guys like you."

"They like you, too Pearl."

I thought of David and felt a stirring in my heart, "I like him too; he's so nice and so sweet to me. He even goes to church with me every Sunday and now knows everyone. They all tell him how lucky he is and he always agrees. Isn't that sweet?" I said as she nodded. "I would love to see him more, but there's too much to be done,"

I took the last bite of my ice-cream and asked. "So I see you and Tommy are going out more. Do you like him?"

"I do," She sighed, "I see him almost every night."

"Well, David and I are going to the movies tonight. I'm looking forward to seeing *Holiday in Havana*. I love Desi Arnaz and think he is such a handsome man," I said as I closed my eyes.

"He sure is, I wish we had Cuban men in Knoxville." We both laughed out loud at that before she went back to talking about the movie, "That's a good movie, you'll love it Betty! It's about winning the grand rumba contest. You should relate to that with all the dancing and the contests you enter."

****

Pearl had been right. "Oh David, I loved the movie! The singing, the dancing, and the costumes they wore." I went on and on all the way home. "I wish I had time to practice more." When we arrived home, he opened the car door and walked me to the front door. He leaned over and gave me a long kiss and held me for a minute in his arms.

****

Later that year, I was awarded a full scholarship to the University of Tennessee. I ran all the way home from the bus stop. I couldn't wait to see the look on Mama's face. *This will change my life and David and I will graduate together and work side by side.*

I even knew exactly ... down to the smallest detail ... what the brick house we would build looked like, in the same way I saw all my dresses that Mama sewed.

AUTUMN BEAUTY QUEEN

Pretty **Betty Jean Clark** of Young High School was crowned Tennessee's 'Autumn Beauty Queen" in a dress she designed and made of thousands of letters and requests received at the Knoxville Tourist Bureau for information on the fall beauty of the Great Smokies. Virtually every state in the Union was represented, for autumn in the Smokies is of national travel interest. As will be noted, Miss Clark utilized envelopes for the shoulderpiece of her gown.

CHAPTER 5

SAEED IN AMERICA

I couldn't sleep; I tossed and turned all night, and knew I must have kept Yubba up. I sensed his uneven breathing. He must be awake, too. *In the morning, I will be going to America!*

Finally, the long-awaited dawn arrived, and I was able to discern the outline of the room. The hotel room held two beds, a dresser, two chairs and an armoire. My gaze softened as I watched Yubba sleep; I knew he dreaded this day. How unfair life was for this man whom I respected, admired, and loved. Sometimes I felt I had lived more than one life. I had to leave behind so many people I loved and cared for in my pursuit of a better tomorrow for my people. I knew I had the will to adapt to change, and I viewed people moving in and out of my life the way I viewed the different seasons. I continued to look at Yubba, wanting to remember everything about him. He suddenly opened his eyes, and our eyes met and locked for a silent second.

How different we looked after dressing. I wore my dark blue suit, white shirt, and multi-colored tie, while Yubba was dressed in his traditional white *gambaz* covered with a gold threaded embroidered abaya.

It was my first time in an airport and knowing that I would be sitting inside an airplane gave me chills, and those chills became stronger as I held on to Yubba. I felt his heartbeat as he tightened his grip before he let me go and turned quickly away.

Having Fou'ad with me eased my apprehension as we both disappeared into the plane. It seemed a lot smaller than I imagined, but the seats were comfortable. We both fumbled with the seat belts before figuring them out and listened to every word the pretty stewardess said. My heart plummeted whenever the plane hit an air pocket, and during the moments of calm, my thoughts went to Yubba. I wondered how he was doing on his long journey back to the Jordan Valley.

My thoughts were interrupted when Fou'ad asked me what kind of plane we were in. I looked at him but before I could shake my head left and right a man sitting across the aisle answered, "A Douglas DC-3, boys, named after its maker, Donald Douglas."

Fou'ad and I never thought that flying would be so loud, so fast, or so scary. We couldn't say a word until the plane landed, and then we sighed in relief, looked at one another, and laughed nervously. After having our passports stamped, we got our luggage, hailed a cab, and asked the driver to take us to the Dorchester Hotel. England was our first stop on the way to America.

The cab driver nodded his head and didn't say a word; we looked at each other and wondered if he understood us. We tried to see everything in the fading light of dusk while at the same time trying to get used to the left side driving. We felt as though we were going to crash at every right turn the cab took. After what seemed like another flight in uncertainty, the cab, to our immense delight, stopped at the right place.

****

So many famous London landmarks to see! Big Ben was first on our list. We spent our days sightseeing. We loved the tower of the Palace of Westminster and marveled at its structure. One church that impressed me was Christ Church, which was one hundred years old in 1949. I went into the church and sat down on one of the benches in the back, bowed my head, and recited a prayer Yumma Om Easa had taught me a long time ago. I knew that Fou'ad didn't know of my childhood. I knew that my behavior puzzled him, but I needed this time to recapture a sense of peace.

The flight to New York was long and bumpy. I tried to stay calm and did not want to admit I was scared. I remember drinking to mask my anxiety, and by the time we landed at New York's International Airport, we were more than ready to be on the ground. We were up at dawn, not yet accustomed to the time difference. Although it was 5:00 a.m. in New York, it was 10:00 a.m. in London, but more importantly it was already noon in the Middle East!

I was awed by the city. A high that day came when we both climbed to the crown of the Statue of Liberty. The view was breathtaking. We had never been so high. The Manhattan skyline left us breathless. I asked Fou'ad if he knew that the seven rays on Liberty's crown symbolized the seven seas and continents and got a nod in response. We walked through Central Park and compared it to Hyde Park in London. We marveled at the opera, hotels, restaurants, and shopping, and both had our first experience on an escalator. We had been in elevators, but these moving stairs were fast and tricky to get on and off. People stood and smiled at us laughing as we got on and off, on and off, again and again until we tired of this new novelty.

I couldn't stand the idea of being on another plane and since Fou'ad felt the same, we decided to take a cab to our next destination, no matter the cost. I mean we were in American after all, how far could Knoxville be?

We headed to the concierge with our idea and he looked puzzled at first; after we explained again, he looked even more puzzled.

"Sorry boys, but no taxi will take you to another state, especially Tennessee. I mean, do you know how many days that would take? I mean, it must be a thousand miles away. I'm afraid to say that flying is your only option, unless you buy yourselves a car and drive it down there yourselves."

Our last flight was our worst; the plane shook and swayed, making us feel sick to our stomachs. We departed the plane on shaking legs and didn't say a word until we were inside the airport.

"Thank God we don't have to be on another plane for four years," I said.

"I hope by then they have built a bridge over the Atlantic Ocean," Fou'ad responded, having regained his sense of humor.

We picked up our luggage, got into a taxi, and asked him to take us to the University of Tennessee.

Looking out the windows, I liked what I saw; green pastures and magnificent trees seemed to come alive as grass and leaves danced to the music of the wind. The cab crossed a little stream, and I admired a bridge that must have stood for many years. Most of all, I loved the many different shades of green, that seemed to sparkle under the perfectly blue sky. I loved the mountains that surrounded us where the greens blended with the blue. It was as if I was back in the mountains of Lebanon, but much greener, magical ones. I loved what I saw, and for a second I wished I was on Soda riding through this beautiful country.

****

We arrived at the Admissions Office and my first impression of the people there was a good one. Mr. Casey, a small man with brown hair and glasses over his blue eyes met us almost as soon we walked in. After shaking our hands, he asked a few questions about our trip, how to pronounce our names and other things. He told us that he had been born and raised in Tennessee, helped us with all our paper work, and later walked us to our dormitory.

I was tired but relieved to be in my new home. He talked a lot and I didn't understand everything he said, but I nodded my head and decided not to ask any questions. He later walked us to the student center and showed us where we would have our meals. Just as he was leaving he told us that the International House was going to be hosting a dinner for all the foreign students next Friday.

We settled in quite easily, and again I felt blessed that I wasn't alone. We were looking forward to the upcoming dinner and hoped to meet other Arab students.

When Friday arrived, I dressed in dark navy pants with a light blue shirt. There were about thirty people when we arrived at the small brick building with a wide porch that opened into a spacious room. A long table to the side held brochures and information about the university and the surrounding area. I leafed through the brochures, chose some, and then walked into the crowd. I spotted two young men who looked Arabic and to my delight, they were. Nabeel was from Lebanon and Jamal was an Iraqi. They had been here a year, and said that they really liked it. They told us that it had taken them a long time to get used to the local accent. We talked for a long time, and we received much beneficial information about where to eat and what to do on the weekends, as well as other domestic concerns. I also met students from many other parts of the world. Satech and Imet were from Calcutta in India; they came to the university to study civil engineering. They both wished to go back to their country, unlike Nabeel and Jamal, who wanted to stay in America and become a part of the American dream. In a short time, all of us became close and met on a daily basis.

"Life isn't easy when we don't conform to the norm, especially when most others are part of the mainstream, as is the case in Knoxville," Satech said, as he made tea for us one afternoon. "I know people are very sweet here, and they are very nice, but I know they hold prejudices, and we as foreign students are no exception to the wrath of that rule." His voice betrayed his strong emotion, and even though I felt bad for him I didn't really know what he meant.

"We need to have fun this weekend; I wonder where we can go and get a beer?" Fou'ad asked when he really wished to change the subject.

Jamal replied, "Tennessee is a dry state, didn't you know that?"

I had never heard this term and wondered out loud, "What does 'dry state' mean?"

"It means it is against the law to sell any alcoholic beverages in the state of Tennessee," Jamal answered.

"Not only that," Nabeel added, "it is also illegal to bring alcohol from a wet state into a dry state."

That night I thought about all that and wondered why Fou'ad got so upset. I knew that we never drank before going to Beirut and for sure could not drink in front of our parents. I didn't think it was a big deal and really wasn't sure I wanted to travel to another state to smuggle alcohol.

That weekend, I suggested going to the Bijou to watch a Gregory Peck movie. He was one of my first favorite actors. I asked if Satech knew how to get to it. He said he did and that we needed to get on bus number 17. It wasn't long after we climbed the steps and sat down until we noticed the bus driver looking at us in an unfriendly fashion.

He then blurted out, "You need to go to the back of the bus."

At first, I wasn't sure he was talking to us and then realized that he was addressing Satech, in particular, and looking at me in an uncertain fashion. I didn't understand. Were we dressed improperly, or was this a bus for Americans only? All of a sudden, Satech sprang up, stood almost in the bus driver's face, and said quietly, "I am an Indian student at the University of Tennessee, and I will sit where I want to sit!" With that, he stormed back a few steps and sat back in his seat.

"What is going on?" I asked Imet as he sat beside me.

He said, "Do you see who is sitting in the back of the bus?"

I looked then, and noticed a couple of black women with two young children and an older, lighter man.

"You mean that black people sit in the back of the bus?"

"Yes, and because Satech is dark, the bus driver thinks he is black and should sit in the back. This has happened before and is very unfortunate."

Now I understood what Satech was referring to the other day when he had talked about prejudices, and it astounded me. It wasn't that I had never heard about slavery. I had read about it, but it is totally different living something and reading about it.

"I thought the American Civil War ended any discrimination."

"It ended slavery, Saeed, not discrimination."

"I believe it is up to every person to think of what is right and what is wrong. How can the color of one's skin make one superior to another? And when do you get dark enough or light enough?" My thoughts were on many of my people and wondered how many would be considered black.

As we stepped down from the bus the drive bestowed upon us another unfriendly look, but we ignored him and stepped onto the sidewalk beside Gay Street. I didn't feel like seeing a movie at that point, and voiced my feelings.

But Satech insisted that we shouldn't let anyone ruin our plans. Inside the theater, I noticed an upper balcony where black people were sitting.

"So I guess this is the back of the bus." I sarcastically asked before adding, "How come the lady in the ticket booth didn't ask any of us to sit in the upper balcony?"

"We already had that mishap on an earlier visit, and I guess she now recognized us as the 'horrible foreigners," Satech said as he gave Imet a knowing look.

The movie was what we needed; it was about a famous writer, played by Gregory Peck, who was lured into gambling by beautiful Pauline Ostrovsky, played by Ava Gardner. The movie was a heavy melodrama that exposed how gamblers can ruin their lives with addiction to the intermittent reward of winning. It had however, a good ending.

The next day Nabeel and I went to the library where I learned that America before World War II had been completely segregated. "Can you imagine that just four years ago it was generally illegal for blacks to attend the same schools as whites, attend theaters patronized by whites, visit parks where whites relax, and eat, sleep, or meet in hotels, restaurants, or public halls frequented by whites?" I looked up from the paper I was reading and sighed heavily.

"Well, you know, such is life. There is always one kind of discrimination or another going on." Nabeel shook his head as he walked away in search of a book he needed.

When he came back, he gave me a quizzical look, "Saeed, why are you so upset? Most of the people we meet here are very nice to us. Come, let's go buy an ice cream or something sweet to eat."

"I'm upset because we are prejudiced against color in our own countries, too."

"No way, Saeed. How did you come up with that conclusion? I mean, I have never met a black Lebanese." Nabeel's face expressed astonishment, with his eyes bulging.

"That's part of the problem, Nabeel. We have few blacks in the Middle East. The majority of blacks live in Africa, and we don't associate those countries with any status. We refer to Europe and America as the advanced countries of the world, the countries we wish to emulate."

"Saeed, African countries themselves think that Europe and America are more advanced than we are. Does that mean they are prejudiced against us?"

"Well, don't we think the lighter you are, the better looking you are?"

"That does not mean we are prejudiced, it just means we all like what is the norm. I am sure in Switzerland they would not think that way because they are all fair."

"I guess you're right. Maybe I'm just sensitive because it feels personal to me."

"Saeed, since ancient times, we have had slavery in the Middle East, as elsewhere. Slavery is confirmed from the very earliest written records, among the Sumerians, the Babylonians, the Egyptians, and other ancient peoples. The earliest slaves were captives taken in warfare."

I realized that he was speaking the truth, "You're right, Nabeel, you are right. Let's go get ice cream."

Saeed at the University of Tennessee

CHAPTER 6

THE COURTSHIP

I couldn't wait to tell Mama that David had asked me to the UT dance! I knew she would be just as excited as I was, and sure enough, she began planning a new dress.

"I can make you a dress out of the red organza, or maybe the white muslin would be better?"

"No Mama, not the red organza. You've been saving it to make something special for yourself. I really don't think I need a new dress."

It didn't take too much for Mama to convince me that a new dress would cost about the same as fixing up an old one, and would be fun to shop for. We talked more and decided to go into town. I felt lucky when we found a deep-scarlet crinoline and matching lace that would be perfect for the Vogue pattern I had chosen. It was a strapless dress with a shelf bodice and a bolero jacket with a rounded collar and cap sleeves. I had saved some money from working and didn't mind spending it one bit.

I couldn't sleep that night and kept thinking about what the dress should look like and what David would think. He had given me his class ring two weeks ago, and I accepted. I could imagine myself married to him and living close to home. I thought about Betty Shepard and how much I missed talking to her. I remembered telling her once that I wanted to live in a beautiful brick house with lots of windows. She and I had even looked at and thought of buying the same pattern of dishware when we got married so we could share when we entertained more than three couples. I lay listening to the night sounds and fell asleep thinking of the gown made of letters and the white orchids Mama had woven into my prom dress. I knew Mama was going to make me another gorgeous dress.

****

Music could be heard the minute we stepped out of the car. I could hear Nat King Cole's song, "Too Young."

"Oh, how I love that song!" I hurried as I held onto David. These events were few and far between, and everyone expected a great time. I wasn't disappointed when we entered the lighted ballroom. All the tables had flower arrangements on them and were arranged in a semicircle around a big dance floor. Elevated on a stage, the band members were all dressed alike in black suits with golden shirts, and they were exceptionally good musicians. David led me to a table with two empty seats close to the dance floor and asked what I wanted to drink. I said RC Cola and watched him go off to the refreshment stand. I remember looking around the ballroom and then I noticed this man. He looked sharp in his trousers, shirt, and jacket. He reminded me of Ricky Ricardo, but with a mustache.

David and I danced almost every dance and I was having a great time. During the evening, from time to time, I would glance at this man and although I saw him dancing with a few ladies, I knew he was watching me. I showed off my dress and my dancing as I twirled in my date's arms. It was getting late and David and I were probably dancing our last dance when I saw this man striding toward us. *Oh, my Lord, is he going to ask me to dance?*

The stranger tapped David on his shoulder and asked permission to dance with me.

"No." David's response was quick and tinged with irritation; I was sure he had noticed this man looking at me all evening.

I sensed this man's uneasiness and thought he was going to turn away when he suddenly looked at me. I smiled at him and felt my heart skip a beat when he tapped David again and said, "I would like to hear the lady's answer."

David gave me a disbelieving gawk when I glided into the stranger's arms and soon twirled away, and then farther away, from him.

****

I couldn't believe that I was dancing with this woman who had captivated my senses. I had seen her soon after Fou'ad and I entered the ballroom. He had talked me into coming, saying it might be a good chance to meet someone. I had gone out with a few ladies and liked southern women. They were sweet, polite, and pretty, but I had not felt strong feelings for any ... until I laid my eyes on her.

"Thank you for dancing with me." I smiled gently as I maneuvered her away from the gaping man. I sensed her nervousness and noticed her reddened cheeks as my brain raced to say something to put her at ease. I thought if she started to talk, she would feel more comfortable.

"You're a really good dancer. I've been watching you all night. Where did you learn to dance so well?" *I shouldn't have said I was watching her all evening!*

"I took ballet and tap lessons, and I love to dance." She answered as she looked up at me for a second. She suddenly asked, looking surprised herself. "Where are you from?"

"Jordan. It borders the Jordan River and the Holy Land."

"Oh my, I've never met anyone from there."

As we talked, the song ended, and I felt she was as reluctant as I was to separate when I quickly blurted out, "I'm sorry, but I haven't introduced myself. My name is Saeed Al-Gazzawiya."

"Nice to meet you, I'm Betty Clark."

"May I call you? Do you mind giving me your phone number?" I squeezed her hands, "I really want to see you again," Just as she was giving me her number, I saw the man she had been dancing with walking toward us, and he didn't look too pleased with the situation. She quickly thanked me for the dance and hurried away.

I stood in the middle of the dance floor, repeating her phone number over and over.

******

Although I went home with David, we both knew that things were not right. I wanted to say something, but I had no idea what. During the silent drive back home, I overflowed with a feeling that rocked me inside out. I had never met anyone like that handsome man.

Mama was up and Daddy wasn't yet back from work when I walked in. David didn't want to stay for a cup of coffee when Mama offered him one and said he needed to go back to work on some homework.

I told Mama what had happened and she wasn't too happy about it. We didn't talk a lot because we heard Daddy's car pull in the driveway. I kissed my parents goodnight and headed up to my room filled with contradicting emotions.

I waited for him to call the next day and raced to answer the phone every time it rang. I kept asking Mama if she thought he was going to call, and knew she was getting a little tired of it, but I just couldn't help it. My mind kept going back to dancing in his arms. I couldn't stop thinking about him. The phone rang right after dinner, just as I was clearing the table. I nearly knocked the dishes out of my hands as I dashed around and prayed *Dear Jesus, let it be him*. I repeated the words until I reached the phone.

"Hello, my name is Saeed, and I would like to talk to Betty, please."

I felt my stomach churning as I tried to sound normal. "This is Betty. I didn't think you were going to remember my phone number!" I blurted out before I could stop myself. I heard him chuckle and felt heat creeping up to my face.

"I was calling to ask if you would like to go to the movies with me this Saturday." His voice shimmered like velvet.

"I would love to go to the movies with you." I was in seventh heaven as I gave him directions to our home.

"I will be there at 6 o'clock. I am looking forward to seeing you again."

"Yes, thank you. Good bye." I hung up and then felt stupid. I shouldn't have thanked him; I should have said that I, too, look forward to seeing him. What is the matter with me?

I walked back into the kitchen with the biggest grin my face could hold. "Oh, Mama, you should have heard his voice. What am I going to wear Saturday?"

"What are you going to do about David, Sweetie? It ain't right going out with this guy when you're wearing someone else's ring."

"I know, Mama, I'll tell David I'm going out Saturday night. Oh, Mama, it's going to be awful. I don't want to hurt David. Oh Mama, he's not going to like this."

"I hate to see this happening. We all like David and we know everything about him. I know he loves you and he would be a fine husband. I just don't want to see you make a mistake."

I knew Mama didn't like the fact that Saeed was from a different country. The next day, I told David about my Saturday night date. It was one of the hardest things I've ever done. I tried to explain how I felt, but he didn't understand one bit. His lips seemed to disappear as he pursed them before saying, "All I can say is that you're making a mistake, a big mistake, Betty. This guy is a foreigner, and God only knows what or how he thinks. He is not like us."

I hung my head and felt terrible. I held out his ring and looked up to see him shaking his head before walking away. He turned just as he got into his car, "I gave you that ring and it will always be yours. You know I will always love you, Betty."

I ran inside, up the stairs and flung myself on my bed and cried.

****

I dressed carefully in my brown trousers and pale yellow shirt; I always seemed to get more compliments when I wore lighter colors. A checkered jacket completed my attire. I parted my short hair to one side, except for one lock that curled over my forehead. I had no problems getting to Betty's place.

By now I knew the customs of dating and I rang the doorbell. The door opened almost instantly. She looked beautiful in a white blouse tucked into the waistband of a striped black and white swing skirt. Her hair was pulled back in a ponytail, tied with a black chiffon ribbon. She looked much younger than the young lady in the red dress twirling around, and I thought that she was even more beautiful than I remembered.

I had always felt somewhat uncomfortable when I met people for the first time. Most acted polite, but in a few instances, I felt they weren't thrilled about their daughters dating men from another country. I followed her into the foyer, which was small and low, before we walked into the living room. Her mother and brothers were staring at me. I walked to her mother, shook her hand and introduced myself first before I said hello to the rest. Betty got really red when her mother asked me my age, but I answered that I was twenty years old. I sensed her relief when she nodded and told me that I was two years older than Betty. She asked me to have a seat. I sat down and answered more questions as I sipped on the lemonade Betty brought me. When I finished, I stood up and said we needed to leave so we wouldn't miss the movie. Everyone walked us outside and her mother told us to have a good time and not to be late.

I opened the door for her as everyone watched then got into my 1946 Ford Tudor Sedan and pulled onto the road. I could see Betty fidgeting with her hands and wondered what in the world I could say to her as Brenda Lee serenaded us with "I'm Sorry." I looked at her and she seemed intent on listening to the words of the song. I told her I really liked that music. She modestly nodded her head and I barely heard her say, "Yes, it is very nice."

"I looked at the movies playing, and I thought that you might enjoy *Giselle*.

She flashed beautiful teeth at me as she said "Oh, I wanted to see that movie!" I noticed her lean a bit in my direction and wondered what it would be like to kiss her.

We found two seats in the center of the theater and sat down to watch the movie. We hardly spoke during the show, but when it finished, I felt she was more at ease as she excitedly talked about it and

70

how wonderfully it ended. I didn't want this night to ever be over and I wanted to hear her talk all night.

"Would you like to go get a milkshake, or do I need to get you home?" I asked hopefully.

"I would love a milkshake." She said as she lowered her eyes as if to inspect her shoes.

As I drove toward the S&W Cafeteria, I talked about Jordan, Yubba, and the tribe. She looked wide eyed as she said, "You mean a tribe like the Cherokees?"

I couldn't help laughing out loud as she laughed with me, "No, it is very different. We live in tents or huts made out of mud and straw. We also dress differently." Then a thought hit me, "Have you ever seen pictures of how Jesus dressed?" she nodded and I continued, "That's how Arab Bedouins dress."

"Oh my, I can't imagine what it would be like to be brought up near the Jordan River."

We talked and laughed for the rest of the evening. She kept asking me questions about Yubba and how I must miss him. She asked how I had felt being in the boarding school. She even asked how it had felt being on a plane for the first time. I enjoyed answering her questions and many made me reflect on how I truly felt. I wanted to answer her as honestly as I could while trying to read her facial expressions. I hated for the night to end. I parked the car, opened the door for Betty, and began walking her to the front door.

"I really had a great time, and I enjoyed the movie. Thank you!"

"I too enjoyed talking to you and the movie was really good too. Will it be okay if I call you tomorrow?"

Her smile and nod gave me the courage I needed to lean down and give her a light kiss. I felt her lips quiver slightly as I felt warmth going up my spine. It took all my strength to stop and walk her to the door where I said my goodbye to both mother and daughter. I had this uncanny feeling that Betty Clark was going to play a big role in my life.

Back in the car, I turned the radio on and thought of those lips.

I could not stop thinking about her and called her the next day. We talked for a good ten minutes and I asked her out again. I didn't

71

want to hang up but I knew that it would be best not to talk too long. I couldn't wait to see her again.

****

Fou'ad and I were supposed to drive to somewhere in North Carolina to buy liquor the next morning. We woke up to snow and I didn't think it was a good idea, but he insisted and I went along. It didn't seem bad the first few hours and we both talked about Lebanon as we drove higher into the mountains. Fou'ad had directions but we still got a little lost before we found the place. We bought four bottles each and headed back after we ate the sandwiches we had made. By then the snow was coming down harder and after a couple of hours, we could barely see the road. I felt the car slip slightly to the right.

"Stop the car Fou'ad. We can't drive in this." My high pitched voice betrayed my nervousness as he stopped. It didn't take long before it started getting cold and we both began shivering. I started to really worry as the snow got higher and higher; I thought we were going to be buried alive. We needed to find shelter so we got out and started to walk. We walked for a while before we saw lights at a distance. We ran up as we blew into our freezing hands and knew we were taking a chance. I had heard that mountain people didn't like strangers and I felt fear as we knocked at the door. The door opened and a man stood staring at us, and asked us what were we doing out in a blizzard.

We explained that we were students studying at the University of Tennessee, we were visiting friends, our car was down the road and we were freezing. We asked him to help us.

I felt God was watching over us when he allowed us into his home. The next day, after a breakfast of bacon, eggs, and biscuits, we thanked the kind farmer and his wife for their hospitality and walked back to our car. Luckily the weather had warmed up and we were able to drive back to Knoxville.

When we arrived safely home, I felt very blessed and decided that if I happened to live in an alcohol free state, then I didn't need to drink. I took each of the four bottles of whiskey and flushed their contents down the commode as Fou'ad called me crazy.

The coming weeks changed my life. I wanted to spend as much time as I could with Betty and I especially wanted to make her happy. Getting to know her and her family brought me more happiness than I thought possible. I knew from the beginning that she was religious and went to church every Sunday. I liked that about her. I liked the fact that she would not let me hold her too close or kiss her too long, yet she quivered in my arms. She told me that they all followed her mother's affiliation and that her father didn't often go to church with them. I didn't understand the difference but I was glad her father was not as strict. I liked him the minute I saw him. He had a genuine smile on his face as he shook my hands. "Have a seat son", were his first words to me. I sat down on the couch next to his arm chair and Betty sat down beside me. He asked what I was studying and how many classes I was taking. I felt his gaze on me even when I talked with Betty. He asked more questions and as I drank the last of my ice tea, he asked me how much I knew about cars. I told him I loved cars and then he asked me if I had been to a football game. When I said, "Never," he said, "We'll have to fix that," as Betty's brothers joined his laughter.

I went to my first football game almost a week later. Ernest and all of Betty's brothers had orange caps on. Her father even had one for me. I had never worn a cap and felt a little uncomfortable at first, but by the end of the day, easily joined in the fun. Everyone in the family was dressed in orange and white University of Tennessee collared shirts. I had on khaki pants and was so grateful that I had worn a white shirt.

We drove down in two cars and found a parking place not far from Shields-Watkins Field. It was larger than I expected and formed a horseshoe with bleacher seating on both sides. At the end two huge steel signs announced the scores. I had heard about cheerleaders and I really thought they were very pretty and very talented in person. They were handing out white and orange pom pons and we all had one to wave when the University of Tennessee team scored. I tried to follow the game and Ernest and Betty both tried to explain what was going on.

The highlight of my first game came at half time when a beautiful sleek black horse strode into the arena and pranced all around the stadium for all to admire. I told Betty about my horse, Soda, thousands of miles away and she squeezed my hand and smiled up at me. We ate popcorn, peanuts and hot dogs and drank a lot of Coca Cola. I told Betty about the first time Fou'ad and I had seen a "Hot Dogs" sign and actually thought it was dog meat. She laughed so hard she had tears in her eyes, and laughed again as she related the story to her family. The weather was perfect and I had a great time with everyone. I felt a part of this family and from then on never missed a game. After a few times, I began to understand what was going on, and enjoyed the game much more.

I enjoyed this sense of belonging. I never realized how much I missed being in a family. Betty's family loved going on picnics and I agreed after my first outing. With time, Betty and I began to go on our own picnics and this became an almost weekly ritual for us. I always enjoyed the drive and scenery. The mountains reminded me of Aley, and I told her about my life and many of my adventures in Beirut.

One night as we were talking, Betty said, "I've never seen a belly dancer. I don't think that sounds like dancing at all."

"Maybe one day you will. I believe you'll change your mind when you see one. It takes a lot of talent and practice to become a really good belly dancer."

I could tell she wasn't convinced and I liked that she was jealous. I knew I was falling in love with her but instead of saying that, I told her I was hungry. She quickly started taking the food out of the basket and laying it on the blanket I had spread near the water. I loved the fried chicken she made and I couldn't eat enough of the potato salad. I loved her cooking and she beamed and thanked me. She sat in front of me as we ate and talked.

These afternoons lulled my senses. "The world that God created for us is a world full of wondrous colors and breathtaking scenery. God didn't just create green, blue, or pink; he gave us an array of greens, blues, and pinks. We live in a world that can take our breath away when we choose to be a part of it, or when we become aware of living in it."

"You should be a poet. I love how you say things." She looked up into my eyes and I could smell her scent. I pulled her closer and captured her parted lips with mine.

Later on, as we packed to leave, she asked, "Would you like to come to church with me on Sunday?"

"Yes, that would be fine." I knew that I should have discussed my religious background with her before, but I didn't know how to approach it. I welcomed her chatter as we drove back. I walked her to the door, kissed her lightly and said "I can't stay because I need to finish writing a paper which is due tomorrow." That was partly true; I had a paper due on Monday. But I also needed to be alone to sort out my own feelings.

I heard Fou'ad in the kitchen as soon as I walked into the apartment. He grinned at me as I headed to the fridge.

"You sure are spending a lot of time with Betty."

"Oh Fou'ad, I have fallen in love with her. I want to be with her all the time."

"Be careful, we are not Americans; our world is different and very far away."

"I know that and have thought about it many times, but I can't help the way I feel"

"How do you think your father would feel? This is not why he sent you to America!"

I had to drink a sip of water before I could answer. I knew he was right but I didn't want to hear it. "I know, but I have met many of her family, and they are good people. I like her mother, and brothers, and I really like her father. I guess the important thing is that I love her."

"If you love her, do you think she will be happy living in our world?"

"That I do worry about, but whenever I bring it up, she says all she wants is to be with me."

"Where will you live Saeed? Surely, you don't think she will be happy in the Valley?"

"No, I don't think she will," I sighed and ruffled my hair to clear my thoughts. Although Yubba now lived in a stone house in the Valley, and not a tent, I knew she would not like to live with my family. The truth was that I too did not wish to live in the Valley.

"I was thinking that we could live in Irbid until I can find the right job and hopefully move to Amman." Even as I spoke I felt confused, "Oh Fou'ad, I wish America wasn't so far away and Yubba could come and meet her. I know he would understand!"

"Wishful thinking, my friend! This is a trip we take once in a lifetime, and it is to get an education. And by the way Saeed, I don't think he would understand. Do you realize that Betty would be the first American woman to marry into a Bedouin Tribe in Jordan?"

Although I knew his words were true, they still struck a chord in me. I nodded and could think of nothing to say. *He's right; I am doing something big. Oh God, why did I have to fall madly in love with her?* He looked at me and sort of shrugged his shoulders.

"Good luck, my friend. Betty is a beautiful girl, and she is the sweetest person I ever met."

I asked him if he was working on his paper as I got my book and sat down to do what I needed for my classes the next day. He said he hoped to finish it in a couple of hours. He asked if I would like a cup of tea and I said that would be great.

It was late by the time I finished my homework and when I went to bed, I kept thinking of Yubba and of Fou'ad's words. I had come to America to get a degree, go back and live with my tribesmen, and make their world better. I had worked hard in my classes and made good grades. I wanted to learn as much as possible and make Yubba proud. I stared at the ceiling and wished for an answer.

I needed to write Yubba about Betty, but knew in my heart that he would not like the idea of my marrying an American woman. I usually wrote him a letter once a month, mostly so he would know that I was well and that school was going fine. I had thought of mentioning Betty a couple of times, but I never did. I knew I couldn't sleep until I did, so I decided to get out of bed and pour my heart out.

My Dear Yubba,
I pray my letter finds you, Yumma Arifa, Yumma Nuzha, my brothers, and sisters in the best of health. I

am doing well and I am learning new things every day in school. Two years have passed and God willing I will be graduating in another two. I count the days to our union and always miss you.

Yubba, you know how much you mean to me and how much I respect and honor your wishes. I am writing to tell you about a woman I have met. I have found the woman God intended for me. After years of wondering who my mate will be, I now know the woman I want to spend the rest of my life with. She is as pure as rainwater and as gentle as a lamb. She makes me complete and happy. Her beauty is not only skin deep. It radiates from within to her exterior, beautiful inside and out. I can't doubt that you will love her when, God willing, you see her. I know you wish for me to marry a girl from my country and faith, but I also know you wish me happiness.

Yubba, I wish for your blessing to make my union complete and holy. I pray that it will arrive soon, for only then will my happiness be complete.

Two years, Yubba, and I will be back with you.

Respectfully and with all my love,

Your son, Saeed

****

The drive to the church was short, and as we emerged from the car, dressed in our best, Saeed commented on the size of the building and said he had expected it to be bigger. I said that Baptist churches were larger and had more people than the Church of Christ congregations and hoped that he knew the difference. As we walked in, I proudly introduced him to everyone; he shook hands and answered questions before I led him into an aisle between the pews. After the pastor came in and preached his sermon, Saeed said that he really liked the singing and told me it reminded him of his mother's singing. He went on to tell me the story of how his father had had to give him up if he wanted him

77

to live. I was mesmerized by what I heard. If he hadn't been so serious, I would have thought he was joking. I looked into his eyes as he spoke of being raised by a Christian family.

"You're not a Christian?" My heart skipped a beat as it raced in my chest.

Saeed scooted closer and held my hand as he looked into my eyes and said, "Before I answer your question, I want to tell you that I love you and the answer to your question is that I am a Muslim."

I had a dizzying moment. *He loves me!* "I love you, too, Saeed, so much." Then I remembered he had said something about himself. "What does 'mulsim' mean?"

"No Honey, m-u-s-l-i-m, Muslim. Islam is the third monotheistic religion, and we believe in the one God and only the one God. We believe in Abraham, Isaac, Jacob, and all his descendants. We also believe in Jesus, and we hold the Virgin Mary in very high esteem. We simply believe that, due to misinterpretations in the bible, God sent the last prophet, Mohammad, to lead the people onto the right path."

"You mean your prophet is a saint?" This was all too strange for me, but I kept thinking that *he loves me.*

"Maybe you can think of him as such, but I don't know." Saeed looked confused as he struggled to find the right words, "I believe we are who we are due to where, when, and to whom we are born. If I had been born into the household that my father put me in, then I would have been a Christian, but we can't pick our destiny."

"Maybe that's why God brought you here." I said as I searched his face for agreement.

"Honey, I love and believe in God. Our God is the same God. I remember being confused the first time I discovered the world had more than one faith."

"When did you discover that?" Saeed was so different from anyone I knew. When he told me about living with a priest and his wife until he was seven years old it gave me hope.

"This means you were raised a Christian, Saeed."

"At seven, I went back to the tribe and began to take Muslim classes with my brothers. Betty, religion to me is one's yearning to connect with the Creator. The more we converse from the heart, the more we realize the differences are minute, and the common themes are numerous. We are concentrating on the messenger instead of thinking about the message."

I tried to comprehend it all as I thought of how I was going to break this news to Mama. I knew she wasn't going to like this. I slept fretfully that night; I kept tossing and thinking of Saeed's words. The next morning I decided to tell Mama what happened. She reacted exactly as I thought she would.

"What do you mean he's not a Christian?" she knitted her brow for a second, "I mean, I know that not everyone is a Christian, that's why we have missionaries. I just didn't figure he wasn't. He seemed comfortable in the church."

Well, I told Mama what Saeed told me about his childhood, and she was awed at the story. Finally she just said "Keep asking him to come to church with us, Sweetie."

Saeed did continue to come to church with us on Sundays and that filled me with hope and more love for him. I wanted to be with him all the time and felt miserable the minute he left me. We saw each other almost every night. He told me he was going to take me to the Regas, the fanciest restaurant in Knoxville, to celebrate our six months' anniversary. I was excited and couldn't make my mind up on what to wear. I could hear Mama talking to someone about Saeed taking me to the Regas. I heard the pride in Mama's voice, and it made me happy. I finally chose a dark green dress, because its pencil style skirt showed my shape. I was putting on my lipstick when I heard the doorbell.

"Hello, there," I said coyly, feeling confident and beautiful. I knew he liked my choice of dress by the look of admiration that couldn't possibly be missed. He told me I looked beautiful and gave me a quick kiss and inched around me to enter the living room. Billy ran and hugged him. He ruffled Jimmy's and Bobby's hair before he gave Mama a peck on her cheek. We stood for a few moments talking mostly about the weather and how unpredictable it was in East Tennessee.

Saeed laughed. "At least you have an idea of what the weather is going to be like. In Jordan, they don't have *any* weather reports, accurate or not."

"How do you know what the weather will be like?" my cousin Patsy asked as she walked in from the kitchen.

"I don't know about everyone, but the tribesmen can tell if it is going to be cold, hot, or if the much awaited rains will come or not. The Bedouins live in nature. A life with no electricity is often a life linked to nature and God's waking and sleeping hours, instead of our own."

The meal at the restaurant was perfect. I wanted to remember everything about this evening to tell Mama, Daddy, and my brothers. It was grander than I had imagined. Dark maroon carpets trimmed with gold shimmered in the lights of beautiful chandeliers. The tables were made of dark mahogany, and beautiful burgundy leather covered the chairs. When I sank into my chair, I felt engulfed by it. I liked the luxurious feeling of this place. We ordered steaks and had iced tea with the meal. The waiter brought our drinks in tall glasses tapered at the bottom. The steaks were perfect, and we enjoyed every morsel. Saeed even ordered the chocolate cake and I loved the creamy texture of it and wondered what they added to make it so moist. I looked up to tell him what a wonderful time I was having and noticed he had not taken one bite out of his cake.

"Is something wrong?"

"No, Honey, nothing's wrong." He squeezed my hand and gave me a smile that brightened my heart, "In fact, everything is perfect. Are you having a good time?"

"Oh yes, I'm having a great time!"

We both started to laugh and I began to feel relaxed. I took a sip of my tea and as I set the glass on the table, I saw Saeed placing a jewelry box in front of me. I looked at him as I felt my face burning; I touched the velvet box and felt the heat transfer to my hands. I carefully removed the wrapping. I felt a churning in my stomach; I had wanted Saeed to propose more than anything. My mind raced as I opened the box and prayed that it was a ring. It was the most beautiful ring I had ever seen! It was a platinum, round, three-stone diamond ring. Two smaller stones flanked the center diamond in an intricate, woven design.

"Will you marry me, Betty?" he asked bent on one knee, staring at me with all the love he had for me; it felt like all I had for him.

"Yes." I could hardly speak through my tears. I started to laugh as tears of joy streamed down my cheeks. Other diners began to clap and I felt I was going to faint from the events of the evening. Instead, we accepted hugs and handshakes from strangers.

I knew Mama and Daddy loved Saeed but I also knew they worried that he would take me to a country far away.

"I know he'll be a good husband, and he'll take care of you," Daddy said, as he grabbed another biscuit and put it on his plate. "I just wish he'd stay in America and not go back to his country."

"Oh Lord, I would hate to have you go far away, Sweetie." Mama said as she gave me a troubled look.

"I don't know why you're worried about something that's not going to happen for another two years. A lot can happen from now till then. He can change his mind and decide to stay here." I looked down at my ring and slightly caressed it before I said, "I love Saeed and I want to marry him more than anything else in the world. I don't know why the Lord had to pick someone from another country. I mean, it takes about a week of traveling to get to the Jordan Valley. Can you imagine that?"

"I know," Daddy said, "I asked Saeed if his parents were coming to the wedding and he told me that it is too far."

"I think that's the saddest part Daddy, because Saeed adores his father. You would not believe the stories he tells me about him. I want to see him because when Saeed is talking about his childhood I feel I am listening to one of the *One Thousand and One Nights* stories." I smiled at Daddy, who shook his head and looked at Mama,

"Your daughter is crazy about him, Lolli. There's nothing you and I can do about that. She'll go with him to the end of the world if he asks her."

"I know, but what about his religion?"

"He goes to church almost every week. That's more than I do."

I knew Mama didn't like that, but I did, and I felt better. "Saeed believes in God and believes that we all have different ways of reaching him." I was repeating what he told me in one of our conversations about religion. "God is capable of making us all similar and alike, and the divine reason for our being different is to watch how we accept the difference and transfer it into acceptance for one another."

By considering Saeed's views, I found that my own thinking was expanding. But I still didn't really want to know too much about Islam. I kissed Mama and Daddy goodnight and went upstairs.

****

Saeed and I were going to visit Grandpa and Grandma Riley the next day, and I was not looking forward to that. I just wished everyone would stop looking at him as a foreigner and would just accept him as he was.

The next day, we headed out to my grandparents' place. The drive was not long, and I hoped Grandpa Riley would be nice to Saeed; I had a good feeling about Grandma, though. She was the sweetest person and liked everyone. Saeed parked and walked around to open the car door for me. Just then, we saw Grandpa come out on the porch and then go back inside. I couldn't believe that he didn't want to even meet Saeed. I felt hurt and anger at the same time as I held Saeed's hand and walked up to the house. Saeed comforted me and said, "It's okay, not everyone likes foreigners."

Just as I was about to say something, I saw Grandpa Riley come out with a shotgun in his hands, to my utter dismay and Saeed's horror.

"No dang furriner is gonna take my Betty away from me." He pointed his shotgun at Saeed who continued to walk toward him.

"Grandpa Riley, you put that gun away, or I'll never come back to see you again." I was so embarrassed. I put my hand on Saeed's arm. "Please don't go up there; he'll shoot you. Let's get out of here. I'm so mad." My hands were shaking and I felt my legs getting wobbly, too.

"Betty, he's not going to shoot me," Saeed said, and despite my words, he continued to walk toward my grandfather. When he was only a couple of feet away, he extended his arm and said, "I was raised by a man who taught me not to run away from something you want. I love Betty and I wish to marry her. She loves you and I want you to bless our union."

82

I'm sure this didn't last more than a couple of seconds, but I felt it was an hour before Grandpa Riley finally put down his shotgun. Grandma Riley rushed over and took it away from him.

"I'm ashamed at ya, acting this way and scaring the daylight out of Betty. Shame on ya! You shake this man's hand."

She hugged me and calmed my shakes as Grandpa took Saeed's still extended hand. We stayed a long time with my grandparents, talking, drinking lemonade, and answering questions. By the end of the evening, Saeed had won them over with his polite and soft spoken ways.

What a story. I still can't believe Grandpa Riley did that! I felt great relief that the meeting with my grandparents was behind us. Now I could concentrate on my wedding.

****

"This is the one, Sweetie! I can see you in it." Mama held the pattern up for me. The cover of the package displayed a lithe female in a wedding dress. The gown modeled an intermediate style ranging from the shoulders of the forties to the narrow look of the fifties. Two rows of ruffles surrounded the neckline in the customary off-the-shoulder style. "These ruffles will show off your beautiful shoulders."

"That is so pretty, Mama. It's what I had in mind, too. I like the shoulders and the sleek look. What material do you think would work best for this design?"

"I think muslin and chiffon," Mama said, as she mulled that over in her mind. "They're not the easiest fabrics to work with, but this is a special dress and I don't mind the extra hours."

I couldn't make up my mind about the exact color I wanted my dress to be.

"It's got to be white. I mean, it is a wedding dress," Mama said firmly.

After more talk, we decided to go with a shade of pearl-white chiffon to adorn the top layer of the dress as well as the veil.

We also decided to tailor an off-white muslin lining underneath the chiffon to give the entire dress some shimmer and just the right texture.

Saeed and Betty

CHAPTER 7

THE WEDDING BLISS

It had been a couple of months since I sent Yubba the letter, and I anxiously waited for a reply. I wished to have his blessings before I got married in two days. The next day, I received the letter I had been waiting for. I tore it open, but as I began reading his words, I felt a constriction in my heart. I didn't expect him to be happy, but the anger in his words hurt my eyes and penetrated my soul. My hands shook when I read the last words:

> *You will no longer be my son, and I will no longer acknowledge you. I will disown you if you marry this woman.*

I stood staring at the sheet of paper in front of my eyes. For the first time in my life, I felt abandoned. I could not believe Yubba would write and send such horrible words. He didn't give Betty a chance; he didn't want to or wish to give her a chance. Of course she was Christian, but so what? The Prophet himself had married a Christian woman.

I had never disobeyed Yubba and I never thought this day would come. I wished I could see him face to face and tell him how I felt. Why did I have to travel so far to get an education? I knew then that it was going to be four years, but I never knew my life would change so much in just two of those years. It was different being in America. I had learned to adapt but now felt confused. I tried to write a letter, but could not continue as I began to cry. I couldn't give Betty up, and the thought of never seeing Yubba again hurt. I wanted to help the tribe. Why was he being so headstrong? I had expected he wouldn't be happy and even thought he would say a few strong words, but to *disown* me? I don't know how long I cried as I held my face in my hands. Finally, I walked to the mirror on top of the dresser and looked at my reflection and said aloud, "Saeed, God is in control and he brought you here for a reason. You will marry Betty and if it is meant for you to go back to Jordan, you will do that too."

Fou'ad could tell something was wrong with me from my red eyes and solemn face. He looked at me with many questions in his eyes. I handed him the letter, and he read as silence filled the room. When he finished, he said he was sorry and asked what I was going to do. I told him I knew that Betty was the woman for me. He asked if Betty knew about this and I said I was going to tell her, but decided not to ruin her big day tomorrow.

******

I tossed and turned in bed as my mind swirled. *Saeed and I will be married tomorrow. I will be Mrs. Saeed El-Gazzawiya.* I liked the sound of that and smiled in the darkness. My body reacted to my thoughts with a wave of heat that flooded my being. Memories of his mouth took control of my beating heart. Louder and louder it pounded; I tried to steady my breath. *I can't sleep; I have to stop these thoughts.* I wiped the sweat from my forehead and laid my palm on my chest and could hear my heart beating as I remembered his mouth on my neck, and I sighed aloud. "Oh my God, I need to sleep, or I won't look good for Saeed tomorrow." At last, sleep came and the morning hour arrived soon after.

I woke up and went down to bathe. When I came out of the bathroom; my eyes fell on my wedding dress hanging on mother's door. It took my breath away. Grandma Riley, Grandma Clark, Aunt Skeet, and several cousins had come bright and early to help. Everyone fussed over me, and I enjoyed every minute. My face had a glow that only inner joy coupled with excitement could bring. I donned my dress as my trembling hands bespoke my heart. The dress cinched my waist beautifully and cascaded down to my ankles in a draped skirt, reminiscent of Princess Elizabeth's. It extended as a modest shadow of a train in waves of chiffon and muslin, drifting between white and off-white fabrics. After Cousin Bobbie put the final touches on my hair, Mama attached the veil. Framing my head, it featured two layers of ruffles that matched the dress and flowed into one layer of chiffon that came to the waistline. Lastly, I took out the string of pearls Saeed had given me last night and fingered them lovingly before Mama clasped them at the back of my neck.

I loved the way I looked! I twirled around to the sounds of "Ahhh" and "Ohhh" coming from family and friends.

Everyone scurried around, piling into cars for the short trip to the church.

****

I wished that Yubba's letter had come after the wedding. It had dampened my spirits and now only a part of me felt excitement at starting a new life with the woman I loved. I could hear my friends laughing from the adjoining room as I dressed in the pinstriped, double-breasted suit I had bought the week before. I wondered for a minute if I would have bought it had Yubba's letter come before that. I knew that life would be completely different without Yubba's money, but I didn't want to think about that either. I touched the black gabardine wool; the material had a subtle, dark gray stripe that ran through it. I put the white shirt on, buttoning it up as I looked at my reflection in the mirror. I could see the pensiveness on my face. *How would Betty react and should I tell her? Would it make a difference to her?* I felt sure of her love and pure heart. *It would only sadden her and maybe make her angry.* I knew this would change our plans about going to the university together. I put on the pants that featured a high "Hollywood" waist, double pleats, wide legs, and a two-inch cuff. The tie came next; it was black, white and red, an infusion of colors. The jacket had large peaked lapels and no rear vent. Finally, I pinned a white carnation to the left lapel, heaved a sigh, and left the room.

"Look at you; you must be getting married or something!" Jamal teased the minute I stepped out of the bedroom.

My friends joined in teasing me. They were excited for me. I was the first to be getting married.

"I wish Satech was here. I will send him pictures of the wedding," I said, suddenly remembering him. He had graduated the previous year and had gone back to India.

"I am sure he will love to receive pictures of your wedding. I am also sure his mother has already found him a bride," Imet said, as everyone laughed. He really missed Satech, and more so because now he had no one he could talk to in his own language. I wondered how it would be when all my friends graduated and left.

I wished that Yubba could have been with me. I had always thought I would be married in Jordan with him by my side. I knew I needed to stop thinking of him. Betty seemed to be able to read my thoughts and I needed to start thinking happy thoughts.

****

"Saeed's here and he has all his friends with him," Billy yelled before he ran back to the front porch of the church to join Daddy.

"He's here; I can't wait till he sees me. How do I look?" I shook as I touched my burning face. Everyone assured me that I looked beautiful.

"This is supposed to be one of your happiest days. Don' let your nerves ruin it for us," Grandma Riley said, as she gave me one of her old handkerchiefs to carry.

"Thanks, Grandma, I've always loved this hanky." I tied it around the fresh forget-me-nots I would carry down the aisle. My dress provided the something new, and I was borrowing my parents' home for the reception. I lucked out on the something blue when I found a sexy but sweet ivory negligee with a touch of whimsical, light blue in the center and under the bust line.

"Something old, something new, something borrowed, something blue ... and a silver sixpence in her shoe." Aunt Skeet gave me a hug as she handed me a copper penny to put inside my left shoe. Everyone was giggling, and I started to relax somewhat.

Daddy wore his black suit, which he had bought two years earlier; it still looked good, and he didn't see any cause to buy a new one. He had on a new, crisp, white shirt Mama bought for him and a dark red tie Saeed had given him on his last birthday.

I closed my eyes and prayed; then I heard a light knock at the door. I knew it would be Daddy and opened my eyes to see him standing at the door smiling with his arms opened wide. I ran into them and almost started crying. I couldn't bear to think I would ever leave Daddy. I stopped my thoughts and just hugged him tighter. While in his arms, I heard the piano music start and knew this was our cue. I laid my hand on Daddy's arm as he walked me down the aisle.

The pastor began reciting *1 Corinthians 13:4* as I walked down the aisle. "Love is patient, love is kind. It does not envy, it does not boast, it is not proud. It is not rude, it is not self-seeking, it is not easily angered, it keeps no record of wrongs. Love does not delight in evil but rejoices with the truth. It always protects, always trusts, always hopes, and always perseveres."

****

I knew that getting married in the church was a must for Betty and I accepted that. I believed my friends thought it bothered me, but little do we know our friends sometimes. I heard the piano and saw everyone turn their heads toward the doorway. My heart stopped when I saw her. She looked like a white tulip blooming for the world to admire. She seemed to float to my side; all I could see was a beautiful angel dressed in white.

The pastor continued, "We are gathered here today in the sight of God and angels, and the presence of friends and loved ones, to celebrate one of life's greatest moments, to give recognition to the worth and beauty of love, and to add our best wishes and blessings to the words which shall unite Betty and Saeed in holy matrimony." I heard the pastor ask who held the rings and Fou'ad came forward. The pastor then said, "Let us bless these rings! Oh God, these rings are circles, symbols that remind us of the Sun, and the Earth, and the universe." My hands shook as I put the ring on Betty's trembling finger. Our eyes met, and I felt the wetness of her tears as she put the second ring on my finger.

"Congratulations! I now pronounce you man and wife." The pastor smiled broadly before he said, "You may now kiss the bride."

I leaned forward as I met my wife's lips with a kiss that sealed our future. I heard applause and shouts of congratulations as we reluctantly moved apart.

****

Mama and I had decided to place the buffet under the stairway to make room for extra chairs and tables. A large low bowl of blue and pink forget-me-nots decorated the center of the table, along with candles in shades of white, painted with forget-me-not sprays. More flowers and candles had been placed all around, giving the place a warm feel. Two cakes adorned the table. One was a three layered, white sponge cake iced with a white flower border. At the top stood a bride dressed in a white gown and a groom dressed in a black and white suit. At the other end of the table lay the groom's dark, fruit-filled cake. Two platters heaped with ham and cheese sandwiches had been placed at either end of the table. Two platters filled with deviled eggs, as well as chips and dips, completed the buffet.

As the guests filled the room, refreshments were offered, while Doris Day's voice singing her hit song, "A Guy is a Guy," played in the background. Pearl was in charge of putting the records on the turntable, and she played many of my favorites including "Heart of Soul" and "Wheel of Fortune."

"Come on, Sweetie, it's time to toss your bouquet. Your friends are waiting." Mama put the bouquet in my hand and called for all the single women to gather around.

To my delight, Pearl caught it.

90

Everything went as I hoped and I couldn't have been happier. After the reception, I changed into a pink and white floral dress before Saeed and I got into his car and headed to the Smoky Mountains. We laughed and waved at people in other cars that were attracted by the noisy tin cans friends had attached to the rear bumper.

I sat up straight in the car, my body on high alert. I couldn't believe we were going to spend the night together; just thinking about it made me flush from head to toe. I didn't stop talking the whole way and later on I asked him if I was talking too much. He said he loved to hear me talk. We reached the inn and went into the office to register. The clerk eyed us suspiciously before he asked Saeed to show him our marriage license

Saeed's face flushed as he fished out the marriage certificate and handed it to the clerk while looking him straight in the eye and said that I was nineteen and he was twenty-one.

The clerk felt Saeed's gaze as he scanned the paper, handed back the document and gave Saeed the keys to the cabin.

Saeed carried the luggage inside as I surveyed what would be our first home for the next week. We unpacked in silence, both in anxious anticipation of what would come next. I went to the bathroom to change into the white negligee trimmed with a touch of blue. I brushed my hair until it shone and applied red lipstick. I looked at myself in the mirror, and liked what I saw. I opened the door and walked into the bedroom.

Saeed had changed into pajamas and was sitting on the chair beside the bed when I came out, he stood up and our eyes locked.

"You are more beautiful than I could have imagined."

His voice caused a fire to sweep through my body. I closed my eyes as his arms encircled my waist. He gently pulled me to him and looked into my eyes.

"I love you, Betty, with all my heart." His lips touched mine, and we both felt the sexual electricity shake us to the very core of our beings.

Dazed and a little apprehensive, I felt him lifting me from the floor and carrying me to the bed. He gently undressed me, then removed his pajamas and pressed his body over mine. I opened my eyes to see him gazing fixedly at me. He kissed me again moving harder against me. I responded to his touch, helpless to do otherwise. He began to kiss my neck, and as he moved further down my body, my senses reeled. When I felt his manhood probing and ready to enter me, fear took over, and I put both hands on his chest.

"Don't be afraid, love. I will stop if you are in pain. I love you, Betty, more than the air I breathe. Relax, relax. I am your husband, and you are my wife."

His words calmed me, as his caresses teased my senses. When I felt the impact of his entry, I whimpered softly. He asked if he was hurting me, and I said I was okay. He slid off to one side and held me tight. "I am the luckiest man alive, and you are the most beautiful woman in the world." We fell asleep in each other's arms.

The week passed quickly for me, every day a new adventure in learning about life with my husband and every night a daring journey into increasing passion and confidence in my ability to pleasure him and be fully satisfied. I felt every inch a lady and even more a woman.

Happily Married

CHAPTER 8

MARRIED LIFE

On our way back to Knoxville, I knew I needed to talk to Betty about Yubba's letter and its implication for our life together. We were on our way to her parents' home, where we planned to stay until we got settled in our new apartment. I didn't know how I would be able to pay for it, or what I could afford. My hands tightened on the steering wheel in an effort to quell the sadness I felt whenever I thought of Yubba's words. I spotted a quiet place to park and drove into a cobbled cul-de-sac without explanation.

"What's going on, do we have a flat tire?" She said as her eyebrows rose a notch.

"No, the tires are fine, but there is something I need to tell you."

"What is it, Saeed? Is something wrong?"

Telling her the contents of Yubba's letter was harder than I thought and more than once I felt my voice faltering. I closed my eyes and finished by saying, "Honey, I don't regret my decision. I just wish I had never had to make it."

"I don't understand … I can't imagine this is the same man that you told me so many wonderful stories about."

The hurt look on her face and her words pained me further. "The world is full of people who refuse to accept what is different." I felt the need to defend Yubba, no matter the circumstances, "Remember your Grandpa Riley's first reaction to me?"

My words hit home with Betty. People oftentimes are struck with the truth when they first fully realize that the way they feel toward others frequently is also the way others see them.

"I guess we're all wary of anyone who is different. I just can't imagine your father feeling this way toward me or my faith. I mean, didn't you say that he had Christian friends and that you were raised by a Christian woman?"

"Yes I did, we love and respect one another, but we don't intermarry."

"Is it against your religion?"

"No, it's not." I lowered my head. I didn't know what else to say. I didn't want to talk badly about Yubba, but I knew Betty felt hurt and insulted.

I felt her hands on my face as she looked into my eyes. "I don't give a hoot what he thinks. I love you, and you love me, and we're going to live fine with or without your father's blessing."

****

The desert wind blew into the majless as the Amir conducted his evening meditations. The breeze was welcomed by all as they silently prayed for a cool evening. The Amir's mind constantly drifted to his son's decision. *Will he marry that woman? Will he come back without her?*

He waited for his son's reply, and when it finally came, he felt the words like the tip of a dagger burying itself deeper into wounded flesh. He couldn't believe Saeed had disobeyed him; this son of his heart, his eldest, Hamda's son.

Arifa knew the Amir was in mourning. At first, she had been outraged at the thought of Saeed marrying a foreigner. She just couldn't understand how he could do this to his Yubba. She knew he was

95

hurting her husband, and that was inexcusable. Arifa also knew that Saeed was to lead the tribe after the Amir passed on, and she knew that would be hard for Saeed with a foreign wife. But when she saw her husband's grief, her heart went out to him. She loved him above her own sons, and to see him hurt pained her.

The elders of the tribe tried to dissuade the Amir from disowning his son and talked to him more than once. He rebuffed any talk about the subject and said,

"From this moment on, my son Saeed is dead. No one is allowed to mention his name."

He stormed out of the majless, his abaya billowing behind him and walked quickly to where his faithful Anter sensed his presence and neighed. Rider and horse rode off leaving dust to conceal their destination. He rode hard and finally stopped where no man, woman, or child could see. He dismounted, went down on his knees, and wept for strength from the almighty Allah.

****

Without Yubba's money, the life I wished to give Betty had taken a new turn. For the first time in my life I was on my own. Yubba had always been there and I took that fact for granted. The adjustment shook me to my core and made me face the fact that I had never taken care of myself, let alone another person. Again, Betty amazed me with her maturity and acceptance of circumstances. Her faith was so strong and her love so true, I could not but feel blessed. When I told her that we couldn't afford the apartment on Kingston Pike, she shrugged her shoulders and said that another one bedroom apartment in South Knoxville would be fine. She even added that it would be *our* first place, and she'd certainly love it .

The new apartment was across the bridge and not too far from her parents or campus. Lolli made beautiful curtains for the windows, and we bought a bed, dresser, sofa, a couple of chairs, and a kitchen table. In about a week, we were comfortably settled. Betty had received a full scholarship to go to the University of Tennessee, and before I entered her life, she had worked to buy a car because her parents couldn't afford to buy her one. She had been working for a year and had saved

96

enough money to buy one when I proposed. She originally thought she would start going to the university with me when we got married. Now she knew her plans were just not practical anymore; we needed more money than I could earn in a part-time job.

"I don't feel this is right for you, you have talked so much about wanting to be the first in your family to get a college degree from the University of Tennessee and how you wanted to be a good example for your brothers. I feel I am the reason ..." I stumbled on my words.

"Don't say another word, Saeed. This is my decision, and I *will* get my degree. I'm just postponing it for a time."

"I still feel that you're the one sacrificing your dream."

"Saeed, you're almost a junior and I haven't even started. It was meant to happen this way. "

I gave in although I felt badly about it. We decided that she would work and I would go to school. After I graduated and hopefully got a job in Knoxville, she would get her degree.

Married life suited us, but money was tight, and I wasn't used to having so little. I didn't know how to budget or plan. But she knew exactly what it meant to be on a budget and to plan not only for the week, but for a whole month in advance. Since she couldn't handle all our expenses plus my school tuition, I took a job at a bakery. Mr. Owens, the owner, liked me. He was polite and hard working. I didn't say much and kept to myself. I would smile, shake my head, and say as little as possible about my private life. I didn't want to say anything about Yubba. It was a subject that pained me whenever I even thought about it. I felt as though one part of me refused another part of me.

Betty found a position as a secretary in an attorney's office on Gay Street. Every day during her lunch hour, she would cycle to the university campus to meet me. She usually packed peanut butter and jam sandwiches, but she occasionally made ham and cheese for a special treat.

****

One evening as I helped Mama in the kitchen, she stopped making the biscuits, looked up, and announced, "I believe I'm pregnant!"

97

"You're pregnant? Are you sure, Mama? Did you go to the doctor, or did you just miss your period?" I chose my words carefully, trying to be tactful. I had been married for over a year now and I hadn't gotten pregnant. I couldn't believe my mama was at forty years old.

"I've missed three periods. I haven't told your daddy yet, but I'm sure he'll be happy. I would love another girl. I miss you, now that you're grown up." Mama's eyes misted and that brought me to her side.

Later that evening, I told Saeed the news. "I wish Mama wasn't pregnant. She's too old, and it could be dangerous. Plus I don't like it when aunts are the same age as their nieces and nephews.

"Why?"

"I don't know, it just doesn't seem right." I didn't want to tell him that I thought I was the one who should be pregnant.

"If you ever go to Jordan, you'll see many uncles the same age as their nieces and nephews, if not younger." He smiled that smile I love and came to hold me in his arms, "It'll be fine, Honey, your mama will be fine."

"I wish I was pregnant Saeed. I'd love a baby!"

"Best words I've heard all day." His voice was like a soothing cream, a smooth balm perfect for my delicate nature.

****

Days passed into weeks and then into months, and nothing much changed. Sometimes we double dated with Fou'ad and Ann. Betty and Ann got along great and everyone thought Ann a beauty. She had long blond hair, big blue eyes, and the sweetest disposition.

"I think Fou'ad is in love," I said one evening.

"I think he fell in love the minute he saw her."

"Just like I did," I said, as I hugged Betty, inhaling her scent.

"Do you think he's going to ask her to marry him?"

"I'm pretty sure he will."

When not with Fou'ad and Ann, we spent almost every evening at Betty's parents' place. We usually stayed until her daddy came home at eleven o'clock. We often stayed later on the weekends since she didn't have to go to work the next morning. I enjoyed those evenings and that made me grow fonder of her family. Although I missed Yubba and thought often of him, I knew that I could live here and start a new life.

One day, as I was busy kneading dough in the back room, Mr. Owens came rushing in, his usually flushed face looking even more so as he blurted, "Saeed, there is a man outside who is from Jordan! I told him about you, and he wants to meet you. Come on out with me. He's waiting out front!"

I wiped my hands on a towel and followed reluctantly. I didn't wish anyone to see me doing this kind of job. My mind raced as I followed him wondering who I was about to meet.

"Saeed! Saeed! What in the name of God are you doing working in a bakery? What is going on?" The olive-skinned, five-foot-five man's dark eyes widened in his tilted round face, giving it a comical look. He rushed past Mr. Owens and almost jumped over the counter in his rush to engulf me in a big hug and simultaneously pat me on my back. I stared into the face of one of my father's friends, Sleman Abid El Hade.

"*A'mmi* Sleman, how good to see you." I didn't know what to think or what to say; I was in total shock, and self-consciously shuffled my feet. "It's a long story." *Oh God, I wish the earth would swallow me whole, this is so embarrassing!* I tried to act normal as I asked, "What are you doing here?"

Sleman would not relent. He needed to know what was going on, and he wanted his answer now, not tomorrow, not even in an hour.

"This man is the son of a *prince*. He should not be working in a bakery!" Sleman said to the open-mouthed Mr. Owens, as he grabbed me and pushed me out the door and into a waiting cab.

I had no choice but to relay the events of my life this past year as we drove to my apartment. I told Sleman in detail about Betty and Yubba's reaction. I stressed the fact that she was working and forgoing a scholarship for my sake.

His concerned face made me feel that he understood, "I know that your Yubba must be heartbroken, for he loves no one like he loves you. After God, he adores you!" He added, "This woman must be special to have the devotion and love of a fine man like yourself."

"Betty deserves even better than me. I told you that she ..."

Sleman nodded, "Yes, son, you said she postponed her education for your benefit. I admire that!" There was a moment of silence as Sleman looked out the window, and then turned his attention back to me. "Listen son, I know if you are hurting one fold, that great man must be hurting tenfold." He talked all the way to my apartment. When we stopped in front of the building, he looked at the place, twitched his face and wrinkled his nose. He stepped out with me and told the cab driver to wait for him. We walked up to the apartment where he declined my offer of coffee.

"Thank you, son, but I only came up to give you money."

"No, A'mmi, I am fine. I will get my degree soon and will be able to get myself a better place." My eyes were downcast as he insisted.

"Son, take this money," he said as he thrust a large wad of cash at my protesting hands. "Please son, your father would have done the same thing for my son. He is a proud man and can't go back on his word. Now, take the money and get yourself another place, and don't go back to the bakery. You are the son of a man I highly admire and respect. You were sent to America to get a university degree, not to live in a tiny apartment and work in a bakery."

Sleman embraced me and we went downstairs where he climbed back into the cab. Once inside, he rolled the window down and shouted, "I want to meet your wife! I will come visit you when you move into a new place."

I burst into the apartment and Betty looked confused as I related the events of the day. She couldn't believe he had given me all that money and asked,

"What if your father doesn't pay him back? We can't spend it, Saeed."

"Honey, Yubba will give it back to him, there is no question about that. It would be a matter of honor. Mr. Sleman wants to meet you, and I know he will love you when he sees you. He will go back and tell Yubba that I married a wonderful person." I smiled broadly at her frowning face, I wanted to dance and sing, and felt happy. *Everything would be fine …* I knew it in my heart, but Betty wouldn't listen and told me that we still needed to wait before we could spend the money.

I went to see Sleman the next day and related Betty's words. "She said she will not move to a new place until she hears that Yubba will pay you back."

He roared with laughter as he patted my back. "She is a special woman, son, and I will have to come and meet her, even though I don't like the place where you are staying."

The next day he came. Betty cooked roast beef and made a chocolate cake. I knew she was nervous and that she fretted about every detail, but I could sense her enjoying herself as Sleman put her at ease with his many and honest compliments that made her glow. He hugged us both when he left.

Six weeks later, I received a letter from Yubba and openly wept when I saw the first three words. *My precious son.*

****

I couldn't believe my ears when Saeed told me we would be moving into the *Nicholes*, the trendiest apartment building in Knoxville. I couldn't wait to tell Mama this happy news.

My face flushed as I ran through the front door and twirled into the middle of the living room and said, "Look at the beautiful hardwood floor, Saeed, and the crown molding on the ceilings!" I ran through the two-bedroom apartment like a child on a playground. "Look at the tiles in the bathroom and kitchen. Oh, Saeed, I love it, it's so beautiful!" I hugged my husband and smiled into his beaming face.

I knew Saeed hadn't liked working in the bakery, and most of all he had hated the fact that I had to support him. I also knew he had gotten so tired of peanut butter sandwiches. But all that was behind us now.

"Honey, let's go get Mama and the boys and show them our new place!" I talked animatedly as I continued to admire the wallpaper in the small alcove of the foyer. As we walked outside to the car, I exclaimed, "Oh Darling, look at those beautiful magnolia trees, aren't they gorgeous?"

"They are breathtaking," Saeed agreed. We stood together for a moment and admired God's creation in this wondrous, flowering tree. Five trees were planted along the driveway, and their scent perfumed the air as Saeed said, "They are actually called Southern Magnolia, and they are considered the aristocracy of trees. I can see why. I mean, they do look majestic, don't they?"

We both admired the glossy, broad-leafed, evergreen foliage. "I was spellbound the first time I saw the large, snowy-white flowers." Saeed added, "Just like I was spellbound the first time I saw your snowy-white complexion. You are my Southern Magnolia!"

It was these moments and such words that made me love this man. I touched my flushed face and said that this was a lucky omen for our new place.

The ringing of the phone jolted us out of bed; it was Daddy saying that it was time. We rushed to the hospital and were met by Daddy and Junior in the lobby. We talked as we drank coffee and waited.

"What do you think, a boy or a girl?" Junior asked, as he paced the room.

"I feel it'll be another boy. She's had four, one after the other," Daddy said, as he lit a cigarette.

"Mama would be disappointed. I hope she has a girl," I said.

Just then a nurse came in, beaming, "It's a healthy girl weighing seven pounds and three ounces!"

Mama was sitting up in bed, smiling ear to ear. She looked tired, but happily tired. "That was one of the hardest labors I've had, but it's worth it. I got me another girl." She said as she hugged both Saeed and me.

Grinning widely, Daddy kissed her. "You got you another little girl to dress and play with. Have you thought of a name?"

"Debra Sue!" Mama exclaimed immediately.

Saeed came forward into the room and hugged Mama. "She will be another beauty, just like her sister."

While sitting with Mama, I held the baby, and had such strong maternal feelings that I found myself crying. *Dear Lord, I want a baby of my own.* I stayed the entire week to help Mama. I missed sleeping with Saeed and hated to see him leave each evening. When the week ended, I was glad to be back in my own place, lying on my own bed, nestled in the arms of my love.

Saeed walked into the bedroom and lay beside me and told me he had missed me and that it had been gloomy without me. He cupped my face in his hands and kissed me. After we were blissfully fulfilled, we held each other and talked. Then he said,

"Honey, we need to go tomorrow and get you registered for college."

I answered carefully. "I've thought about it a little more, and I think it would be best if I start in the fall. A new year with all new students will be better than beginning midyear. I wouldn't know anyone if I start in the summer."

"I guess that makes sense," he agreed.

"You got a letter Honey, it's on the table."

He eagerly tore it open and began to read. I knew he waited each month to hear from his father. He would read the letters and then he would translate them to me. After he folded it and put it back in the envelope, he looked up at me and said,

"All is well, everyone is healthy and the crops are doing great. He can't wait until we come and he sends his regards to you." He said with a smile, "Do you remember me talking about my horse, Soda?"

I nodded and said I hoped that she was fine.

"Well, she has foaled and Ra'ad wondered what I would like to call her."

"Who is Ra'ad?"

"He is the best horseman in our tribe and I entrusted Soda to him when I left." He seemed deep in thought before he said, "I will call her Amar."

That evening, as I nestled in Saeed's arms, I complained that I was having another mild headache. He thought I was reading too much. He had noticed that I squinted when I looked at things. He wondered if I might need glasses. I didn't like that idea and told him that I could see quite well, but agreed to go to the eye doctor the next day. After checking my eyes, the doctor confirmed Saeed's words. I sure didn't want to wear glasses. It reminded me of my first grade teacher. A week later, we came back to pick up my new glasses. I put them on, looked in the mirror, and didn't like what I saw.

The doctor saw my disappointment, cocked his head to one side and said, "Now, look at your father, and let him tell you how pretty you look."

The look on Saeed's face was comical and it was hard not to laugh out loud. When we got home he went to the bathroom and locked the door. He seemed to stay in there forever, so I knocked and asked if he was okay. He said he was fine and that he'd be out in a minute. But when another ten minutes passed I banged on the door and threatened to break it if he didn't come out. Within seconds, the door opened and he stood before me. I took one look at him and started laughing. I doubled over with laughter, unable to stop at first, but I finally wiped the tears from my eyes and gave him a big hug.

"Oh, Saeed, I love you with or without your mustache. But you do look a lot younger, my handsome, dashing prince."

****

"Honey, when are you going to register for fall classes?"

I put down my fork and looked him in the eyes, "I don't know what to do. I mean, you're graduating at the end of this year and I haven't even started."

"That's why you need to start." He patted my hand and I went on, "Will you stay here until I graduate?"

"Honey, you know I can't stay. I'll go back to Jordan when I get my degree and then I'll come and visit you in the summer."

I saw the uncertain look on his face; I knew it must have mirrored my own. I couldn't imagine living without him.

"I will come back for your graduation, and then we can both go to Jordan. But you need to start."

"I'm not going to be working in Jordan. A degree would do me no good."

"It's not about working or not, Betty. It's about a dream you had. Remember?"

"I do, but I'll only enroll if you promise to stay here with me."

He got up and got ready to go to class. He came back into the kitchen as I was cleaning up, kissed my cheek and said, "Betty, I still

104

think we can do this. I'll come and visit." I started to say something but he quickly added, "It's your decision. I love you, but I have to go."

I stood by the sink, closed my eyes, and prayed for guidance. I instantly knew that I wouldn't stay in Knoxville without him. Two days later, Saeed introduced me to the Hadads, a Christian-Palestinian family who had immigrated to the states in the 1940's. I liked them and thought they were sweet and hospitable people. I had my first taste of Arabic food and Arabic customs at their home, and enjoyed both.

"This is hummus, a very traditional dip, made from chickpeas."

"What are chickpeas?" I asked, as I timidly tasted it. Everyone laughed. "Mmmm, I like it!" I added, truthfully.

I spent my days trying to enjoy this time in our life. I spent a lot of time at Mama's and loved taking care of little Debbie. She was so cute, with her big brown eyes and curly blonde hair. I wondered how my children would look. Would they be olive skinned like Saeed or fair like me? I also knew that with each passing day, I was getting closer to leaving Knoxville and scarier than that was leaving America. I wished I would get pregnant. A few months later, and after two and a half years of marriage, I knew I was with child. I thanked the good Lord and waited until my period was two months late before I told Saeed.

We had finished our evening meal and were drinking a cup of coffee on the sofa when I said that I believed we were going to have a baby. He beamed and told me that this was the best graduation gift I could have given him. Days later, Saeed graduated with a lovely ceremony attended by Mama, Daddy, Junior, Jimmy, Bobby, Billy, and little Debbie. Camera bulbs flashed as everyone took pictures. Saeed, dressed in his cap and gown, proudly smiled for pictures with us. He later took pictures of the campus to show his father when we returned to Jordan.

The next couple of months were hectic as we planned for our departure to Jordan. I wished it was only going to be a little jaunt, but how do you plan for such a momentous trip? I felt like Columbus must have, excited at this wondrous journey and fearful of what might unfold. Anxious or not, I knew I had a ton of things to do before I would be ready. Our lease was going to be up that month and Saeed wanted to extend it a couple of months, but I suggested that we stay

105

with Mama and Daddy until we left. I said that Mama could help us with packing and getting ready. She was already sewing me a pregnancy wardrobe to take with me. Saeed thought it a good idea and encouraged me to buy everything that I may need since he wasn't sure what Amman had or didn't have in the way of western clothing. I knew he had not been back to his country in four years and although he said that Amman, the capital of Jordan, grew larger daily, he wasn't sure what that meant in terms of stores, fashion, or, specifically, maternity clothes.

Daddy tried to talk Saeed into staying until I gave birth, but Saeed thought that would be too long to sit around and wait. He assured Daddy that Amman had good hospitals as well as skillful doctors. Later in the evening, he must have thought of Daddy's words and asked me if I would rather stay in Knoxville until the baby came. I hugged him and knew why I loved him so. He was so sweet.

"Only if you're staying with me; I don't want our baby born without you, and I know I don't want to be flying without you.

"I can't stay, Honey, I just can't. My father has been waiting to see me for four years. It is times like these when I wish I didn't belong to a tribe."

"And I know you couldn't be more proud of belonging to one either." I decided to change the subject as he gave me a tender look, and asked him about our plans for when we got to Jordan.

"I know that we'll have to live with my father in the Valley for a few months before I can hopefully get a job and move us to Amman or Irbid."

After some thought and many deliberations, we decided to travel by sea in order to take all our belongings and, of course, our most prized material possession, Saeed's new car. His father had sent money to buy the car of his dreams, a two-tone, green Buick.

"Are you ready to go pick up our car?" I knew he hoped for a smile, and I sure wasn't going to disappoint him either.

We loved our car, "It's so pretty. I just love it! I can't wait till we get back home. Mama and the boys are so excited. That's all they've been talking about. I'm going to take them for a ride and show off the car. We'll go visit Grandma Riley and Grandma Clark."

Time seemed to fly by. I helped Mama with the cleaning and cooking, and she helped with the packing and reminding me of what I might need.

"You still need to get more socks for winter, and don't forget to buy cigarettes."

"You're right, Mama. Saeed said I won't be able to find cigarettes that I can smoke. They must have really bad cigarettes over there."

"I reckon so, Honey. You'd better buy as many as you can take with you."

I guess the thing that weighed most heavily on my heart was leaving Mama. I'm sure I said this to Saeed a thousand times, "I don't know what I'm going to do without Mama. I don't think I've ever bought a dress in my life. Mama makes all my clothes, and that's why they fit so perfectly."

"Honey, I'm sure you'll find a good seamstress in Jordan. Maybe she will not be as talented as your mother, but hopefully close."

His worried face made me wish I'd stop saying things like that. "You're right, I shouldn't think such thoughts. I need to concentrate on the task at hand."

"By the way Honey, I thought of a couple of more people I want to get a present for."

"I don't think I know of anyone who has more family than you," I laughed as I thought of the many gifts we were buying. I really enjoyed that because Saeed would always tell me a thing or two about them and that made me feel like I knew them. "Who is it this time, a sister, a cousin?"

"Neither, this is for Fathma. I have known her all my life. She was my late mother's companion, and when my mother married my father, she came with her."

"She must be old,"

"Yes, but she didn't look it the last time I saw her."

As the weeks progressed, I started having morning sickness and found it harder and harder to do all the work in the house. I sort of worried about Mama being all alone with four boys and wished Debbie was older.

The Graduation

CHAPTER 9

CROSSING THE ATLANTIC

The day finally arrived: March 13, 1954. I couldn't believe it had been two months since we moved in with Mama. Saying goodbye was harder than I ever thought it would be. I kissed and hugged everyone trying hard not to cry. I lingered especially long in Mama's arms. "I love you, Mama, and I'm going to miss you all so much."

Mama started to cry as she hugged me tightly, "I hate to see you go, Sweetie. I just hate it."

The first day felt like we were on vacation as I watched the terrain change, but by the second day, I noticed that I hadn't seen any Church of Christ churches. We reached New York City on the third day and the weather quickly changed, turning cold with strong winds blowing. I had read and heard so much about this city. That evening, we went to see *Rhapsody*, a play starring Elizabeth Taylor, and I savored every minute. I couldn't believe that I was actually seeing her in person. The next day we went to Radio City and toured the United Nations building. Going back to the hotel, I was amazed to see people ice skating in the open, and they were actually wearing skating suits.

Back at the hotel, I wrote Mama a long letter about our trip, and yes, how I already missed her. The next morning we set out to the harbor and it was a hectic scene. People going and coming from all directions, luggage, cars, carts. You name it and it was all around us. I even heard different languages and thought for a moment that I had already left America. We finally found our passenger ship and I couldn't believe the size of it. It looked like a floating hotel. We went through a couple of lines and Saeed signed various papers before we headed up the gangplank and shook hands with the captain, who stood greeting all the passengers.

We strolled around the deck and admired the woodwork inside the foyer where other passengers milled around, looking at various aspects of the ship before Saeed asked if I would like to go downstairs and see our cabin. I nodded, and he held my hand as he helped me down the narrow stairs. Disappointment flooded my face when I entered our room and saw bunk beds.

"Remember, they couldn't guarantee one bed." Saeed, too, was displeased, but he focused on the positive for my sake and I appreciated that. "The room is bigger than we expected, and look at this closet. This is pretty large."

The room was spacious enough to accommodate a full-length mirror and two chairs with a round table between them. I went into the bathroom, and I liked the fact that it had a shower and a reasonably roomy layout. I wished we were sailing that night instead of the next morning. We slept fitfully and were up early. After showering, we joined all the passengers on deck as the ship set sail.

I stood watching as America disappeared over the horizon. The weather was bitterly cold, and the wind tossed my hair into terrible disarray, but I wanted to stay on deck until the shorelines completely disappeared. I looked at the many passengers milling around the deck and noticed that most, if not all, were drinking. For the life of me, I couldn't understand why people drank alcohol. Didn't they realize that it made them talk louder and laugh for no good reason? I had little tolerance for this kind of behavior. I noticed a couple standing beside me who weren't drinking and I started up a conversation. Marley, who had light brown hair and dark blue eyes was from Arkansas. She was of medium build and seemed very sweet and polite. Ali was Egyptian with thick, curly, black hair, dark brown eyes, and a complexion a little darker than Saeed's. He was outgoing and friendly.

Saeed tried to persuade me to go downstairs, but I didn't want to be in the cabin. Instead we went to the game room where I bought a candy bar and checked out a book to read. The Captain came in and told us that a movie would be played every night after supper. I was really happy to hear that and after we enjoyed our first supper on board, we watched the movie *The Caddy*. It was a comedy starring Dean Martin as a golfer and Jerry Lewis as his caddy-manager. We both laughed out loud at their antics as we shared some popcorn. We went back to our cabin but got little sleep because the ship heaved in rough seas. Only one night away and I felt so far away from home already.

The next morning we found out that the weather would improve and hopefully that meant smoother sailing. We were also told that a dance had been organized for that evening. That put a smile on my face and I wondered what to wear. I decided on a party dress that Mama made me in gray-green velvet. It had a ribbed bodice decorated with pleats and loose panels of wool fabric in front and back. Saeed loved it and gave me many compliments that made me blush with excitement. Dinner was good, but I couldn't wait for the dancing to begin. I had a great time and danced to each and every song.

The next day, I was talking to Marley and told her that apart from the tea room and the game room; there was nothing else to do, except for the bar, which was where most of the passengers spent their time.

She said, "I see your point. I suppose drinking does make the time pass faster. I'm sure they sleep better at night than we do. How are you faring? I mean with being pregnant and aboard a ship."

"I suppose my pregnancy hasn't been too bad; just a little morning sickness. The hardest thing to get used to is the monotony of the hours. Every day is like the day before."

"I hear you, loud and clear. I tell Ali that every night." We laughed as we went into the bar to buy some candy.

Everyone looked forward to the movies after dinner. They were especially good conversation pieces the next morning. Some nights, they played older movies or ones I had already seen, like, The *World in His Arms*, but I still enjoyed them too. I loved romantic movies and they always reminded me of Saeed and myself. I also loved mystery and western movies. Saeed once told me that I would go to any movie. The women enjoyed the movies more than the men, who preferred to go to the bar or the gaming room. Saeed, on the other hand, stayed by my side most of the time and would only leave on occasions when he knew I felt okay and that I was sitting with people I liked.

A week had passed and I can't say why I was feeling so pensive on our way to breakfast. I knew Saeed sensed it; it was like he could read my mind sometimes. He tried especially hard to sound merry as he talked about how fast the week had gone by.

"I feel like I've been on this ship a month." I tried unsuccessfully to sound light, but I felt lousy. I ordered eggs and pancakes. The eggs weren't cooked right. I felt so tired and wished we were back in our apartment. I felt tears stinging my eyes.

"Betty, we can ask for another order of eggs. Honey, please don't cry."

"I'm sorry, I just can't help it. I miss Mama, Daddy, Debbie, and the boys so much. I miss the mountains and the trees, especially the magnolia trees. Remember the ones at our apartment?"

"Yes, I do, and I want you to think of the two seedlings that I plan to plant as soon as we get to the Valley."

"Where are we going to plant them?"

"On the land my father will give me. You see, Honey, one day I want to have a house in the Valley. That way when we come to visit and see our land; we will have a place of our own. I want to plant the trees where we will build our house one day."

"That sounds really nice." I tried to sound as cheerful as possible.

We went back to the cabin where I rested for a couple of hours. I then rearranged the luggage and read for a spell. My current book, *The Caine Mutiny*, told of Herman Wouk's life aboard a destroyer minesweeper. I felt as though I had been transported into another world echoing my predicament, even though it took place in the Pacific Ocean instead of the Atlantic. I lay my head against the chair, closed my eyes, and placed my palms on my belly. *I am so glad that you are traveling with me. I really hope you are a girl. I feel that you are a little*

112

girl and I will name you Susan Beth and we will be best friends. Just like Mama and me. Please Lord, make my baby a little girl.

Saeed convinced me to go down to the gaming room and play checkers with Marley and Ali. We were having a good time and were in the process of playing a third game when Ali looked up at me and asked in his cheerful way, "Betty, are you Catholic?"

"No, I belong to the Church of Christ."

"Church of Christ!" He had a perplexed look on his face as he tilted his head sideways and asked, "What does that mean?" He continued without waiting for my answer, bypassing his wife's smoldering look. "Houses of prayers should be built in the name of God, not in the name of prophets." Ali gazed at me and, although he could see I was getting nervous, it was obvious that he would pursue the subject doggedly.

"Christ is the Lord, and the church was built in his worship." I tried to sound confidant and calm. "Christ was the one who shed His blood on the cross to save us from our sins." Ali interjected, "God is the savior, and only He."

At that moment, Saeed came back from fetching two glasses of lemonade and caught a few words. He looked at me and I knew he sensed my discomfort.

Ali looked up at Saeed, "I was discussing religion with your wife. I have never heard of a Church of Christ."

"It's big in many southern states, such as Texas, Alabama, Kentucky, and of course, Tennessee. Right, Honey?"

I knew Saeed wished to include me so I could practice how best to answer this question that would surely be asked in Jordan.

I took his lead and went on, "Yes, Tennessee has many congregations. I did notice that as we drove up to New York, I didn't see any Churches of Christ. My daddy is Baptist, but Mama isn't." I felt better as I talked about it more and explained to them the subtle differences.

"Betty is a very religious person. All her family is religious, and she believes very much in her faith. That's one reason I love her." Saeed reached out and squeezed my hand as he continued, "In the end,

113

it is who our faith makes us and how religion shapes our behavior that is important."

With that said, everyone went back to playing checkers. Saeed and I didn't say anything to one another about what had transpired in the game room. I felt that we had become one in heart and soul, and there was no place for religion in our bed.

The next day we met Ali and Marley in the breakfast room, and all went well. In fact, Ali tried especially hard to be pleasant to me.

"We need to go to sleep early tonight so we can get up in time to see the Rock of Gibraltar. I have never seen it and have read so much about it." Saeed leaned forward against the rail as he smoked a cigarette on deck.

"You know what I'm really excited about?" I was silent for a second and then said, "Seeing land! Two weeks of looking at water has really tired me. Honey, I can't wait for tomorrow to come." I tucked my hand under his elbow and squeezed it as hard as I could.

"Excited about tomorrow?" Ali asked, as he and Marley walked toward us.

Marley gave me a hug and complimented my dress before she sank down on one of the chairs strewn about the deck and looked at the horizon.

"What were you two doing?" Ali asked, in his usual curious fashion.

"I bought some books about the places we're going to visit on our way to Port of Beirut," Saeed explained, holding the cover of the book up for Ali and Marley to see.

"I'd be interested to hear. Do you mind if we sit and listen?" Marley asked politely.

"Of course not, but don't let me bore you."

He must have read for at least twenty minutes. All I remembered was that The Rock of Gibraltar was the most famous rock in the world, is in Spain, and stands at the crossroads of the Atlantic Ocean and the Mediterranean Sea. I only wanted to see land, period.

The deck was filled with passengers wishing to see land; of course that was my opinion. But I guess some were up to see this monumental rock. I stood with the others enjoying the scene and tried to see the invisible line that separated the Atlantic Ocean from the Mediterranean Sea.

Now that I could see land, I wanted to be on it and off this ship. I couldn't have been happier to hear the Captain announcing a day trip tomorrow. Saeed's excited face softened my heart and I knew that he must really be tired of this ship, just like I was.

I thought that the first step on land would feel really different, but it didn't. What caught my attention was the landscape. Roads, trees, birds, houses; everything looked beautiful. I enjoyed the day and walked hand in hand with Saeed. I had a weird feeling in the pit of my stomach, as I felt far away from home. For the first time on this trip, I felt the reality of not being able to go back. *I can't get in a car and drive home. I am in the middle of a world I know little about.* When I got back to the ship, I quickly went into our cabin and cried.

Saeed heard me crying as he walked into the room, and asked, "What happened? Did someone say something to you?"

"I miss Mama so much." my voice wavered.

"You haven't written to her in a long time. Why don't you sit and write a long letter, Honey? I'm sure she's wondering why you haven't written. You know that she must miss you as much as you miss her. You can tell her that you have crossed the Atlantic Ocean. Come on, Honey, you will feel better afterward."

I wrote Mama an eleven-page letter; more like a journal than anything else. I poured out my feelings. My words were trimmed with a sad lining, knowing that with every new place I saw, the farther I would be from home. But Saeed was right; I did feel a whole lot better after writing.

Dear Mama, Daddy, & all,

> *I hope everyone is fine when you get my letter. I'm sorry I haven't written earlier, but I have been tired and not in the mood. Saeed pushed me to write. He thinks it will make me feel better.*
> *I hope it does.*

115

I went on to talk about the trip and the movies we had seen. I then wrote that we had set foot in Spain that morning. I closed the letter with the following:

> *I feel so far away from everyone, Mama. I wish I could be with you. I wonder what you are doing, what you are eating, and what you are saying. I never knew that I would miss everyone so much. Saeed is being so sweet, but I don't think he understands how I feel. I guess he is used to being away from his family. I don't know if I will ever get used to this. I wish I was going back home, instead of heading to Jordan. I even miss the way the trees smell and the sound of our southern birds. It has been so horrible just seeing all this water around us. Even the air is salty. I'm so glad we are finally able to see and spend time on land.*
>
> *Write soon. We will send you a telegram from Beirut.*
> *Give our love to all,*
> *Betty and Saeed*

After dinner, the captain proudly informed us that tomorrow we were going to see the L'Escolo de la Mar, which is a Marseilles folk-dance group founded in 1854. Everyone applauded the news as we discussed tomorrow's plans.

Saeed talked about his friends who had gone to study at the Sorbonne and wondered if they had fallen in love with French women, or were they on their way home alone. At night as I cuddled in his arms, he heaved a loud sigh. I asked him what the matter was. His voice was low and I strained to hear him. "I really worried about you this morning, and it's times like these that I wonder if I am doing the right thing for you."

I quickly assured him that he was, but he hugged me tighter and continued, "I know it's the best thing for me, but am I being selfish, and please don't answer that Betty, let me finish. I am taking you to a world that you will have a hard time living in. I know I plan to get us out of the Valley as soon as I can, but I wonder how soon is too late. I

116

love you so much … " His voice faltered and I almost started crying, but instead put on my best smile and held his face between my palms.

"Saeed Gazzawiya, you stop that this minute. I know I miss Mama and everyone. I miss them very much, but if I had them all and you were missing, I would be ten times more miserable. I know that I would cry myself to sleep every night." I felt his breathing calming down, "You are the love of my life. You are my destiny and there is no changing that. Do you understand?" I joked as I started to kiss all over his face. His laughter brought happiness to me and our lovemaking was the medicine we both needed to ease our hearts and worries.

The next morning, we eagerly explored this beauteous city. I wanted to see everything and eat everything, too. I told Saeed that I had overheard passengers talking about a pastry called *naiveté* that I wanted to taste. He asked more than one person before we located the place where I had my first taste of a French sweet and the first glass of milk since we had left New York City. I couldn't drink enough. The pastry tasted heavenly and melted in my mouth. I told Saeed that I could eat ten of them. He laughed, shook his head, and told me that he was so glad that I was having a good time and that I could eat ten of them if I wanted to. We walked hand in hand and enjoyed the many shops, and for the first time I bought French perfume: *Chanel No. 5*.

"This smells even better than *Jungle Gardenia*, and I never thought anything could smell better than that. I can't wait till I go back to Knoxville to show it off." I admired the delicate bottle nestled in the beautiful package. I carefully put a few drops behind each ear, on my wrists and on the nape of my neck.

"How do I smell?" I leaned toward Saeed, who took a deep whiff.

"I love it! We should get you more than one bottle. I don't think they sell this in Jordan. We'll take five bottles please."

I also loved the silk scarves and bought two of them. The first was red with black and white prints of flowers on it. The second was a dark olive green with a geometric design in gold and royal blue.

I loved the *L'Escolo de la Mar* dance group. Their costumes were colorful and so authentic, and the music was lively and different. They twirled while performing intricate leg work that I enjoyed enormously. I clapped until my hands hurt. Afterwards, we rode the trolley, which stopped and let us out in front of the most beautiful cathedral I could imagine. We went inside, hand in hand. I lit a candle and Saeed said a prayer. We returned to the ship about 2:00 a.m., knowing tomorrow would be another busy day.

We woke up in a different city in another country. The ship had docked in Genoa, a seaport in northern Italy, as we snoozed in our swaying beds. Saeed insisted that we see the cemetery of Staglieno and said that it had been built thirty-one years after Napoleon banned burials in all churches and towns. I thought that was so interesting and really liked the cemetery because it was filled with giant cypresses and cedars. I stood under the trees with my eyes closed, listening to the sound of the wind as it blew softly through the branches overhead. My mind compared the sounds with those I used to hear standing under pine and maple trees back home. I opened my eyes and found myself staring into the brown orbs of my love.

"Why does the wind sound different when I'm standing under one tree than when I'm standing under another?"

At first Saeed didn't understand what I meant, and then it dawned on him. "The leaves are different from one tree to another. When the wind blows through them, depending on the formation, it will generate different sounds. I guess something like wind instruments and the different sounds they make." He stood by me for a moment and listened to the music the wind produced. The trees seemed to converse in a different language.

"Is this it for today?" I asked.

"We, my lovely lady, are going to go to a restaurant the Captain recommended. He said they served the best spaghetti he had ever tasted."

****

"I have never had spaghetti before," I said between mouthfuls. I asked the waiter for the recipe, and turning to Saeed added, "This is really good; different from macaroni and cheese."

You know, Italy reminds me of Mount Lebanon."

That got my attention as I put the recipe back in my purse. "Oh, that sounds nice. Will we see the mountains?"

118

"Of course; you have to go through them to get to Jordan."

"That's a pretty name, *Le-ba-non*. I like the sound."

The next afternoon, Saeed and I, as well as eight other passengers, boarded a bus for the famed Leaning Tower of Pisa. We listened as the driver related the history of the tower in his wonderful accent. After departing the bus and taking pictures in front of the leaning tower, Saeed and I declined to go up the stairs of the tower.

"You really should go up the stairs; each year we say we will no longer allow this. Maybe next year, not allowed." The bus driver told us.

"Why don't you go ahead, Honey? I'm sure the view is breathtaking from above." I hated for Saeed to miss this because of me.

"I really don't like heights much. Besides, I would rather sit with you and talk."

"What does my love want to talk about?" I casually asked, but then I saw the look on his face, and asked again, "You're not still thinking about our conversation last night, are you, Honey?"

"No, no Honey. I've just been meaning to tell you a few things so that when we get to Jordan, you will know a little of what is going on. For example, when I greet my father, I will kiss his hand three times, as is the Bedouin custom. It is a sign of respect," he added, as he saw the look on my face. "There are so many tribal greetings, especially if you are the leader. Some tribes will take each other's hands and while still holding them, we gently bring our foreheads together allowing our noses to barely touch." When Saeed saw me wrinkle my nose, he began to laugh, and seconds later, I joined him.

Later, we visited the Cathedral of Pisa and went walking to enjoy the Italian sights. The evening ended as other evenings in these beautiful ports - we had a wonderful dinner at a delightful restaurant. Later in the evening, we talked through much of the night, and I thanked God for my blessings. Nothing mattered except the two of us, soon to be the three of us. I drifted into a much-needed sleep in his arms in the small bunk bed.

The next day we watched as the ship docked in Naples in the early afternoon. The view was beautiful, and the houses on the hillsides created a charming scene. Although I enjoyed all that I saw, the drastic changes of scenery, language, food, and people made me subconsciously alert. We had only a couple of hours for walking and looking in a few shops. We spent most of that time sitting at an outside café eating the softest ice cream - called gelato.

The next day was cloudy and cold. We passed the channel between southern Italy and northeastern Sicily. I watched the ferry service cross the strait that linked Messina with the Italian mainland, and thought, *what a different way of living!*

Back in our cabin I sensed Saeed's apprehensiveness. We talked and he said that he'd been gone for four years and feared that he had formed new habits, likes, and dislikes. I said that everyone changes in four years, but I was sure he would be fine. Some things don't change.

The last two days were spent in preparation to land in Beirut. Everyone copied addresses and promised to stay in touch. "I can't believe it has only been eighteen days! I swear you'd think we've been on this ship at least a month." My stomach felt queasy with both pregnancy and the knowledge that a new, strange life lay ahead.

All the passengers were on deck when the ship landed in Beirut, Lebanon, at 6:00 a.m. We could see people waiting on the dock, but we couldn't disembark until two hours later.

Saeed pointed out his father, Arifa, brothers, sisters, and some thirty other relatives. He explained that everyone in the tribe was related in some form or fashion. They looked strange from a distance, reminding me of American Indians, standing solemn and still. They dressed alike: the men were in some sort of long robes, and the women mostly in black dresses. I couldn't see details, but I waved, smiled, and tried my best to look happy. I had on one of the new dresses that Mama had made me. It was dark jade green, matching my eyes.

Leaning Tower of Pisa, Italy

National Museum of Natural History, Paris, France

CHAPTER 10

THE JORDAN VALLEY

My footsteps slowed as we descended the gangplank from the ship. Saeed hurried forward as if he had been jolted back to the past the moment his eyes fell on his father. He held my hand and I felt him pulling me past unseen faces to reach him.

"Yubba! Yubba!" He let go of my hand as he bowed his head to kiss his father's extended ones.

"Saeed!" His father instantly lifted Saeed's head to look into his face then engulfed him in a warm hug as he showered him with kisses. For a second, he looked like a little boy instead of a man who was going to be a father himself. I stood and watched him as he turned and greeted Arifa, kissing her hand. She, in turn, kissed his head and cheeks. At that moment, I felt his hand touching mine and gently guiding me toward his father and Arifa.

In his sixties, the Amir presented an imposing figure. His flowing garb and headdress added height to his actual six feet two inches. A gun lay strapped over his shoulder, and a long dagger shone from a belt around his waist, giving him a medieval air.

I froze, feeling as though I couldn't move toward him. Our eyes met for a second and we just stared at one another. My thoughts went back to the letter he had written Saeed before we got married and I quickly chased them away. I took one tentative step and then I saw him smile; his eyes were gentle and warm. I went to him and slipped into his open arms and started to cry. I don't know how long I stayed in his arms, but he held me and patted my back and said something to me. I didn't know what he was saying but it sounded sweet. I didn't know why he evoked such strong emotions in me. He smelled of aged apples and other unrecognizable spices. I knew that this scent would be forever etched in my memory. I felt embarrassed and after what seemed an eternity, he handed me over to Arifa who kissed and hugged me as she talked to me in Arabic. I smiled and nodded and looked at this woman with a tattoo in the shape of a small cross between her eyebrows. She had a lovely complexion and more dots tattooed all around her lips and down her chin. Two small tattooed crosses made the woman's pretty dimples more noticeable. I wondered why Saeed had never mentioned tattoos. I noticed that all the women had tattoos in different designs, but all were lovely. I glanced back at Saeed, and although we were separated by a few people, I heard him say that he had to go get the car and our belongings.

Arifa patted my shoulders and hugged me again. I knew she wanted to welcome me. Then I saw her calling to others as she gestured them forward. A young boy came over; he looked seventeen or eighteen years old. He was dressed in trousers and a shirt; he had dark hair and dimples like his mother.

"Hello, my name Talal. Saeed brother." He shuffled his feet.

I was so glad to hear English that I almost started to cry again. I smiled at him as I heard Arifa talking to him.

"Mother is habby you here, and she your mother now." Talal beamed as he added, "She love you!"

I remembered Saeed telling me that five of his brothers went to a boarding school in Amman. Mamdouh was the only one who stayed with the tribe and studied only Arabic and religion classes. He was the second-born son and the Amir wanted him to stay with the tribe to help Saeed when he returned. It seemed so complicated to me and I wished I had listened and asked more questions. I was grateful for their presence as we moved to make way for other passengers and their luggage. I saw Saeed making his way toward me and I headed to meet him. He asked me to go with his brothers and said that he would join me as soon as he got our luggage. He abruptly moved away from me and was surrounded by men, all shouting and laughing at once. I didn't even say one word to him. I felt lost and alone.

"Bitty," Talal tried to say my name as he tapped me on the shoulder. "You come to coffee shop." He smiled and added, "Very good coffee shop." I walked with the others to an outdoor café. It was pleasant enough and had several tables with umbrellas overlooking the ocean.

I tried to be pleasant to everyone, but felt terribly alien and alone. I was thousands of miles from home; far away from anything familiar. Saeed's brothers and cousins were trying to converse with me, but their success remained limited. They laughed a lot during their good-hearted trials, and this endeared them to me.

"You wants water and lemoon?" Mehyadeen asked. He was the third son by Arifa; he, too, had dark hair and dark eyes. He looked similar to Talal but had a much darker complexion and no dimples.

Talal heard his brother's attempt at conversing and said something in Arabic that made everyone laugh, including Mehyadeen. Talal then turned to me and said, "He speak bad English. You like lemoonade?"

I nodded my head as everyone jabbered and laughed and poked at Mehyadeen. In some ways, they reminded me of my brothers, and just thinking about them so far away almost made me lose control and start to sob brokenheartedly. Finally, after what seemed like days, Saeed, his father, and a group of men came to the café.

Saeed searched my face for clues of what I was feeling. I gave him a brave smile his father didn't miss. I knew I had to be strong for him, for myself, and for our baby. As I walked beside him, I yearned to touch his hand, but I knew that a public display of affection was not acceptable here.

"Honey, are you okay? Is everyone being nice to you? This all must look really strange." He attempted a smile that didn't quite make it.

"I'm doing okay, everyone's being so nice to me." It felt strange seeing our car in this foreign land, and I wondered if it felt as lost as I did.

"I hope you don't mind sitting in the back seat with Yumma Arifa?" He said as his father got in the front seat.

I didn't mind at all, in fact, when we were in Knoxville, Daddy often sat in the front seat while Mama and I sat in the back I appreciated his worry and knew that he too was under his own sense of newness.

"What a fine machine this car is! It's almost as though it drives itself. You are hardly exerting any effort." Saeed translated his father's words, who then said, "Look how people are staring at us; they must think we belong to the palace." He chuckled out loud. I started to laugh as well; he was right, people were staring.

Arifa then started to talk quickly and very loudly, but when I saw her giggle, I assumed all must be well.

"She thinks the car rides like the wind. She is telling my father that she doesn't feel the road under her." Saeed and I locked eyes in the mirror before he added, "I'd feel a lot better if I saw those dimples!"

The Amir and Arifa were quiet as we talked. I realized that it wasn't easy for them either. They didn't understand a word of English and must have felt exactly like I did. At that moment, in a strange way, I sort of understood why Saeed's father was against the marriage. Having a foreigner among them was not going to be easy. I looked out the window and was pleased to see that we were heading up the mountain. I noticed that, in a short time, the climate quickly changed from the warmth of the coastline to the colder, snowy, peaked mountains. My mind drifted to the Smoky Mountains.

The view was breathtaking. Almost as soon as we reached this winter wonderland, it was time to leave it. As the car descended the mountain, the scenery once again changed, and I admired all the wildflowers that lined the streets as if to welcome me into their midst. I soon closed my eyes and pretended to be asleep. This way, I could

126

listen to the others without feeling so apart from them. I heard Saeed and his father talking as I lulled my mind to rest, as I gradually slipped off to dream of another, more familiar stretch of land back across the Atlantic Ocean. Saeed's words woke me up after about three hours.

"Welcome to Damascus, sleeping beauty!" he said cheerfully. "This is the oldest continuously inhabited city in the world. I always thought that interesting. Don't you?"

"Yes, that is interesting." I looked out the window and tried to take an interest in this ancient city and did notice that its architecture was stunning. Although they spoke in Arabic, Saeed tried to translate what was being said. He said that they were discussing the fact that in the past four years, nothing had changed. It was as if he had been here yesterday.

We were registered at the Omayad Hotel and I was impressed when we entered the foyer. The place was beautiful and had more brass than I had ever seen, but it was cold. When we got into the room, it had no hot water. Saeed took one look at my disappointed face and said,

"Honey, did you want to take a bath? I'm sure you have missed baths since the ship had only a shower."

"Yes, that would be really nice."

I turned the hot faucet on and cold water came out. Saeed came and tried both faucets, but he could only get cold water. He took one look at my disappointed face and said,

"I will fix that, Honey. I am sure they can bring hot water."

After a phone call and many buckets of hot water, I sank into the tub and thanked God for Saeed's insisting on doing this. I didn't realize how much I had missed having a bath. I closed my eyes and relaxed. Twenty minutes later I felt like a new woman. When I walked out of the bathroom, Saeed was standing in front of the balcony and turned when he heard me. He opened his arms and I ran into them. I don't know how long we held on to each other. No spoken words were needed. We were where we both belonged, with each other.

"Honey, I have to go down and eat dinner with everybody. You can stay here and I'll order food to be brought up to you."

I thought for a minute but decided to go down with him. Everyone seemed tired and after a quick dinner we returned to our

127

room. I nestled in his arms in bed, and Saeed asked what I thought of his family.

"They're nice but not like I expected."

"I'm glad that you think they're nice. They all think you're the prettiest thing they ever laid eyes on. So, what were you expecting?

"I really don't know, I guess I didn't expect them to look so different. I mean, Arifa and many other women were dressed in similar, but beautiful traditional clothes, whereas some of your sisters were dressed in the same way that I was."

"Well, Honey, most of the people who live in Amman or Irbid dress like the western world. If you go out to the villages or the desert, then people are dressed in the traditional manner. Noffa and Wadad go to school in Irbid, so they dress that way, but my older sisters never went to school and so they dress like Yumma Arifa."

"By the way, Saeed," "Why didn't you tell me that women here had tattoos?"

"Tattoos?" he look perplexed for a few seconds before he stated to laugh, "Oh my Gosh, you know, Honey, I never thought of that. You're right, they are tattooed. Only the older generation has them. They didn't have makeup back then and this was used instead."

He tightened his arms around me, "Honey, Yumma Arifa and some of the women are going to go to the famous Damascus Bazaar. I think you would love it. Would you like to go with them?"

"I would love to!"

"If you see something you like, just let Yumma know. She will buy it for you."

****

I woke up to the sound of Saeed talking on the telephone. He hung up just as I opened the curtains enjoying the scene of a busy street with a continuous procession of donkeys. It was good to be on land and not have water to look at. Saeed asked if I was hungry and I said I was starving. I knew that everyone would be waiting for us and I wanted to look good and decided to wear a black-and-white-striped dress with a fetching design.

At breakfast, I enjoyed all the little plates they placed in front of us, and I tasted everything. I also had a wonderful chocolaty drink served in a tall glass patterned with gold designs. I noticed how delicate and light it felt when I lifted it up to my lips. After breakfast we headed to the marketplace.

A high, domed ceiling of engraved wood and brass covered the marketplace. Little shops, all warmly lit, sat shoulder to shoulder. The owners smiled from benches in front of their shops as they blew smoke from long flexible tubes connected to glass containers. I admired heavily embroidered tablecloths and mats in one shop and bought two sets, one in gold thread, and another in silver. I also admired the local women dressed in their black dresses and scarves that brought attention to heavily made-up eyes and mouths brightened by lipstick. I walked in a semi-daze as I absorbed the smells of coffee, smoke, and incense, reminding me for a fleeting moment of the Amir.

I motioned to Arifa and pointed at the men smoking their pipes.

"*Sheesha!*" She said laughing.

"Sheesha," I repeated and laughed.

I especially loved the heavy velvet fabrics, and bought a burgundy shawl-jacket embroidered with gold. As I gazed at bracelets, I heard someone speaking English and turned around and saw a man and a woman. They were much older than I, and both had stark white hair and blue eyes. I introduced myself and told them that I loved their accent and asked if they were British.

"Yes, we are dearie, and I'm sure everyone simply adores *your* accent. Why, it sounds like you're singing instead of talking. Where are you from?"

"I'm from Knoxville, Tennessee."

"Never heard of it, but a lovely accent nevertheless. My name is Jane, and this is my husband, Walter. Whatever brings you here, dearie?"

We talked for a few minutes and I did my best to introduce them to Arifa who laughed as she shook the woman's hand but merely nodded at the man. He didn't seem bothered by that and I guessed they knew more of the customs than I did.

The day had been exciting, and the evening meal was another enjoyable experience. The food kept coming, plate after heaping plate of spiced vegetables, meats, and fish. At the end of the meal, waiters brought sweetened hot tea served in dainty glasses with gold designs.

At last, it was time to head to the Jordan Valley. I was a little uneasy and didn't know what to expect my new home to look like. The caravan, consisting of four cars, took off and drove for an hour before reaching the border region of Syria and Jordan. Saeed, his father, and most of the men walked ahead of the cars and began talking to the Syrian customs officers. I watched as they talked and stamped everyone's passport. One of the officers came to my window and waved while he looked at my passport. I smiled and waved back as Arifa said something through the closed window. Minutes later, we stopped at the Jordanian customs where they stamped our passports again.

The landscape began to change. With each mile we drove, going from mountains to desert, the greenery diminished. I was startled to see a large group of men on horseback riding toward us. They were screaming, with rifles blasting the night every other second. I let out an involuntary shout as the gunshots mounted. Saeed's father was saying something, and Arifa laughed. Saeed turned to me and shouted, loud enough to be heard, "It's okay. These are tribesmen welcoming us home. The rifles are like fireworks. No one will get hurt."

What a way to welcome us home. I was lucky not to lose my baby! The crowd grew larger as the noise increased, and as Saeed drove in the midst of this madness, I just knew he was going to run over someone.

"We're home!" Saeed's words were strained in spite of his effort to sound positive. I heard the tension in his voice, and knew he was trying to make me feel better. I felt badly because I realized that Saeed, too, was overwhelmed.

We passed through two black steel gates at least ten feet tall and twenty feet wide. The minute Saeed stepped out of the car, the robed men dismounted and whisked him off. *What if someone shoots him?* Eerie noises echoed my inner fear, and loud shrieks cut through the dark night.

I lost sight of Saeed and felt swallowed by a barrage of noise and sweat that seemed to envelop the hot air and my very being. I stared openly at the women who were making strange noises with their mouths. It looked as though they moved their tongues really fast as they screamed, making this eerie, wailing sound. They reminded me of American Indians and the war chants they make in western movies. I wondered, in my daze, if they were actually doing the same thing, except that this sound was used in times of celebrations.

Hundreds of women and children surrounded me, shouting, staring, laughing, and pushing one another to get a closer look at me. All wished to touch and kiss me multiple times on my cheeks, forehead and even my neck. I tried my best to remain calm and not go running off into the darkness, screaming for Saeed to rescue me. Arifa tried her best to protect me from all the attention, and she barked at many to stay away, but with such an uproar, that was not easily accomplished. At some point, I was taken into a big room in the front of the house. There I smelled the appetizing aroma of food and realized I hadn't had a bite since morning. I thought I would finally have some peace when I was guided to sit on what looked like mattresses pushed together into a square. Beautiful rugs covered the floor, and a low table stood in the middle of the square. Saeed's youngest sisters, Noffa and Wadad, sat on both sides of me, and I thanked the Lord for their protective presence. Two women entered the room, one carrying a pitcher and a bar of soap, and the other carrying a small basin. They came to me and I took the soap and lathered my hands as one poured the water. I then dried my hands with the towel the second woman gave me. The procession went on until all the women had washed their hands. I then saw four women carrying a huge tray laden with rice, meat, and the skull of a lamb.

"Mansaf," A woman sitting beside Saeed's sister said, as she pointed toward the tray. She was dark, with small eyes, and for some odd reason looked familiar.

An elderly woman broke the skull by cracking it with a pestle and offered me the coveted brain. I felt I shouldn't refuse, but I was sure I would vomit if I ate it. After a moment of silence, I sensed all eyes on me again; I wasn't sure what I was supposed to do. Then Noffa motioned with her hand. She was about my height and had jet black hair, black eyes, and skin lighter than Saeed's but darker than Arifa's. Although when they were in Beirut, Noffa had worn a skirt and a loose shirt, I noticed that she now had donned the traditional black dress and scarf. I guessed Noffa's age to be about fourteen or fifteen. She put her thumb, middle, and index fingers together and gestured toward her mouth.

She must be telling me that I needed to start eating so others could follow, but I didn't see any utensils to use so I followed her lead and managed to put some of the rice and nuts into my mouth. I had my first taste of the Mansaf and liked it. Although the women washed their hands, I didn't feel that was adequate preparation for eating out of the same plate, no matter the size. The women were using their right hands as they expertly rolled the meat into the rice and gently squeezed it over and over until it resembled an ellipse. Then they slid it into their mouths. I knew I wasn't going to attempt anything like that. I just wanted to eat enough to drive the hunger away.

After we ate, we washed our hands again. Moments later, other women brought in a big brass pitcher and a heaping pile of small, porcelain cups. They poured a tiny amount into a cup and gave me the first sample. The liquid smelled like coffee and I liked the taste, but it was the strongest coffee I had ever tasted. I handed it back, and the woman poured me another sample. I shook my head and put my hands out. She looked strangely at me and said something before she moved on. Minutes later, Arifa tapped me on my shoulder and motioned for me to follow. As we were going up two flights of broad stone stairs, I felt like using the bathroom. I gestured my need the best way I could. She yelled something to a woman, who quickly came and escorted me to another room with a hole in the middle of the floor flanked by two big footprints made of porcelain. I closed my eyes and couldn't believe it; I actually laughed when Saeed tried to explain this to me. Now, I wanted to cry, but instead, I carefully placed my feet on the two footprints and did the best I could. For a brief moment, I had a vision of falling into this hole and disappearing forever.

As I headed back to Arifa, it dawned on me what she was trying to do and I was touched. Everyone wanted to see me and so she led me

132

to sit on a chair on the side of the roof. I felt grateful and for a while enjoyed the solitude. I watched the women below from my new vantage point. Many squatted around the big rice trays, still eating with their hands. Every once in a while, they would look up at me and wave. I tried to close my eyes and rest, but the night air had a chill to it, and after a couple of hours, I felt tired, hungry, and very lonely. One of Saeed's older sisters came to get me.

I hoped I would see Saeed soon.

The kissing launched the minute the women spotted me. Some pushed others away from me as I was taken to the middle of the crowd. The older sister motioned for me to get up on a table. I almost laughed out loud. But sure enough, they had a big armchair propped on a large table in the middle of a huge ballroom filled to capacity with women, girls, and children. There wasn't much I could do except oblige my new family. I was helped into the chair as people circled it singing. This must have lasted an hour before Arifa looked up and our eyes met. I yawned and covered my face. Minutes later she was shouting orders and I was helped down from the table and taken to one end of the room, then into an adjoining room. Relieved to see our luggage there, I knew this meant the room must be ours. Two women in the room were lighting kerosene lamps that sent a soft glow into the dark corners. I shivered, hugging my jacket. The women stood next to the luggage, and I guessed that they wanted to help me. I gestured to the trunk that had most of our clothes, and after I unlocked it, they started to unpack our things.

The lovely bedroom suite was oak with triangular designs in two-tone wood. The huge bed had a beautiful headrest, and there was a massive closet which would easily hold all our clothes. I looked around and saw a vanity with a dainty, velvet-upholstered chair. It immediately became my favorite piece in the room. I sank into the elegant chair and looking at my reflection in the mirror, saw a stranger looking back at me. I looked so pale, and my eyes looked larger than usual. I closed my eyes and placed my hands over my face. I felt a hand come to rest gently on my back, and I turned to look up into the eyes of a woman who always stayed close to Arifa.

"*Thrya, Thrya.*" she pointed to her chest as I repeated her name, all the while nodding and grinning.

"Tha-ree-a?" I tried my best and she smiled even wider, nodding her head happily. I liked her. She was a little shorter than me, brown eyes with dark skin that reminded me of the color of a buck. She pointed to her mouth, and I hoped she was asking if I was hungry. I nodded as she scurried away, returning shortly carrying a tray heaped with different kinds of cheeses, olives, and bread. The bread was nothing like I had ever seen before - large, flat, thin loaves. The bread was hot to the touch and smelled so good.

"*Shrak, shrak.*" She pointed to the bread.

I looked at her, and slowly repeated the new word. "Shhhhhraaak." She laughed out loud when she heard me speak in Arabic. I laughed, too, and for the first time since arriving, I felt a small window open in my heart, along with the barest glimmer of hope that I could someday adjust to my love's world and even be happy in it.

At some point, sleep overtook my wish to wait until Saeed came. In the drowsy state between wakefulness and sleep, I heard the door open and saw him silhouetted against the door. Before I could go to him, he moved swiftly across the room and held me, stroking my hair in the gentle, loving manner that always made me feel so very special and so loved. We held each other; too much to say, too exhausted to attempt, and too scared to start. We closed our eyes and drifted to the world of slumber.

When I opened my eyes the next day, he was gone. My disappointment was so strong I almost cried, and then I saw a letter on the dresser. I sprang out of bed and ran to unfold the piece of paper quickly, almost tearing it apart.

Good Morning My Love,

I feel there is so much to explain, but I have no idea where to start. I would have loved to wake you up and talked to you. But you looked so peaceful. I can't imagine what must have gone through your mind. I myself was overwhelmed and can only say, I love you. I love you. I love you.

I have to go now; my father is waiting to take me on some tribal errands. I will try not to be gone all day, but I can't promise anything I don't know.

Your Loving Husband, Saeed

****

I hesitated at the door for a second, wondering if I should wake Betty. I could hear her steady breathing and wanted to go hold her, but I knew that Yubba and the others would be up. Most of the household got up to pray the Morning Prayer at dawn and by now should be having breakfast. I looked at the letter on the dresser and hoped that it wasn't too short.

When I entered the majless, Yubba's face lit up and he had the broadest smile as he stood up to hug me. Ya'goob quickly brought me a cup of coffee. I slowly sipped it and felt guilty at wishing Betty and I were back in Knoxville. I later went to use the bathroom before heading out and thought of what Betty must have felt when she used it. I quickly went to Noffa and asked her to make sure to fill the brass tub for Betty to take a bath in the evening if I wasn't back, and prayed to God that I would be back by then. I walked outside with a rush of excitement in my chest. I could hear her neigh before I saw Soda being led by Ra'ad. I ran and hugged her neck as she nickered and bobbed her head up and down, nudging me.

"She is happy to see you; she would let only me or the Amir ride her." Ra'ad's voice overflowed with pride.

"She looks great, Ra'ad, I knew you would take good care of her."

Ra'ad glowed at the compliment. I turned to Soda, stroked her neck and said,

"So you're a mother now!"

"She was like a daughter to me in your absence," Ra'ad said "The Amir had to see her every day. He wanted you to be happy when you saw her. God is great that you are back safe and sound." At those words, Ra'ad disappeared and shortly returned with the filly. She was over a year old and as gorgeous as her mother. Ra'ad helped Yubba and

135

I mount our horses. He stood watching us ride out of the gates as I waved to him.

As I rode beside Yubba, all the familiar feelings of belonging to a tribe came back. Riding as if the wind was trying to race with you across this vast emptiness of cherished land was a feeling I missed and had not forgotten. It was not like being back on holidays and summer vacation. In four years we form and forget different habits. Not living with the tribe all the time made it an adjustment every time I came back. City life was different than the nomads', who lived a simpler way with few luxuries. I would have surely enjoyed a shower, but I should not even think of such things now.

The day flew by as we had meeting after meeting with other tribal leaders. Many were concerned with watering their land as well as taking care of their livestock. Yubba talked about sharing the various water wells among different tribes. He said that depending on the time of the year, different wells were fuller than others. I listened more than I spoke, wanting to learn how to deal with such problems. I felt bad about leaving Betty. I knew she must be dealing with more than I could have explained. Describing one thing is totally different from seeing or living it. We can only imagine that which we do not understand, and I knew I couldn't relate everything to her. I loved her with all my heart and would never regret marrying her, although I knew that I had brought her to a world that I hoped she would never regret coming to. I looked up at the sky and prayed for her patience and love.

By the end of the day, I felt all my muscles aching. As much as I had missed being on Soda, I knew I would pay for this tomorrow.

****

I stared at the words "gone all day" and sighed heavily. I willed myself to be okay. I knew Saeed had to do a lot of things with his father. I put on my robe and walked to the bathroom. When I came back, Noffa and Wadad stood inside our room with a breakfast tray. They watched as I ate scrambled eggs, cheese, tomatoes, and honey. Every now and then, they would say something in Arabic and laugh. I asked for coffee, and Noffa was able to understand. Wadad ran out and came back with the small cup and brass pitcher. She poured a little of the dark coffee into it

136

and handed it to me. I liked Wadad and thought she was very pretty. She had light skin like her mother, Arifa, dark brown hair, and large brown eyes. She was tall and slender with regal features. I guessed her to be around thirteen years old.

After breakfast, Wadad took me on a tour of the house. It resembled a medieval castle, with one big room with other rooms branching off. There were only two corridors; one led to the indoor toilet, which no one but the immediate family was allowed to use, and the second to the kitchen. I walked into the kitchen and everyone stopped working, smiled, and stared. I smiled back and looked at the kitchen; big pots lay in one corner and two cupboards occupied another. One was filled with large jars containing different cheeses, olives, pickles, and other items I didn't recognize. I couldn't see a refrigerator or an oven. Four young girls squatted as they cleaned a mountain of rice. At the other end of the room, an open door led outside. This part of the house was situated on the left side of the building. As I stepped outside, I could smell smoke as well as hear the crackling of the burning wood and I saw many open fires on which women were cooking. Enormous pots sat directly on many of them. I assumed that they were doing the laundry at first, but when I walked a little closer, I could smell the lamb cooking. I then realized, from the smell, that this was what I had eaten yesterday. I stood and watched the women stir the lamb with huge ladles. As I approached them, they stopped what they were doing to openly stare and giggle. A little to the left, I noticed other women squatting and kneading a doughy substance. An older woman cooking the shrak bread caught my eye. Tall, slim, and black, the woman had chiseled features and generous, pink lips. I wondered how they made the bread so thin. I watched as she rolled the dough out onto a floured surface and then tossed it up in the air until it became wider and thinner. At a certain point, she spread it out on a round metal griddle shaped like a shallow dome. I watched as she peeled the bread from the sides of the griddle and expertly flipped it. The loaves looked like giant pancakes. I wondered how she could balance herself in that squatting position. I noticed her dress was tied at her knees so that it wouldn't get in her way. She looked up, our eyes met, and she smiled broadly, displaying two gold teeth. She rushed to greet, hug, and kiss me. *"Fathma,"* she pointed to her chest as she started talking in Arabic. I suddenly remembered that Saeed had bought her a gown. I tried to say her name before I hurried back to fetch it. Fathma saw me approaching and stood watching me. When she realized that I was walking toward her, she hurried to meet me. I handed her the gown saying, "Saeed, Saeed."

She seemed reluctant, almost embarrassed. She covered her face with her hands momentarily and then extended them and took the gown. She tapped on her chest several times and said something as she bobbed her head up and down. She gently caressed the gift, looked straight at me with glistening eyes, and smiled proudly. She twirled to show off her gift, talking and laughing at the same time. I was so moved and knew that I liked Fathma.

Back in my room, I rethought the idea that I should wait for Saeed to give out the gifts. I pretty much knew who was who from the many stories I had heard about them before we bought the gifts. It went wonderfully well; everyone loved the gifts and many tapped lightly on their chests with one hand. I concluded that gesture must mean "thank you." I felt great!

I had my second taste of lamb and rice at the noonday meal, and this time I liked it way better, thanks to unpacking the silverware and plates. I tried a little jameed and thought I would love to eat this in a bowl. After eating, everyone quieted down. Arifa and many of the women rested on the mattresses in the big hall. I went back to my room and resumed reading *The Foundling*, a romance by Georgette Heyer. I loved the story, and it transported me to yet another world that brought a welcome distraction into my bewildered present.

A knock on the door jerked me out of a restful slumber. It was Arifa motioning to me to get dressed. I noticed she had on a beautiful, dark-green, velvet jacket. I hoped this meant we were going somewhere. I got up, brushed my hair, put lipstick on, and grabbed my red wool jacket. I saw Wadad, Thrya, and a couple of the other women waiting at the door. They began walking, and I went along with them, welcoming a change in my day. For the first time I noticed the surrounding scenery. The village was situated atop a hill in front of the big house; the Jordan Valley spread to the left, and the view uplifted my soul. I noticed that the people lived in mud and straw huts that were domed or squared. Women, children, and some older men began to come out of the huts to greet Arifa. I could see that everyone kissed the back of Arifa's hand, but I would not let anyone come near mine. We went into several huts, and in each one, the hosts served us either very sweet hot tea or the bitter coffee. I tried to drink a little of what was offered because they seemed so happy that we were visiting. Little children stared at me and I smiled and waved at some. I watched as the women took out tobacco from sachets and rolled them in thin paper. I politely declined when they offered me one, and wished I had gotten my cigarettes. I was tired when I got back to my room and I hugged Noffa from sheer happiness when she had two women carry in a brass tub filled with hot water. As I relaxed and thought of the day's events, I decided that I wanted to learn Arabic and I wanted to learn it fast.

I looked at my watch and knew it would be dark soon. I thought of Saeed on a horse at night and didn't like that one bit. I knew I was getting hungry and wondered if I should order something when I heard a light knock at the door before it opened.

"Saeed! Oh God, I'm so glad you came back before dark!" I ran into his open arms and kissed him.

"Honey, I've been riding all day, and I'm sure I don't smell nice. I'll go take a bath and ask for supper. I'll eat with you tonight."

"Oh, thank God. That would be so nice. I took my bath in here today."

"It's easier in the bathroom since it's closer to the kitchen. I'll be back soon. Love you." He kissed me softly and slipped out the door.

I was sitting in the armchair beside my vanity reading when he returned.

"Honey, I hope you don't mind, I gave the women their gifts today."

"I'm glad you did. You picked out most of them anyway. I'll give the other gifts out tomorrow. I already said goodnight to Yubba."

A tap at the door announced our supper.

"I asked for a glass of warm milk for you, Honey," Saeed said

"Is it camel's milk?"

He was laughing as he said, "No, it's goat's milk. In fact, the white cheese is also made from goat's milk. We don't use camel's milk. Remember the *labana* you had at the Harbs'?"

"Oh, yes, didn't they give me that yesterday. I liked that, and I like the milk."

"I thought you would. I am so glad that you are okay. I worried about you all day, but I should have known that you are my courageous Southern Magnolia! How I love you."

"I love you too, so very much, and by the way, when are we going to plant the Magnolia trees?"

"Hopefully in the next couple of days."

"You never mentioned that they shoot rifles in the air, or make those horrible sounds with their mouths, which sounds just like war cries to me."

"No, the *zagroota* is a happy sound; it is loud, but it has a happy note to it. You can't compare it to war cries. They sound more like a scream. You'll get used to it, and with time, you'll be able to tell the difference."

"And, you never mentioned that there would be no silverware! If I have to eat with my hands all the time, I'll starve to death."

He laughed out loud and told me that he had thought about that while riding with his father. I went on to tell him about the long hours on the roof, then on top of the table. I then confided in him and told him that at times I felt like they were both kissing and laughing at me.

"Honey, they would never laugh at you. Bedouins are simple people who show their emotions. They were happy to see you. I feel bad for all that you had to go through because of me, but life is learning new things and growing from our experiences."

Saeed talked more about the customs and culture; he said that now that he was back, it was easier to see what needed to be explained.

"Your mother took me on a walk, and we went to visit the same people who I had seen here. What's that custom about?"

"They consider it a great honor to be visited by the Amir's wife … and by you, of course. You are the guest of honor."

"Everyone we saw kissed your mother's hand. I think they would have kissed mine, but I kept them folded."

"That's something Bedouins do. Like I told you, children kiss their parents' hands, and it's a sign of respect."

"Do they kiss your hand?"

"Yes, as a sign of respect because I am the eldest son." I knew my question made him feel uneasy and he tried to make me understand. "I try to discourage them by quickly removing my hand. With time and education, these customs will disappear. One has to be patient and allow everyone to change at their own pace."

My brow creased as I remembered something. "By the way, what's the word for 'no'?"

"*La'a*, or you can just shake your head from side to side."

"La-Ay. Did I say that right?"

I asked about *sheeshas,* and he explained that they were water pipes that made the tobacco taste better and cooler. I apologized for asking so many questions and knew he must be tired, but he told me that he loved my inquisitive nature and hoped that I would continue to ask and learn about his new culture, or more appropriately, *our* new culture.

"You know, Honey, I've really never been gone this long. When I told you I thought the festivities of our return would calm down and life would be normal, I guess that meant one thing to you and another to me. When I was gone all day, I felt I was letting you down. You know, I'm clueless myself in many ways. I really don't know what it's like being a tribesman. I've spent more time in boarding schools."

"Don't talk like this. You know you are not letting me down. I want you with me but I understand."

He took off his watch, wound it, and turned to me with a sly smile. "I forgot to tell you that Yumma Om Easa said you are as beautiful as a gazelle."

"You mean the woman who raised you? I didn't see her; I guess I wouldn't have known who she was. There were so many women. I hate that I didn't recognize her. What did she look like?" My disappointment flooded my voice and face.

"She's small, with the prettiest round face, and eyes that laugh all the time. I thought you might have noticed her since she wears a big cross around her neck."

I vaguely remembered. "I thought I saw a woman wearing a cross, but I quickly dismissed the idea. I want to meet her and I also want to meet your sister, Shamma. I still can't get over the fact that her own father shunned her!"

"My father is kindness itself, and yet he did this to Shamma. All I can say is the desert affects its inhabitants, and they adopt its dryness at times." He took his slippers off and climbed into bed. I soon wrapped myself in his arms.

"When you hold me, all seems well, and I know I can deal with whatever life throws at me. It's when you're gone that I yearn for a life that's an ocean away."

"Betty, when I was young, I yearned for a woman to love who would love me. You are that woman. I want you with me. I'm complete only with you. Maybe I thought I could move mountains for you but didn't realize that only God can do that."

The next day started much better when Saeed had breakfast with me. As Thrya was taking the tray away, Saeed told me that he was taking me to the River Jordan. I jumped up and clapped my hands as Thrya laughed and asked Saeed what made me so happy. He translated and she said something as she left the room. Saeed said that she told him I looked like a happy child. I really liked her, and I hoped to be able to speak to her one day.

It took less than five minutes to drive down to the river. We parked and began walking.

"It's about a two to three minute walk, Honey, but you will enjoy it this time of the year."

I heard the sound of the river before I actually saw it. It wasn't as big as I thought, for I could see the other side, but it was still a flowing river. Trees which I didn't recognize lined both sides. They weren't big either but had a nice scent and some had little white flowers. I slowly descended to the bank and dipped my hands in the water. Cupping the clear liquid to my face, I said "I can't believe I'm standing at the River Jordan. The water is so refreshing. I can't wait till I go back and write everyone about this. Oh Saeed, I feel so peaceful."

I looked up and noticed a man in the distance; he squatted and gazed at nothing, it seemed.

142

"I see them do that for minutes that would stretch to an hour, if I could watch that long."

"What are you talking about?'

"See that man crouching? He looks like he's watching an invisible television."

He chuckled lightly "Oh, he isn't looking at anything specific. He's listening to the sounds and smelling the air. He's enjoying being alone."

"Oh, I see. Well, I can relate to that, but if they're such sensitive people, why are they so loud all the time?"

"When you're brought up in the desert, there's no echo to bring your voice back to you. Your voice will travel away from you. Desert people have to actually speak loud and thrust their voices into the wind in order to be heard and to get other people's attention. Another reason could be that they live in a communal manner, and everyone wants, or is expected, to hear what everyone else is saying."

"I guess that makes sense, and I can see wanting some quiet time. Do you think he can see us?"

"No, the trees above are obscuring us from his sight."

He guided me to a huge Poinsettia tree where he spread the blanket he had brought. I sat down and admired the view, the river, the trees, and my love.

"I know that it's not easy when I leave for the whole day, Honey, but time will pass quicker if you start to interact with everyone. They all love you and want to please you."

I looked at my shoes and thought, they will need cleaning when I get back. I didn't know what to say to him. How can I interact with people I don't understand?

"Honey, look at me!"

I looked up and sighed, "I guess I can spend more time with Seetah, I really like her and Mamdouh. I also like her two sons Tayseer and Yousif. How did Mamdouh meet Seetah?" I thought I saw Saeed grimace.

"Seetah's father is our uncle."

"You mean they're cousins?"

"In our culture, cousins are the first choice for marriage partners. It strengthens the family line."

Saeed explained that in the tribal world, everyone grew up together and knew his or her place in the hierarchy. The relationship among members was close, and many viewed themselves as distant cousins.

"I heard Thrya call Arifa *Amma*; doesn't that mean she is her aunt?" I returned his puzzled expression

"Oh no, Honey, all the tribal people call Yumma Arifa Amma. It is out of respect. Yumma Arifa as the head mistress of the tribe takes care of everyone's needs and wants. Many call me *akouya,* which is 'my brother,' or *Ammi,* which is 'my uncle.'"

"I think I know what you mean. So many things are different, but I will work at getting to know these things." I hadn't understood why they called me *amty* or *okty*. But now maybe I did. *They must consider me family. Officially one of them now!*

We talked about going back to Knoxville for a visit the next year. We each smoked a cigarette, and I felt content. On our way back, he took me to another hilltop that overlooked the land and asked me what I thought of it. I told him I absolutely loved it.

"I think this is the land I will ask Yubba to give me." He came over and hugged me before he said " and tomorrow I will plant both Magnolia trees on this side because I can see our future home here." He quickly added when he saw my worried expression, "Not our permanent home, Honey, our week end home." I lit up with pleasure and hugged him extra tight.

After driving for a few minutes, he stopped the car in front of one of the huts in the village. It was little larger than most, and I looked at him quizzically before he said,

"I know you met all my sisters, but I wanted you to visit Shamma. It'll make her feel special.

"I'd love to." I recognized the woman coming out and said,

"That's the woman who was sitting beside Noffa. She said *mansaf* when they served the food. I thought she looked familiar. She does somewhat resemble you."

Saeed didn't have time to react as Shamma ran over and started kissing both of us. She called out to her family, laughing and obviously pleased. I allowed her to kiss and hug me to her heart's content. Saeed said something to her that appeared to excite his sister even more.

"I've asked her to come have supper with us," he explained.

Shamma practically leapt into the car with two of her three sons. The chatter in the backseat was nonstop until the short ride ended in front of the big house. As we walked into the great room, Saeed's father was watching. Shamma advanced slowly into the room, her head down. Saeed stood by his sister and patted her back. Saeed's father welcomed her and patted the heads of her boys as they kissed his hand. Shamma's face turned red and she looked as excited as a child. I wanted to hug and kiss her myself.

*** *** ***

The Amir ate in silence as he watched Saeed interact with Shamma. Suddenly, he felt a pang in his heart as he noticed Shamma laugh and try to hide her mouth with her hand. She reminded him of Hamda, and his heart raced so furiously it brought a cold sweat to his forehead. *She's got Hamda's way of hiding her mouth with only three fingers. How long has it been since I've seen that gesture? Hamda's blood is in this woman, Saeed's sister and my daughter. She didn't cause Hamda's death; she simply had the misfortune of not dying.*

*** *** ***

We had been here almost ten days and life in the Jordan Valley was pretty much the same from one day to the next. Everyone convened with Yubba in the afternoons to discuss matters of interest, or to simply be there. I guess it was their way of staying connected and knowing what was going on. I thought it was boring many times, but it would get interesting when there were disputes since Yubba's council acted as the judiciary court and everyone went along with his ruling. They also discussed marriages and other civil matters, which were settled in one sitting, with the quarreling parties hugging at the end. I tried to relate these events to Betty so she could have a sense of what I did when away.

145

"When you depend on others for your survival, you can't have ill will or bad feelings among tribesmen. Many times disagreements are settled by marrying offspring to strengthen bonds between tribesmen."

I knew she was not going to like that but I wanted her to understand the world she was living in.

"Saeed. I hope you don't have any part in marrying off a poor girl to someone she has no wish to marry."

"Honey, girls are asked if they wish to take someone as a husband. And no, I don't interfere with those things. I listen most of the time."

"Was Shamma asked?"

I looked at her for a second and thought it so sweet that she would worry about my sister. I pinched her cheeks before I answered,

"As a matter of fact, she wanted to marry this man and I helped her. You can't deny he's handsome." I turned a little more serious, "I won't deny that some are in marriages they would rather not be in, but I can't fix the world. I can hardly have supper with my wife every night."

****

"I went to visit your uncle Abid El Gader today with Arifa and *Wadad*." Saeed's eyebrows lifted up and I knew he must know what I was about to say, "I don't like to be judgmental Saeed, but some things are hard to ignore. I mean, you should have told me. I was appalled. Your uncle is living with *three* different women under the same roof. I thought the third one was his daughter, but no, they were all his wives."

"I'm sorry, Honey, I guess there are many things that I should have told you. I didn't think that they would affect us. These are exceptions to rules, not everyone has multiple wives, especially in the city."

"But you should have told me, Saeed."

"Betty, life is tough in the desert, and many times a woman would rather be a second or even a third wife to a well-to-do man than be the only wife of a poor man."

"Surely you don't believe that?"

146

"No I don't. I guess I'm just trying to justify some of the things that I don't have all the answers to." He held my hands and said very seriously, "If I had told you all the customs that I thought would offend you, would you have still married me?"

"Without a moments' hesitation. This has nothing to do with how I feel about you."

We agreed not to argue about things we both didn't like. For Saeed's sake, I tried to be civil. With time, I befriended the wives and got to know them, especially the first wife, *Wath'Ha*, who received much respect from the other two. I spent more time with Seetah and played with her boys. I also began learning a few words and everyone was really helpful, but I always missed Saeed.

Two weeks later, Saeed took me to visit the woman who had raised him, Om Easa. We reached the village in about thirty minutes. He parked in front of a gate made out of wood attached to a mud wall surrounding a little courtyard. I could see a structure made out of mud and straw tucked in the far corner with the standard wooden door. A couple of olive trees, a small well, and an old wooden bench adorned the otherwise empty courtyard.

A small woman emerged with outstretched arms and hugged Saeed, who kissed her hands as she showered his face and head with her own kisses. Then she turned to me with open arms. I smelled a pleasant, earthy scent as I hugged her. She ushered us into her home and hurried to spread a clean blanket on the mattress so I could sit. I sat and surveyed the place. The ceiling was slightly domed and low. A couple of pictures of the Virgin Mary hung on the wall with some Arabic writings. Saeed, watching me and said, "They are verses from the Bible, Honey." He patted his Yumma's hand as he translated for me.

We were drinking tea when a young man came into the house. Saeed introduced him as his brother Omar, after he kissed and hugged him. Omar smiled and shook my hand. I enjoyed the afternoon and laughed at the many stories they told about Saeed. I could tell they loved him and were proud of him. Later, we all went into the little Christian church across the street. Father Easa's face lit up when he saw Saeed, and he hurried forward to hug him. A small man with gentle features, he wore a brown cassock with a head covering. I lit a candle for each member of my family as I kneeled in prayer beside Saeed's Yumma. I felt wonderful and at peace with my life.

When it was time to leave, Father Easa, Omar, and Yumma all stood and waved until we were out of sight. I closed my eyes and lay my head back.

"I can see you there, Saeed; I can see a happy boy laughing. You know what? I've really missed spending time with you. Now, I can barely get a half hour out of you before you fall asleep from sheer exhaustion."

"I miss you and I miss those days too, Honey. But don't forget that I was a student then. If we had stayed in Knoxville and I had a job there, I would be gone all day, too."

"Well, then I would be busy going to school."

My words hurt him. I could see the look in his eyes and I quickly regretted saying them, "Aww, Saeed, I'm sorry. I just have so much to tell you and so many things to ask. I'm frustrated and lonely." I started to cry.

He didn't try to stop me but just held me and stroked my hair. He kept telling me he loved me and that I was his entire life. All of a sudden I started laughing. I was wiping my eyes and laughing. The look on Saeed's face made me laugh even harder. "I am so sorry, Honey, but I can't believe I'm crying when I had a great day today. It was wonderful to meet the woman who took care of you and to be inside a church that you spent your younger years in. It was a magical day and I should be laughing, not crying. I love you so much and I know that I will be happy in this world, *our* world."

The next afternoon, I had yet another craving; this time for an apple pie, and wondered aloud if we could make one. Saeed thought for a minute before he said that we could at least try.

Thrya and Fathma both looked up when we walked into the kitchen. They were pickling olives and stuffing them into big glass jars. Saeed asked for apple, sugar, starch, cinnamon, flour, butter, salt, and one lemon. Everyone wanted to see Saeed in the kitchen because Bedouin men don't cook. Saeed knew he was making a commotion, but then again, he enjoyed being different. Arifa, Wadad, Noffa, Seetah, and others watched him help me with the pies. When finished, he took them to the bakery because there was no oven. We baked eight apple pies, and only burned one. I had a ball, an absolute super time.

Later on, Saeed, his father, Arifa, I, and other members of the family sat on mattresses in the outside *majless.* We talked, drank *gahwa*, and ate apple pie. The East and West blended in a tapestry of acceptance and love, and this was only the beginning for this Bedouin tribe as they welcomed me and my American cuisine.

A few days later, as I was heading to the bathroom for my daily bath, I noticed two ladders, one at each end of the tub. I stood perplexed until Noffa came in with two girls, each holding a bucket of water. They signaled to me to stand up, and they alternated dousing me as I faked pleasure. I didn't have the heart to tell them I preferred the tub to this shower. I couldn't risk hurting their feelings, they were all so happy. They even hung a curtain for my privacy. That meant so much since I knew they hardly had any privacy in their lives.

I was touched by all the ways the women tried to please me and make me feel at home. Arifa even concocted Arabic pancakes, which she dubbed *luzageyat,* or "sticky things." She used hot shrak bread and drenched it with ghee and sugar. It was really good and became a favorite of mine, although it did not replace my craving for pancakes.

"One good thing about luzageyat is that it's affordable, and so, my love, you have introduced a wonderful treat that many will be able to enjoy. How about that? Oh, by the way, Yumma Arifa wants to make you a traditional dress."

The next day I asked Thrya about my dress by pointing to myself and to Thrya's dress. I wasn't sure she understood but nevertheless followed her as she led me to the back of the house. I saw many women of the tribe working on a native traditional dress, and I felt such warm emotions for each one of them. They were all working on a dress for me. From then on, I often watched as they embroidered the little cross-stitching, sitting side by side as they talked, laughed, or simply worked in silence. To everyone's delight, I tried to do the stitching and discovered that it was hard and very meticulous work, but I did do a little. When it was finished, Wadad told me that it had seven thousand stitches in it and took one hundred hours of work. I lightly touched the embroidery with my fingertips as I admired the beautiful colors: red, white, blue, green, turquoise, and orange. The dress was black with long, tapered sleeves, and it covered me completely. The embroidery was three layers deep on the sleeves, with a plunging neckline, meant to be worn over a shirt or sweater. I loved it, and wore it with pride.

Although people surrounded me much of the time, I still had time to work on my Bible lessons, which always brought me peace. I also wrote long letters to my family in which I spilled my anguish and my strong wish to be back home. As I wrote, I often cried from the sheer grief of not having them near. One morning when we were sharing breakfast in the privacy of our room, I blurted out,

"I sometimes feel you're a different Saeed than the one I met and married."

"Of course I'm not a *different Saeed*." He sounded irritated, but then he looked at me and said, "I guess I am a little different. I've always strived to belong in places where I didn't fit. I'm a forlorn hand forever searching for the perfect glove."

"Oh, Saeed, be serious."

"Betty, I am. When I was in the States, I began to think like an American, and tried to integrate. We can all do that, and with time, it becomes part of who we are. Just like getting a tan. It becomes a part of our skin color, and when we are unable to sit in the sun, it goes away, but the minute we are exposed to the sun again, it returns." He saw the exasperated look on my face and tried again. "Now that I'm again a part of *this* life, I feel I need to change in order to adjust. Honey, not only did I forget what it was like having a suntan, but I'm actually getting sunburned!"

I felt bad for my love and vowed to try harder to understand what he was dealing with as I sorted out my own feelings. I prayed for strength, patience, and wisdom to know what to do and what to say. I talked to Susan Beth and told her that I couldn't wait for her arrival. She was going to help me bridge the divide. She was going to be the first half American, half Jordanian Bedouin. I laughed as I referred to my baby girl as my Hillbilly Bedouin baby.

****

150

Betty and I had only been here for three weeks, but I had to agree with her, that it seemed more like three months. I sat in the majless with Yubba listening to the government officials as they explained the government's intent to buy three fourths of our land in order to build a dam and a canal. They were not able to say another word because Yubba stormed out of the majless followed by the rest of his group. The government officials looked at me for answers. I felt uncomfortable but felt it was my duty to listen to the full offer as I motioned for them to stay. The highest official was a man from another well-known tribe who had gone to the same school as I had. He had the highest respect for Yubba, but went on to explain that the efforts were led by the United States who wished to build a dam that would be able to irrigate up to thirty thousand acres. The problem is that our tribe owned almost all that land. The United States would foot the bill only if more than one tribe benefited. King Hussein believed it was in the country's best interest.

After they left, I took a sip of coffee and looked up at a Royal Poinciana tree in full bloom, as though searching for an answer among the brilliant red blossoms. I knew Yubba was proud, but his world was changing and unless we got on the wagon we were going to be left behind.

I asked where Yubba was and Ra'ad said that he had ridden in the direction of the river. I mounted Soda and went searching for him. I looked at the land and my heart swelled with the pride and love I had for it. I feared that losing so much would kill him. I banished that thought. After riding for a while, I saw Anter tethered to a tree beside the river, and then I spotted Yubba standing tall as he watched me galloping toward him. I dismounted and for a long time we just stood there, neither knowing what to say. At last Yubba broke the silence,

"The government is retaliating against us, son."

Yubba was reliving a past I was too young to have witnessed, but I knew the story well. During World War I when the Middle East was under Ottoman Empire rule, Abdullah, King Khalid's grandfather, sought to build political unity by merging the Bedouin tribes into one group. He formed the Arab Legion with help from the British and in 1946, the parliament proclaimed Abdullah *King*. This changed the

151

name of the country from the Emirate of Transjordan to the Hashemite Kingdom of Jordan. The El-Gazzawiya tribe refused to be part of the consolidation.

Under the Ottoman Empire, the Jordan Valley had been a municipality and Yubba had been its Prince. Under the Kingdom of Jordan, Yubba was the head of the Gazzawiya tribe. Relationships were not great with King Abdullah. But after his assassination, his son Talal became king, and was more liberal, and for that reason he formed a close friendship with Yubba. When King Talal abdicated in favor of his eldest son, Prince Hussein, Yubba was not happy, and made his sentiments clear. The tribe kept thinking that was why King Hussein wished to take our water rights away and undermine our power in the valley.

"Yubba, the King isn't retaliating against our tribe. Jordan has a limited amount of water, and we're the only ones benefiting from the river. The dam will make it better for more people." I tried to approach him in another way, "Yubba, it will make it better for us too as we would be able to plant better crops on all the land we keep, instead of its being grazing land for the sheep."

"What do you suggest son?"

"I believe that we could grow bananas on our lands and that an acre of those will yield the same profit as ten acres of vegetation."

Yubba listened but was quiet. He finally said it was time to go back as his evening duties would start soon. We rode together; I felt his heaviness and it weighed on me. I excused myself and went to see Betty for a few minutes before I joined him in the majless. She was reading her bible and her face lit up when she saw me. I hated to have to tell her that I had to go back and most likely spend hours in the majless. I gave her a summary of what was going on. I knew that she needed to know in order to understand and be patient. I kissed her and said that I loved her before I left.

I really wanted to convince them of my idea, but failed miserably. In the end, it was Yubba who announced that we were going to plant bananas on one plot; that silenced all. After everyone left, Yubba motioned for me to stay. He told me that he wanted me to be more assertive with the elders and hoped my idea would prove successful. I bade him goodnight and prayed that it would be.

Betty was in bed when I opened the door. I thought she was asleep, but as soon as I slipped between the sheets, she was in my arms. Everything was forgotten as I inhaled her scent and for the next hour we both drifted into a world of utter bliss. Later, as we both smoked a cigarette, I related the events of the day. I told her that the tribe didn't have any trust in me. Betty said that she had every confidence in me and I thanked God for her in my life.

I explained that the next few weeks would be hard on both of us. I had to oversee the planting, watering, and taking care of the banana crops. We had never grown trees before and this was all new to everyone. I had to make sure it would succeed. I could tell by Betty's face that she dreaded being alone all the time, and I promised her that we would move to Irbid within a month, no matter what.

Betty looked at me in a strange way and when I asked her what was wrong she said, "My God Saeed, I don't want to be here, but I have no idea what Irbid looks like either. What if I dislike it more than here?"

"I can't imagine that, Honey."

I looked at her for a second and we both started to laugh.

****

One of my happiest early days came the same week Saeed began planting his banana crop. One afternoon he happily announced that a couple of Americans who were working with the Jordanian government to cultivate the Jordan Valley would be dining with us the next day. I couldn't sleep that night from excitement.

I loved the Grays and the Reynolds the minute I saw them. Both couples were much older than Saeed and I. Mrs. Gray had short brown hair, hazel eyes and wore glasses. She looked to be in her fifties while Mrs. Reynolds seemed a little younger, with blue eyes and light brown hair. They were so kind and knowledgeable about the Bedouin ways. They raved about the Amir's house in the Valley and the beauty of the stone. They also remarked on the stitchery of Arifa's dress when she welcomed them and said that one could always tell a woman's status from the amount of stitchery on her dress.

I talked, listened, laughed, and couldn't have been happier. I hated to see them leave, but they promised to come back and visit. They also made Saeed promise to bring me to Amman to visit with them. Saeed and I talked about how wonderful they were before I told him more great news: I had learned that an American missionary doctor was living in Aj-loun and running a hospital.

The next day, I dressed carefully for my first visit to Doctor Stevens. I wore my dark- green gabardine dress, which was quite warm. Saeed had two boxes filled with vegetables and fruits from the valley to take with us. The drive from the valley into Irbid was pleasant, and Saeed drove around the city so I could imagine my new home. The city was smaller than I had hoped, but still had a downtown and some stores. The houses were built out of stone and looked nice. I noticed that half the people dressed in western clothes and that made me happy. I couldn't wait for the days to pass.

What took my breath away was the drive to Aj-loun. We drove fifty miles north into the rolling highlands of the country's highest mountains. The road climbed steeply, winding through about seven miles of oak and pistachio woodland. I could see beautiful pine trees leaning precariously on one another for support against the strong winds that came from the north in the winter months. After this breathtaking ride, my spirits soared even higher when I sighted the hospital nestled in the middle of this forest. Once inside, we walked to the end of a clean, well-lit corridor and turned right, into a waiting room. We were soon ushered into another room where I was face to face with the doctor. Tall, lean, and smiling warmly, Doctor Stevens wore glasses that made his ears look larger and his hair thinner, but I liked him at first sight.

All seemed well with my pregnancy and after prescribing a medication to calm my nerves, Doctor Stevens led the way outside the hospital and into a side garden. We continued along a path to his house to meet Mrs. Stevens. Mariam was as tall as her husband and as sweet; and had a charming Southern accent. They were in their early thirties and had no children of their own. I loved their place and it felt like

154

being back in the States. She made southern-fried chicken, mashed potatoes, green beans, and ice tea. Doctor Stevens said grace and I thought of Daddy saying grace in a faraway land. After the meal, we both laughed as we related some of the stories of this new life. We hugged when it was time to leave, and made plans to spend the next Saturday evening together so that I could attend services with them on Sunday.

As we were driving back, Saeed said that we were going to Amman the next afternoon because his father had an audience with the King. He also informed me that we were going to stay the night with good friends of his fathers' who also had a son studying in the states. Saeed added that while we were there, he was going to get me a Jordanian Passport. I welcomed the news and was excited about seeing Amman soon.

That night I slept peacefully and said a thank you prayer for Doctor Stevens coming into my life. I felt blessed that he would be delivering my baby.

The drive up the mountain to Amman was enjoyable. I liked the city and said it was more modern than I thought. Most of the houses, built out of gleaming white rock, sported little gardens containing various vegetables and flowers.

"I like Amman much more than Irbid," I said and Saeed agreed, but added, "Irbid is not that bad, Honey, and it's picturesque with its hills and meadows.'

"Yes, but I wish your father had bought the two acres in Amman instead of Irbid." I looked around and exclaimed, "I'm so glad to see most people dressed in Western-style clothes. I've missed that!"

The only thing I didn't like was the cold weather. Amman was so cold I had to keep my coat on all day long.

After lunch, we headed to a government office to get a Jordanian Passport for me. The official requested pictures, our marriage certificate, and my American passport. After giving him what he asked for, he told us that my passport would be ready the next day. We stayed with friends of the family, the Dabanis, and their home was impressive. It boasted four bedrooms with two bathrooms, and a kitchen with an oven and a refrigerator. The living rooms and dining room were spacious and wonderfully warmed by large heaters. The Dabani family was friendly. They had three daughters who spoke some English. They showed me pictures of their brother, Ali and his beautiful American wife, Linda. The visit put me in a great mood, and I hoped that one day I would live in Amman and be friends with Linda.

We came back the next day, and the government official happily gave me my Jordanian passport and said, *Mabrook*, which means congratulations. He then handed me my American passport ... in two pieces. I couldn't believe my eyes. I stood shaking and looking up into Saeed's equally shocked countenance. He started to fuss with the official who just stood and stared at us before we stormed out of the building. I felt totally lost without my passport. How could I go back home without it? I was trembling as we entered the American Embassy and asked to see the ambassador. Minutes later, we were ushered into his office, and I nervously told him what happened. He was not happy and said they had no right to assume I was relinquishing my American citizenship to become a Jordanian. He took my torn passport and two pictures I had with me and told me not to worry, that by tomorrow afternoon, I would have my American passport back. He patted my hands and smiled into my relieved face and told me no one can take that away from me.

The receptionist at the Embassy told us about a supermarket that specialized in foreign products. I couldn't believe my eyes when I saw peanut butter, Nescafe, American cookies, candy, and other foods I missed. I bought everything and Saeed encouraged me to buy multiples. But my best surprise was when I found sliced bacon and ham. When we were in the car Saeed asked me not to let Noffa or Wadad eat the pork. I gave him a puzzled look and he explained that Muslims are not allowed to eat pork; that it is forbidden. He said that he really never thought about these things and ate bacon, ham, and pork chops. He thought that due to cleanliness issues long ago, pork had not been good safe meat. He said that the Jews also were not allowed to eat it. That really didn't make sense to me, and I asked if they would mind if I ate it. He shook his head and said that I should eat what I want to and that they would love me just the same. He kissed my nose as I thought how lucky I was.

Later in the day, Saeed and his father had their audience with the King, and the dam was further explained along with the promise to give Saeed a position in the Ministry of Agriculture. The king said it would not happen this year, but would next year.

Saeed knew that I was fervently praying that our move to Irbid ... our first move ... would happen soon He took this opportunity to persuade his father that we needed to move. He told him it would be good to have a place in Irbid just in case he got the job early. He also told him it would be easier to oversee the building of the Amir's house in Irbid. At the end of the day, Saeed received the okay to rent a house for us and I couldn't have been happier. This hectic day sure turned out to be a nice one after all. I thanked the Lord for all my blessings.

Knowing that I would be leaving the tribal home in less than a month helped me to be patient with the people and their customs. It allowed me to take a deeper look at their ways and encouraged me to learn the language. I visited with Shamma and Seta; I enjoyed playing with their young ones and couldn't wait till Susan Beth came. I was five months pregnant and in another four months I would have my own baby.

One of the scenes I never tired of was the women fetching water from the well behind the house. I often walked with Noffa and Wadad to the well and watched as the village women came in a procession to fill their jugs before they headed back home. Here I could see how they all depended on each other; one woman alone couldn't lift the jug without losing a good amount of the water. It took two to position the jug squarely onto one woman's head. At first, their gawking bothered me, but now I tried my best to let them get a closer look at me, and I welcomed their smiles.

Living in tents also intrigued me and I never forgot the fact that Saeed had lived in one when he was young. I told Saeed that I would really like to see a tent where a family actually lived. He said that would be easy and after about an hour of travel, we arrived at a huge tent and were greeted by the many families who resided in it. Situated at the bottom of a hill with trees lining the back as well as the side, the tent exuded a welcoming aura, and I was surprised at the warmth when I first entered. The unique smell, Saeed explained, was the tent itself, and further explained that it changed depending on the season and the rain. I noticed everyone taking their shoes off before entering, and I did the same. The floors felt much like hard wooden floors. Mattresses lay in an open, rectangular shape, and plush pillows had been placed all over. A fire burned in the middle of the rectangle, with coffee pots resting on the flame. I was ushered through a cloth divider into another section of the tent. I went through two other rooms until I finally overlooked the trees I had earlier noticed bordering the back of the structure. Awed by the expanse, the cleanliness, and the décor of the tent, I sat on the mattresses and watched a woman working on a loom in the open, just outside the tent's door flap. I rose and stepped outside and she greeted me, displaying a mouth with many missing teeth. She showed me her loom consisting of two beams of wood that rested against four tent stakes pounded into the ground. Yarns were wrapped in a continuous figure eight around the beams.

It looked deceptively simple until she let me try to weave. I sat on the ground, pushing and pulling, beating and plucking, as everyone joined me in laughing. This dense cloth was made to withstand the severe sandstorms, wind, and general wear of nomadic life. She showed me how to spin the strong, heavily twisted yarn on a simple hand spindle. She sat with a distaff of twisted bunches of goats' wool tucked under her left arm. She held the spindle in her right hand and turned it quickly in her open palm, guiding the stream of fleece from the distaff with her left hand. I hadn't realized I would receive this extent of an education in making tents, but I appreciated the hospitality and enjoyed the Mansaf and the coffee. I also thanked God that Saeed's family didn't live in a tent.

Arifa

159

Seeta, Arifa, Noffa, Shamma, Wadad

The Amir, his brothers, and a tribesman

Noffa, Susan, Betty, Thrya, and Tyseer

Betty, Mrs. Seal, Mr. Seal, others eating a Mansaf

CHAPTER 11

SUSAN BETH

When I went for my July check-up, Dr. Stevens suggested that I come and stay with them in late August in case I had an early delivery. I welcomed his idea and when the time came, packed with care, not sure how long I would be there. I hugged Arifa, Thrya, Noffa, and Wadad and promised that Saeed would bring them up as soon as I had the baby. Wadad pleaded to come with me, but I reminded her that she had school.

The drive was pleasant as usual and when I arrived, Miriam had a room all ready for me. We spent the days walking under the beautiful trees and eating wonderful food that we prepared. Many evenings we sat on the screened porch and talked. I took this time to ask her perspective on many things.

"What do you think of the *Ramadan* holy time, Mariam?"

"Well, I know that our Lord Jesus also fasted, foregoing all food and drink except water. What I don't understand is why these children fast when they are so young."

"Oh Mariam, I so agree with you. I felt sorry for the children and noticed that they became quieter as each day progressed." I took a bite of my apple pie and a sip of my coffee as I remembered that first night

162

of the fasting month. "I thought I was dreaming the first time I heard someone beating on a drum in the middle of the night."

Marian and I both laughed as she recalled her first time hearing the drummer whose job was to wake people up to eat in the middle of the night in preparation for fasting the next day.

"You know, I discussed fasting with Tereza, a Coptic Christian I met in Irbid, and learned many new things. Observation of Great Lent means giving up many foods like meat, dairy products, fish and wine, praying and going to Church more; it also means giving alms to the needy and working on becoming a better person. What struck me as strange was that they permitted oil and wine on Saturdays and Sundays. I know Mama would be surprised at the wine part when she reads all this."

"I can imagine her surprise when she reads it." Mariam winked before she added, "As I was when I heard that years ago."

"Wadad asked me if I was going to fast and before I could answer Noffa said I didn't have to since I am pregnant. I am not going to fast even when I'm not pregnant. Saeed got so tired and so very weak. I felt so sorry for him."

"Did you discuss this with Saeed?"

She looked concerned as she waited for my answer and I quickly said, "I sure did ... and he told me I never have to fast or do anything I don't wish to do."

She patted my hand and told me how lucky I was. I agreed and wished he was with me.

As the fasting month progressed, I got into the spirit and thought that it reminded me somewhat of the Christmas season. Adults were more giving and less boisterous. Children enjoyed all the attention they got while they fasted and I liked that everyone ate together after sundown. Best of all, I loved the sweets. I told Mariam that I had told Saeed that it's like the eggnog and the fruitcake at Christmas. I shook my head and said that Saeed was really happy and thought that I was doing a good job at connecting my two worlds and that we needed to keep linking a chain in order to find as many similarities as possible. The more connections, the fewer prejudices. Marian liked that.

"One good thing came out of Ramadan," I continued, "You know how, at the end of the fasting, they celebrate with a three-day feast where everyone wears new clothes?" I asked, as she nodded her head.

"Well, Saeed took me one Friday to Amman where I found a striped red-and-white muslin fabric I loved and Arifa introduced me to a tailor who I immediately liked. He's short, slim, sweet- natured, and has delicate, long fingers that he waves in the air as he speaks. His name is Iyad; he loved the fabric and turned it into a strapless dress cinched above the waist with a flowing skirt below that accommodated my belly. I was really happy with the results. I thought of Mama and knew she would agree that he was a good tailor. Do you have a good tailor?"

We would talk almost every night since Dr. Stevens stayed late at the hospital. I hoped I wasn't talking her ear off, but she always laughed and told me she enjoyed our conversations and loved to hear my stories.

I talked about how nice it was seeing all our Christian friends coming to say Happy Feast to us. But I did say that three days of festivities was a bit too much. I couldn't imagine three days of Christmas. I don't think anyone could! We both agreed.

I was about to tell Mariam about going to Tereza's all-girl party where they taught me how to belly dance and told me that I had done a good job. I decided not to because I wasn't sure how she would feel about belly dancing.

Mariam asked how I felt about *Eid-Eladha*, the Feast of Sacrifice, which came two months and ten days after the end of Ramadan. It was the beginning of the *Hajj*, the yearly pilgrimage to Mecca. The feast honors Abraham's willingness to obey God, even when that meant sacrificing his son. The reason she asked was because she knew that Saeed's father always sacrificed many lambs to ensure that every person in the tribe had a piece of meat to eat. I closed my eyes and missed Saeed again as I remembered how he had tried to tell me that I would not enjoy this feast as much as I did my first one. I had insisted on going because I hated to be without him, but when I got to the valley and saw the vast number of lambs waiting to be sacrificed, I wished I hadn't come. Marian looked at me and I could see her face twitch. I almost cried when I told her that Saeed had anticipated my reaction and had arranged to take me to Wath'ha who had promised that I would see nothing of what was going on.

While I was waiting for my Susan Beth, I read a lot and missed Saeed even more. We talked on the phone in the evenings, but with an operator listening, our conversations were short and unfulfilling. Saeed came to visit twice a week, and we always had a great time. On one of his visits, after an enjoyable picnic, we discussed naming our child. The birds whistled, the wind blew, and the sky showed off fluffy white clouds. I knew that in the Arabic world, everyone's middle name was their father's. That way everyone knew who your father was. Although that made sense, I still wanted to give my children second names. Saeed said that I could pick the girl's name, but if it was a boy, he wanted to give him an Arabic name. We laughed as I tried to say some of the names, and we decided to pick a name I could pronounce.

On September 4th, as I was walking, I experienced a sudden pain in my abdomen. I put my hand on my stomach, felt the second wave of pain, and knew it was time. The labor was long and hard, but I felt better the minute Saeed walked into the room and gave me a kiss even while I heaved from the pain. After eleven hours of labor my baby girl arrived. Tears of love, exhaustion, and relief flowed down my face. For a moment, I missed Mama, but that didn't take away from the happiness I felt as I gazed down on my child. She weighed seven and one-half pounds and had a head full of light brown hair. She looked darker than I am and her eyes were a dark blue, and I wondered if they would later turn light blue like Mama's. Saeed hovered nearby as the nurse dressed her in a white, long-sleeved gown and wrapped a woolen baby blanket around her.

"What are you going to name her?" He asked, as he kissed the baby's forehead.

"Susan Beth." I looked at my love, "Saeed, are you unhappy that she is a girl?"

"Not at all, Honey, in fact, I wished for a healthy baby, but in my heart, I knew that a little girl would be better for you. At least that way you would be able to have her more to yourself. I wished for Susan Beth."

165

The Amir and Arifa came the next morning to see us. He came to my bedside, and gave me one of the long hugs which I always appreciated. Arifa gave me a big hug, too, and showered kisses on both me and the baby. She laughed and said that I looked like a full moon, which is considered a great compliment, as she gave me a wrapped box. I opened it and found two golden bracelets; one for me and one for Susan. The nurses and staff laughed as they brought in box after box of fruits, vegetables, and different candies.

"What is all this? You'd think I'm staying a month!"

"That is Bedouin generosity. My father wanted to show his thanks to Doctor Stevens for taking such good care of you."

Arifa wished to hold Susan, and I handed her the baby. She kissed Susan's head and took her to the Amir, asking at the same time why the baby wasn't wrapped properly.

"The doctor says that it restricts the baby from moving naturally," Saeed explained.

"But it will stop them from being bowlegged!" Arifa exclaimed. Then I heard her voice rising as she laughed and looked quizzically at Saeed, who said, "This is the way Dr. Stevens wants us to wrap her." He changed the subject then, saying, "Yubba wants to hold Susan. He has rarely held any infants, and never a girl."

Arifa laid Susan in her grandfather's arms, where she looked so small. The Amir admired the baby and then said something to Arifa, who translated for me: "He says she is beautiful just like her mother."

I fought back tears. I knew he had wished for a grandson, and I was thrilled that he held my baby girl with such obvious delight.

Saeed took picture after picture in the next couple of days that he stayed with us. I was so glad he didn't leave with his father and Arifa. His presence was a godsend, especially when I started getting visitors the next day. People from the Valley as well as from Irbid came with gifts and chocolates. Yumma Om Easa and Omar came and she gave me a cross she had made herself from blue turquoise stones. I lovingly fingered it and gave her a big hug. I remained at the hospital for another week and Noffa came and stayed with me.

Susan's birth changed our lives and Saeed tried to be home more. He said that he never thought being a father would be so much fun. He missed her the minute he left the house! I told him that we both missed him the minute he walked out the door. "I think Susan knows you are gone when she no longer sees the camera," I joked. Saeed was forever taking pictures of Susan and me. In the evenings, we watched the slides and ate pie with family and friends.

Noffa and Wadad stayed with us on the weekends and it was always busy. They wanted to eat fruit pies, cobblers, and cakes. They screamed with delight when I said I was going to make pineapple-upside-down cake or coconut cake. They loved everything I cooked: hamburgers, hot dogs, biscuits, and chili. I laughed out loud as I remembered the noises of delight they had made the first time they tasted a doughnut. I enjoyed those visits but when Saeed told me that the children didn't want to go back to the boarding school and wanted to stay with us all the time, I didn't like that.

"Honey, just until the school year is over. They love you and want to be with you."

"I don't want them to love me like that," I said. I didn't like the sound of my words, but I couldn't help it. Saeed hugged me and I inhaled deeply, drawing in the essence of this man I loved so much. Susan started to cry and I went to comfort her. I held her for a long time and walked around the house. After a while, I nursed her and put her to sleep. I read the bible and prayed as I kneeled by the bed. I thanked God for Saeed, Susan, and my many other blessings. I thanked Him for friends who helped me along the way. I especially thanked Him for the Grays. They were like having another set of parents and they treated me like their daughter. I went to bed looking forward to going to Amman the next day.

We first stopped at the Supermarket and bought every American product they had, then Saeed dropped me off at the Grays' who lived in a compound that housed nine other American families. It had one gated entrance that led to the many houses lined up in rows opposite one another. Every house had a screened-in porch overlooking a little flower garden. Mrs. Gray told me that her neighbors loved my visiting and loved my laughter. I hugged her and told her how dear she was to me. We talked and I told her that I couldn't wait to come and live in Amman.

167

"Be glad that Saeed is not trying to change you like a lot of other men try to do." She knew a few foreigners married to Jordanian men.

"I know. I'm blessed to have him. That's why I love him so much."

"Some of us have wondered, my dear, what his people think of the way you dress. I mean, I see you in sleeveless dresses, jeans, and even shorts." Mrs. Gray had a quizzical smile, and I almost laughed.

"I only wear shorts when I'm home or in your compound. Saeed did express his wish to his father about not wanting anyone criticizing or trying to change the way I dress, eat, or behave. I have to admit, they've been good about it."

"The Bedouin culture is more tolerant with outsiders. Maybe because they see few of them, and outsiders are novelties. Keep in mind that they're harsh with anyone inside the tribe who may wish to change or not follow their rules."

****

Driving back to Irbid, Saeed told me he had to go see about the banana crop; he said that they were not doing well. He asked if I would go and spend the night with him at the Valley and promised me a picnic by the river. This was a deal I couldn't refuse. It was hard getting up the next morning since Susan had kept me up a good portion of the night. After a quick breakfast, we got ready. I put on one of my sleeveless dresses and dressed Susan in an almost identical dress. As usual, I enjoyed the drive and being in the car with Saeed. We stopped by Yumma Om Easa and everyone made eyes over Susan. Father Easa said a prayer of protection over her as I lit candles inside the one-room church before we continued on our way to the Valley.

After hugging and kissing, the Amir wanted to hold Susan in his arms. I saw the tribesmen's look of astonishment before they started to laugh out loud. Later that evening I brought it up to Saeed. He told me that I had brought change and had done much good for many. He then said,

"I have prayed on how to approach these issues of unfairness between men and women. Now I see that you are the answer, Honey. You and Susan."

"Susan and I?" I looked at him as I raised one brow.

"I'm serious; you have inspired women to dress differently. Noffa and Wadad always used to dress in the traditional dress when they were not in school. They no longer do that. Haven't you noticed that even Yumma Arifa smokes foreign cigarettes now?"

I started to notice more of the ways in which I was having a positive effect on these women, and it humbled me as I said a prayer of thanks. They watched my every move and I made a point of talking about why I didn't wrap Susan like a mummy and bathed her daily, even in colder weather. I breastfed in private, feeling it was inappropriate to do in public as the women of the tribe did. I couldn't understand how they could be so conservative and yet breastfeed in public! Even Saeed had no explanation for that.

Although Saeed had a lot to do, he kept his promise of a picnic by the river. It was like the good old days, we sipped our ice tea as we ate fried chicken and cole slaw. Susan's first picnic was a great success. When we got back, we joined the others in the majless. The Amir looked at me and said something, waving his hands in the air. Everyone fell silent as Saeed translated that his father was offering me three hundred acres of land if I would convert to Islam. I was momentarily stunned, not knowing whether to be insulted or amused. I got up, gave him a big hug, looked into his eyes and refused his generous offer. I think it was then his turn to be momentarily stunned, but I did see respect in those wise eyes before he hugged me again.

As the days passed, I still missed my own family, but a little less. With Susan in my life, I had her to concentrate on. I was beginning to adapt and understand the culture.

One evening Saeed said, "Remember, Honey, when you would stay in your robe, thinking that would indicate your displeasure, and ...

I interrupted, giving him a sour look. "I know … I know. You don't have to remind me. I thought that by staying in my robe, I was giving guests the impression that I was very uncomfortable with them being in my house. I tell you, your people are crazy." I couldn't hold back my laughter as he began to sing Patsy Cline's song, "Crazy."

The next day Saeed came home early and said he had something to tell me. At first I was worried, but he quickly reassured me that it was not bad news, but that he had to go to Amsterdam for two weeks for an agricultural convention. I wasn't happy with that news but felt a whole lot better when he said that he had made arrangements for me to stay at the Gray's while he was away.

Life would be much better if we were living in Amman. I wondered when we would move. We had been in Irbid almost a year and Saeed had not gotten a job yet or started building the house. I told him I needed to nurse Susan and went to our bedroom. I sat on the edge of the bed and started crying. I felt down and missed Mama so much. I didn't ever hear the door open, but I sensed Saeed's presence. I looked up and there he stood looking at me. He came slowly to my side, held me, and said how sorry he was. I stopped crying and lay in his arms. He asked if I would like to go to Beirut for a couple of days before he left for Amsterdam. How I love my husband. I dried my eyes and told him that I loved him. He looked so pleased with himself.

We had a great time in Beirut. This port city, with its beautiful hotels, reminded me of Florida. I loved the array of restaurants with American food that we both had missed. Hamburgers, hotdogs, and even milkshakes! I wanted to order the whole menu. I also thought Lebanese food such as *kubba, tabula,* and *manageesh* were very tasty. I even wished aloud that Saeed had been born a Lebanese, and my love jokingly answered that he too wished that.

The highlight of that trip was seeing Nadia Gamal, a renowned belly dancer. I could not take my eyes off her as her hands and hips moved in unison with the music. I absolutely enjoyed every minute. Shopping was another delightful experience that Beirut provided, and I bought lovely clothes for Susan and me. While out browsing in various shops, we discovered the Elfa Supermarket that dwarfed the Rainbow Supermarket back home.

The next morning, back in Irbid, I got up to Saeed's nervous tone as he talked to Noffa. I asked him what was going on. He looked awfully disturbed as he said,

"There is sad news, Honey. I wanted to be the one to tell you about it. It's not your family," he quickly added, as he saw the alarmed look on my face. "Wath'ha passed on while we were in Beirut."

"Oh, how terrible! How did she die?" I felt tears start to course down my cheeks.

"She set herself on fire when she found out my uncle was about to wed her maid." Saeed hung his head.

"Oh, my God! Oh Saeed!" My hands shook as I covered my face and cried.

Noffa came in at that moment and, once she knew what we were talking about, came and hugged me and began to relate the horrible details.

"She locked herself in her room, threw the key out the window, and then doused herself with gasoline." Noffa's eyes widened and brimmed with tears as she continued, "Wath'ha lit herself on fire; she kept screaming and screaming as she pounded on the locked door until she died." By then, both Noffa and I were openly crying. I felt my heart breaking as I thought of this gentle woman who I had come to love. I refused to go give my condolences to Saeed's uncle and I told him that I didn't care if his father did not approve. Saeed hugged me, caressing my back and told me that he would always support my decisions. He said that I was his backbone. The next day, he even told me that his father and Arifa respected my action. It didn't bring Wath'ha back, but I showed my love to her. I will always miss her.

****

Saeed drove while I talked, and Susan slept all the way up to Amman. As we neared the Gray's home, he said that it would be great weather to go to Jerusalem the first weekend he was back. I leaned over and kissed him. I had wanted to go to Jerusalem. I know Saeed was trying to make me feel better and it did help, but I still grieved for Wath'ha.

Mrs. Gray helped me settle into the guest room. We later had supper on the porch and enjoyed a wonderful lemon meringue pie for dessert. Morning came too soon, along with breakfast, kissing, and hugging, and then Saeed was gone. I stood and watched until the car left the compound. I knew I was going to miss him dreadfully.

I turned around and Mrs. Gray said as she tried to comfort me, "Two weeks will pass in no time. We've been invited almost daily to a barbeque, lunch, or dinner, not to mention all the card games going on.

This is the time for you to learn how to play bridge, my dear. You will enjoy that so much. As for today, after lunch, we will walk to the embassy and see a movie."

Although I had a wonderful day, I broke down and wept at night when I nursed Susan and thought of Saeed so far away. I cheered my soul with thoughts of tomorrow's Sunday service, held at Mr. and Mrs. Jenkin's home three houses down.

Noffa or Arifa called every day to see how Susan and I were doing and to ask if we needed anything. I was pleased that they thought of us so often. The next week, the Amir, Arifa, Wadad, and Noffa drove up to visit. They brought every kind of fruit and vegetable available, chicken and lamb, and a gold bracelet for Susan. Wadad and Noffa ran to hug me, and they took Susan in their arms, kissing her all over. I was so touched that I began to cry.

Days passed with many interesting and fun activities, and I would have been blissfully happy if I hadn't missed Saeed so terribly. We had never been separated this long since our marriage five years ago. Two days before Saeed was supposed to arrive, Mr. Gray walked in with a telegram from Saeed saying that he extended his stay another two weeks. I almost cried; I was so upset. Susan looked like she was about to walk any day now, and he would miss that.

Mrs. Gray patted my hand, saying, "Now, dear, it's not that bad. This way, you'll get to come with us to the ambassador's party next week. You'll like it!"

"Oh, but I have nothing to wear, and who will take care of Susan?"

"We'll think of something, and besides, in another two weeks, you'll become a pro at bridge. Why, you're already a good player."

The next day Noffa called, and I told her that Saeed had delayed his arrival day. I was happy to hear that the family planned to visit the next day, and asked for extra clothes for myself and Susan, including my black-and-white, floral-print sheath for the ambassador's party. I genuinely looked forward to their visit and was disappointed when Wadad didn't come because she had a bad cold. Again, they brought vegetables, fruits, lamb, and a beautiful new dress for Susan, which they had purchased in Damascus.

The Amir's disappointment at Saeed's delay equaled mine, and we expressed our mutual feeling with extra hugging and a lot of waving arms and body language. He played with Susan and hugged her, saying she smelled exactly like Saeed. I really expected a show of disappointment toward my staying another two weeks in Amman, but none came. I began to understand the true Bedouin nature of acceptance, pride, and love.

The party at the ambassador's house was the highlight of my stay. It was like being in a movie. Everyone was so elegantly dressed, and the music and the dancing were perfection. When Mama made this dress, I didn't know if I would ever wear it. Life was so unpredictable.

The four weeks finally came to an end, and on his last visit, the Amir presented Mr. and Mrs. Gray with a beautiful, hand-woven rug that they loved.

****

Although I was busy from morning till sunset, I thought of Betty and Susan every day and every night at the convention. It was my first official visit as the Agricultural Engineering representative for Jordan. I was excited and wished to learn as much as possible. I paid extra attention to the lectures that dealt with climates similar to Jordan and the Jordan Valley in particular. The only regret was not knowing about this trip early enough to have arranged for Betty and Susan to fly to Knoxville for a couple of weeks. I spent my free time admiring this lovely city and wishing Betty was with me. I did some shopping and wanted to buy everything I saw that I thought she would like.

When we got the news that the convention was going to be four weeks instead of two, I felt terrible. Writing the telegram hurt because I could see what Betty's face would look like when she read it. If I had felt badly not knowing about this trip earlier, I felt doubly bad then. I kept telling myself that she could have spent four weeks with her family. I chased those thoughts away chiding myself for a habit that does no one any good. They were both taken care of and I knew Betty loved the Grays and she would be fine; but I still felt guilty.

Day after day I researched the best crops to grow in the Valley. In the end I was not happy with my findings. Bananas were not the answer; citrus would be the right crop. Jordan had almost no citrus farms but it would yield the best profit for the longest time. I just hoped Yubba and the elders would not hold the banana crop against me. Finally, the four weeks were up and I was going back home to my wife and child. I missed them so much that I hardly slept that night from the anticipation of seeing them; Yubba too.

****

"Oh, you found my Chanel No. 5! Oh Saeed, you got me four bottles. That's so sweet; I will give Shamma one. She always wants to smell like me." I sniffed deeply as Saeed pulled gift after gift from his bag. Susan sat in the middle of the bed, laughing out loud. He also bought me two handbags, a gorgeous burgundy satin dress, two pencil skirts, four sweaters, and an exquisite silver necklace with matching earrings.

"Oh, everything is perfect. I love Susan's clothes! I can't get over these beautiful colors and designs. Even the toys are different." My happiness couldn't be measured with words. The minute Susan fell asleep we were in each other's arms, making up for the long lost weeks. Finally, exhaustion overtook us. Sleep was wondrous, filled with the knowledge that I would see Saeed when I woke the next morning.

Saeed and I had plans to go to the States that summer, but after being away for four weeks, he couldn't leave again so soon. He told me that Susan and I could go, but I decided that I would not go until we could go as a family. He said he might be able to travel with us next spring.

Saeed kept the promise he made me before he left for Amsterdam and one week after he came back we were on our way to Jerusalem. The drive was shorter than I expected. It was only about sixty-five miles - less time than it takes to get to Chattanooga from my parents' house.

Saeed had arranged for a guide to help steer us to the most important places of interest. He was not only thinking of me, but also of the Grays. Once we finished breakfast, Khalil, our guide, met us at the door of the hotel. In his early thirties with olive skin, dark hair, and dark eyes, he had a hooked nose that didn't seem to belong with the

174

rest of his delicate features. We headed first to the Chapel of the Ascension, which was a short drive from the hotel. We entered through the ornate gate, and walked into a paved courtyard. Mrs. Gray and I walked together as the men trailed a little distance behind. Khalil strolled alongside and provided a wealth of information. We were speechless and awed by all we heard.

"First thing to know is that several religions contributed to this wonderful place. It began in the Crusades era, and then the Muslims added these." Khalil pointed to the stone dome and a beautiful octagonal drum. "If you look at the walls, you will see the expert carvings depicting capitals from the twelfth century." He indicated two winged birds."

"Oh, they have four legs. I wonder why they carved and painted such nonexistent creatures. Saeed and I saw many of these carvings in Rome. Remember, Honey?" I spoke louder to get his attention. He turned slightly and agreed as we entered the chapel.

"This is a *mihrab*, a resonator for the voice, shaped to bounce the sound back and magnify it. The *imam*, or the prayer leader, stations himself inside to lead the congregation in prayers, indicating the direction of Mecca in the south wall," Khalil continued as he pointed to a slab of stone on the floor, "This imprint is the right footprint of Christ." He paused for a second. "The left footprint is in the Al-Aqsa Mosque, not far from here."

At this point Saeed came closer and gave Susan a kiss, "You are getting heavy, big girl. I know Mama is getting tired." He said as he took her from me.

We viewed the burial crypt and listened to Khalil's fascinating information. "All monotheistic religions have different beliefs concerning this burial spot. Jews believe it contains the remains of Prophet Huldah. Christians believe it holds the remains of Saint Pelagia. Muslims believe it holds the remains of a holy woman, Rabi'a Al-Adawiya. Nuns now live inside.

I couldn't imagine such devotion or more love for Christ. I didn't know why it affected me so, or why the nuns were on my mind for the rest of the day. To voluntarily never see your loved ones seems such a heavy price! I glanced up and saw Saeed looking at me, and my heart raced. We saw the Church of Our Lord and the Church of All Nations, and I learned that the name came because twelve nations contributed monies to build it. We admired the countries' symbols inlaid in gold in the ceiling.

Khalil then said, "It is also believed that Jesus prayed here on the night of his arrest, which is why it is also called the Basilica of Agony."

His words shook me to my core as I realized that I was actually walking where Jesus Christ once walked, lived, breathed, and talked. In this shared state of peace and tranquility, we stopped for lunch. We sat under the branches of an olive tree and sipped on lemonade before digging hungrily into the food the minute it was placed on the large round, brass table.

"A penny for your thoughts," Mrs. Gray said as I fed Susan some of the roasted potatoes.

"Just thinking how my life changed from meeting Saeed. I never dreamed I would visit Jerusalem or live so close."

"Isn't that the truth, my dear! We never know how one person may change our life. I never thought I would see so much of the world either, when I was your age."

Next we visited the Virgin Mary. I noticed Susan fidgeting in her daddy's arms and knew she was becoming tired. He rocked her as he walked, and I was so thankful that she was such a good baby and that Saeed was such a good daddy. We entered the dimly lit vault where walls, blackened by centuries of smoke, gave the place an air of great antiquity. Khalil stood still, as if turned to stone, before he quietly informed us that this was Mary's tomb. We all stood in silence as I thought of Mama and wished she was with me. Finally, we were on our way to the Church of the Holy Sepulchre. Khalil went on in a low voice. "It stands on a site that covers where Jesus was crucified and the tomb where he was buried. Of course, due to these important facts, it has been a pilgrimage destination for hundreds of years."

We admired it and then followed Khalil, who stood in front of the entrance. "This is the right entrance door, which was blocked after 1187 A.D. as part of the Muslim control of the site when the Crusaders had been defeated. Inside the entrance sits the Muslim doorkeeper."

"A Muslim man is the doorkeeper of the church?" Mrs. Gray's surprised voice mimicked my own face.

"That makes no sense. Is it because the majority of the population is Muslim?" Mr. Gray asked.

We all looked at Khalil, who quickly pointed out, "Peace is the only reason a Muslim has the keys to the church."

"Peace? You would think that would cause disputes, not peace," Mrs. Gray interjected politely.

Khalil went on, "You have to remember that the holiest site in Christendom is not owned by one sect, but is equally important for many denominations who each believe theirs is the only right branch. The main guardians were the Greek Orthodox, the Armenian Apostolic, and the Roman Catholic churches, with the Greeks holding the lion's share. Later on, other churches such as the Ethiopian Orthodox, the Coptic Orthodox, and the Syriac Orthodox became partners with lesser responsibilities."

"What do you mean by 'lesser responsibilities'?" I asked.

"Like the responsibility of keeping the building and shrines in good shape. Since there were many groups, their times were regulated in the common areas."

"Oh, I see. Thank you." I was astonished at how little I knew. Overwhelmed by my emotions, I exchanged glances with Mrs. Gray as we followed Khalil up steps to the roof.

"This is the holiest site in Christendom. The body of Christ lay under this slab, and this is where, three days later, he rose from the dead."

It all seemed so surreal, as if I had been transported to a different time. Overflowing with emotions I was silent until we were back at the hotel. I was spiritually subdued by the impact of the day. I began a long and detailed letter to Mama.

Much later, Saeed felt me crawl into his arms, waking him from a deep sleep. When he asked if I was tired I answered, "Yes, but happy. However, I still can't imagine why there are so few Christians here when everything began and is still here."

Saeed yawned and thought about my words. "Most were Christians until Islam came, some five hundred years after Christ."

"You mean they conquered them and made them become Muslims."

"No, churches were *not* converted into mosques, and religious freedom was given to all as long as they paid the taxes. They . . ."

"What if people didn't have money to pay the taxes?"

"I'm sure that was an incentive to convert in some cases." Saeed yawned and kissed me.

Soon I fell into a deep, restful sleep, and dreamed I was showing Mama the city of Jerusalem. All of a sudden, Daddy came out of the Nativity Church with Saeed, and I ran to hug him, saying, "Oh, Daddy, I thought you couldn't make it. I'm so happy. I'm in a blessed place!"

Saeed, Susan, and Betty in the Jordan Valley

Susan

CHAPTER 12

DONNA JEAN

I couldn't believe time passed so much more quickly since I had Susan. She turned one today and I threw her a party. I had no idea that Bedouins didn't celebrate their birthdays, not even the children's. Noffa and Wadad had never had a birthday party. Why, they didn't even know their exact date of birth. They excitedly helped me make and decorate the cake, jello, and sandwiches. I loved them for their love and effort. I invited many relatives and will never forget the looks on their faces when they saw the decorations and the lit candles. When Saeed came to take pictures, I started laughing out loud. Everyone became so still the minute they saw him with the camera. They all stood and smiled into the lens the whole time. I will always laugh at that memory.

Next spring came and Saeed couldn't come with us to the States as we had hoped. I thought long and hard about going alone with Susan, but I hoped to get pregnant again. I wanted to have another daughter so Susan would have a best friend and confidante in this world. I knew my daughter was never going to be like her cousins or other little girls in this country. More than anything, I wished for Susan to have a sister with whom to share her genes and dreams. In the end, I

180

decided to not go either, and stayed in Jordan. Mrs. Gray thought that I made the right decision and that made me feel better. I was thankful for having such a wonderful person in my life, but I really wished I had someone my age to be friends with.

God must have been listening when I made that wish because I met Linda soon after. Saeed had business in Amman that would require him to stay there a few nights, so we stayed at the Grays. While we were there Saeed said that Ali had arrived in Amman and we should go and welcome him home. He said he was sure his wife would love to see another American.

I liked Linda the minute I saw her. She was a little taller than I, with dark blonde hair and twinkling blue eyes, and pregnant. We hugged and talked as if we were old friends. I guess one thing that helped was the fact that she too was a southern girl. She hailed from Alabama.

"You have a little girl, how wonderful. What is her name?"

"Susan Beth,"

"Where is Susan? I can't wait to see her!"

"She is with a good friend of mine, Mrs. Gray. You'll love her when you meet her. She is the sweetest person on earth. She thought there would be too many people for Susan, so she took her home to take a nap."

"She sounds like a dear indeed," Linda commented.

I had a good time the next day when Ali's sisters threw a party for Linda. They brought sandwiches, cakes, and music. The women played record after record of Arabic songs, some that I had heard in Irbid. I showed Linda how to belly dance, and she laughed out loud, duly impressed with my skill.

"I love all sorts of dancing. The first time I saw belly dancing was in Beirut, I was spellbound," I told her.

"You must be a quick learner." Linda watched as I began to show more moves. "I love that move with your hands; I'd like to learn that myself." She began to wave her hands as her hips moved.

"One thing for sure, you can't be sad when you're dancing. What you need to do is remember to follow the beat," I said "It's the same all over the world - the beat moves the body."

The next day, I further impressed everyone with my ballet and baton moves. Linda stared at me as I conversed with the others in Arabic, and I noticed that she didn't smile much. "Linda, try to smile at everyone, or they'll think you don't like them. They're sensitive that way," I said gently.

We spent as much time together as we could, but living in different cities didn't make it convenient to visit. I was more flexible than she was because of Saeed's easygoing nature. But, I didn't enjoy staying at her house; I preferred to stay with the Grays.

"If it's not one person barging in, it's another. They don't understand she needs to have some privacy. And whenever Ali is home, he wants her attention all the time." My cheeks flushed with irritation as I told Saeed how I felt.

"Honey, Ali is a good man. I have known him almost all my life, but his family is very conservative and so is he. I know he loves her, and that's who he is." I told him that I was upset because I had tried to convince Linda to go see Dr. Stevens and Ali had argued with me. He wanted her to go to a Doctor Ma'Ahir in Amman. He said Aj-loun was too far away and he didn't want his child delivered at 'no Baptist Hospital.'"

"I mean, how could he say that when Linda is Baptist?"

Saeed tried to placate me, saying Ali had some valid points. "After all, Aj-loun is more than an hour away, and Dr. Ma'Ahir is a great physician. "

Our friendship grew quickly and we tried to see each other as often as we could. I sometimes spent the night with her. Although I always stayed another night at the Gray's because they meant so much to me. Linda came to Irbid and spent one or two nights with me whenever she could, and we always enjoyed those times talking, baking, playing games, watching slides, and being with Susan. We talked about the States and all the things we missed. I hated to see her leave, and Susan always cried.

Linda asked me if I would come and stay with her until she had the baby and I agreed. She was a couple of years younger than I and I knew that my presence would be a calming thing for her. Linda had a younger sister and two older brothers. I knew she missed them as much as I missed mine. But after only four days at her place, I missed being with Saeed, although he came every other day to visit. I was so thankful when three days later, Linda went into labor. She had an easy delivery and gave birth to a healthy boy she and Ali named Khalid. Everyone was happy and Ali was ecstatic. Two days passed, and I was ready and eager to go back home. I missed the family, too. I was actually happy to be driving back to Irbid!

Several days later, we went to the Valley where Saeed took me to the piece of land overlooking the Jordan River where he had planted the Magnolia trees. One was not looking good, but Saeed said it would be okay. I hoped he was right; I couldn't wait to see a magnolia blossom. I stood and looked at the land. It was a little elevated allowing one to see for many miles. I could even see the big house. I loved it. He then told me about his plans for a citrus farm.

"The majority will be different varieties of orange trees. But I will also plant grapefruits, mandarins, lemons, and clementines."

The next day as I was sorting Susan's clothes, I overheard Wadad scolding Susan for something she had done. Wadad wasn't loud or mean, but I felt the blood draining from my face. I quickly explained to Wadad, as Noffa listened, that no one was allowed to say one word to Susan. I continued in a gentler manner by saying that if Susan does something wrong, and it is possible, because she is a baby, you need to come tell me or Saeed what happened. We are her parents, and we are the only ones who can reprimand her.

"I'm sorry! I love Susan very much. I love you, Auntie Betty." Wadad was almost in tears. Noffa glared at Wadad, giving her an "I told you so" look.

I hugged her, "Auntie Betty loves you too, Wadad. I just want to teach you right and wrong, so when you grow, you will be the best mother."

Many women and men in the tribe observed the way Susan was raised, and they implemented what they saw in their own lives. I spoke to Susan when she did something wrong and explained to her why she shouldn't do one thing versus another. Susan represented an important milestone for the tribe. She was the first daughter to be treated with as much importance and love as if she had been a boy.

A few weeks after Khalid's birth, I found out I was expecting my second child. I couldn't have been happier, for we had been hoping I would get pregnant again. I wanted another girl. I thought that Saeed would be hoping for a boy, but he said that he didn't care as long as the baby was healthy. I went up to Amman for Thanksgiving where I stayed the first night at Linda's. We had a wonderful time together as usual and in the afternoon Ali's mother came to visit. She admonished Linda for not pinning an amulet on Khalid's top. When she left Linda looked at me and said that Ali's mother had asked her to keep it on him as long as I was visiting. I laughed out loud,

"They believe that these stones protect from evil eyes. Ali's mother thinks I'm envious because you have a son and I have a daughter. Wait until I see her tomorrow and tell her that I'm praying for another daughter so Susan will have a sister!"

Linda hooted, "I'm looking forward to that."

After lunch, Susan and Khalid fell asleep while I read to them. Later Linda asked me about removing the hair on her legs with a sticky gum that Ali's sister had made for her.

"Oh, yes," I said. "It's called *A'eedah*, and it's made by boiling sugar, water, and lemon juice. Come on, I'll make some for you, and you can watch."

After cooking the concoction and allowing it to cool for a few minutes, I scooped it up and kneaded it in my hands until it became pliable. I then spread it on Linda's legs and, waiting only a moment or two, yanked it off, showing her all the hair follicles stuck to it.

"Ouch, that hurt!"

"I know, that's what I thought too, the first time I did it."

We both laughed as she practiced a little more. I helped her, and we both waxed our legs from the knees to the ankles.

The next day we had a wonderful time with other American families at the Gray's compound. They cooked turkeys, some stuffed with bread and others with cornbread. The ladies cooked an array of side dishes, including mashed potatoes, green beans, corn, yams, and rolls, along with lemon pie, apple pie, coconut cake, and chocolate cake. Everyone helped cook, eat, and clean up the hearty mess. As they all sat drinking coffee afterward, I talked about my experiences.

184

"Things are not as bad when you know what to expect or when you understand why something is happening. I remember the first time I had Mansaf, or the first time I drank the *Gahwa Sada*. Little things, like shaking a cup, can make a big difference. We need to form a committee that visits the new American women in Jordan. That way we can introduce them more gently to the habits and the cultures of this region."

Mr. Seals, an American sitting next to me, encouraged me to follow through. "I already know of a couple of Jordanian men who are still studying in the States and who have married American women. In a year or two, they will be coming to live here. I think you have a great idea, Betty. When you move here, you should work on that."

Three weeks before Christmas Linda called and sounded so distressed. It was her first Christmas in Amman and Ali had told her she could not have a tree. After discussing this with Saeed and telling him I would like to ask her to stay with us during that time, I asked her to come. I felt blessed when Linda said that she and Khalid where going to spend Christmas with us. Saeed and I went all the way to Aj-loun to find a tree. He promised to plant two rows of pine trees around the perimeter of our citrus farm. That way we'd have many trees to pick from each Christmas. Linda and I had a marvelous time decorating the tree as we sipped hot chocolate.

"You're so lucky to have a man like Saeed. Ali said that he would never let me have a Christmas tree."

"That's horrible, Linda. He can't be serious. You had a tree in the States, didn't you?" I couldn't help my anger and I felt so bad for her. "I'll always have a tree, and you can spend every Christmas with me." I handed Susan one of the ornaments and she gazed at the silvery frosted ball and pointed to the little Santa nestled in the middle before she hung it on the tree. I hugged my baby, promising her a Christmas tree every year.

"Yeth, Chrithath tee." Susan was trying to speak at one year and four months of age.

"Are you going to speak English with her? Ali thinks it's confusing to speak two languages at once. He thinks Khalid should learn Arabic first."

185

"Where does he come up with all this nonsense? Of course I'm going to speak English to her, and so is Saeed. Everyone else speaks Arabic to her. Your children will not be able to speak English like a native if they don't learn it as babies. Have you never wondered what is meant by 'mother tongue'?" I plugged the Christmas light cord into the socket and lit the tree.

Susan and Khalid began to laugh and clap their hands. They sat on the carpet and stared at the lights until they both fell asleep. Ali came to our house on Christmas Eve and complimented us on the tree. I asked him why he didn't want Linda to have one and he said that since he was the eldest, he should be a role model. That didn't make sense to me. Saeed, too, was the eldest. One look at Saeed's face made me say no more.

We all exchanged gifts and then I found a card that Saeed had placed among my gifts. He loved to surprise me, and he smiled as I opened it. The writing on the card read: *We are going to go to Cairo in two weeks*. I ran and hugged his grinning face before I begged Ali and Linda to come with us. Ali said he needed to help his father start building their first factory.

"I'm sure there will be plenty of other trips," Saeed said, and he took the final picture of the evening: Susan, rocking her little doll.

My thoughts were on Susan, who we left in the Gray's care, when the plane landed in Cairo. The airport there was large, compared to Amman's, and I noticed many foreigners and heard different languages as we waited to have our passports stamped. The immigration officer was friendly, a warm smile remaining on his face as he welcomed us to Egypt. Outside, I was glad to see the sun shining as Sameer, one of Saeed's friends who had attended school with him years ago, greeted us. After hugs, laughter, and still more hugs and pats on the back, Sameer turned his full attention to me. He held his hands out and took mine in a hearty handshake.

"Welcome, lovely lady, to my beautiful city. My brother has indeed brought a flower to his country," he said as he kissed my hand.

I liked this charming man who was about Saeed's height and build; he had curlier hair and light hazel eyes. Saeed looked happy to be with his friend as they joked together all the way to the hotel. The drive took about half an hour, and I liked everything I saw. Wide streets lined with palm trees, beautiful bridges over the Nile River, and exquisite statues everywhere. The tranquil scenery testified to the wonder of rivers and all that they add to a landscape. I also liked the hotel which overlooked the Nile. Sameer explained that the Tahrīr Square, behind the hotel, was a hub of tourist activity. It was full of things to do and see; of course, the most important was the Egyptian Museum. I admired the lobby's walls, embellished throughout with gold leaf and painted Pharaonic images. I thought it breathtaking.

After checking in at the desk, we went upstairs to freshen up before meeting Sameer again for dinner. I loved our room which overlooked the Nile. I walked out onto the little balcony and breathed in the beauty. Saeed followed and hugged me as we stood there for a while before I thought of my baby again and told him how I missed her. He suggested calling the Grays and I happily agreed.

Hearing Susan's voice and being assured by Mrs. Gray that she was fine enabled me to enjoy my first evening with Sameer and his wife Suhair. She was tall with jet-black hair and slanted, dark brown eyes. She wore a stylish black cocktail dress with a matching coat, and I was glad that I was wearing a dress Saeed had brought me from Amsterdam. They took us to a nightclub with excellent food and another superb belly dancer, Samia Gamal. Her body moved to the music in such a synchronized manner that I couldn't take my eyes off her. Saeed's words way back about seeing a real belly dancer came back to me and I now understood that there was great art in belly dancing.

After checking with the Grays the next morning, we were off to the zoo a short distance from the hotel. We walked on the paved mosaic pathways and across miniature bridges. After a couple of hours, Sameer and Suhair took us to a Swiss-owned café called *Groppi*. It had a quaint garden with ornate steel chairs and tables. I really liked it, especially their wonderful ice-cream.

Sameer jokingly asked Saeed if he wished to see the Agricultural Museum. Suhair explained that it used to be the palace of Princess Fatma, the daughter of Khedive Ismail. She also said that it was the first museum of its kind in the world. I enjoyed it but not half as much as Saeed did. He even said he could have stayed there all day. But we both equally enjoyed the Egyptian Museum which opened its doors in 1902. It housed magnificent treasures from different Pharaonic dynasties. I could have stayed there all day.

The following day we saw the Citadel, which had a number of museums, ancient mosques, and other interesting sites. I couldn't imagine people had actually lived inside these walls. The view was spectacular; we were able to see the Pyramids as well as all of Cairo. I noticed people praying in this ancient Mosque and wondered why we pray in different ways.

"I wish Jordan was more like Lebanon or Egypt," I said to Saeed in the airport. I was having a great time but missed my baby very much. He mimicked my sentiments.

Susan seemed to have grown in only one week! She was overjoyed to see us when we returned, and clung to me until we reached Irbid. It felt good to be home. I didn't mind that the family was waiting when we arrived. By now, I was calling Arifa "Yumma Arifa," as Saeed did, and she loved the way I said it. We gave out the gifts we bought for everyone and they all seemed happy. Susan jumped up and down, from one lap to the other, and finally fell asleep in Arifa's lap.

Linda and Khalid came over the next week and stayed for a couple of nights. We decided to go to the Valley for the day. I put on a sleeveless dress and Linda looked surprised, saying that Ali's mother had told her that it was not proper to wear sleeveless dresses in public. I told her that Saeed's family was not really bothered by the way I dressed. To them I am not a Bedouin, and they didn't want to change me. I added, "To Ali's family, you need to be changed in order to fit into their society, into what they think is correct. City dwellers have made up a set of rules they expect people to follow."

"I really think the biggest difference is who Saeed is, and not who his family is," Linda offered tentatively.

"I guess you're right, Linda. I'm blessed to have Saeed, but then, too, it can't be all him. Okay, here's another example. What happens to Ali's mother and sisters or whoever is there when the call to prayer is heard?"

"They go pray?" Linda tilted her head to one side and looked at me.

"I'm talking about how they all start calling each other so they can all pray behind Ali's mother, who is usually looking at us and trying to make us feel bad because we aren't joining them."

"What does that have to do with anything? Ali said when you pray in a group, God gives you double the blessings."

"Bedouins are different. I've seen many slip outside unnoticed to go pray under a tree or beside the creek. That's more like our praying, and I think when I sit and read my Bible and pray, they see my love and devotion and accept it."

I was really upset that Linda was speaking in Arabic to her child and I thought a minute before I said something to her. She said it wasn't worth the fight.

I was adamant. "It is absolutely worth the fight, Linda. Can't you see how this will affect your relationship with them when they grow older? I mean, you speak good Arabic and so do I. But can you honestly express exactly what you mean?" She didn't answer, simply hung her head. I felt bad and asked her if she could at least speak English to him when Ali wasn't home. I for one, always spoke English to my daughter.

Later that evening, Saeed came in late, and I knew he had had a couple of beers. I didn't like it when he drank. He said it relaxed him but that made no sense to me.

"It's the same thing as cigarettes, Betty. People say they smoke because it relaxes them. Why do you smoke?"

"I enjoy it! And it's not against my religion."

"Betty, The Grays are God-fearing people who go to church on Sunday, but they still drink alcohol. There's a difference between having a couple of drinks and being drunk.

I didn't have an answer but wished I did. Why did Saeed have to always say things that just made sense ... why?

Once again, I was happily settled in Aj-loun. I enjoyed my time with the Stevens and took long walks with Susan under the beautiful trees. Saeed came up every three or four days and stayed a couple of

189

nights with us. Those were my favorite times. The Stevens also enjoyed him, and Miriam made special dishes when he came.

"If the baby doesn't come soon, I'm going to gain more weight than Betty in her pregnancy," Saeed joked as we all laughed.

****

Miriam and I were talking about drinking. It seemed that I often thought about it because I knew Saeed enjoyed it and that I had a problem with it. As I was talking, I felt water rush down my legs. *Oh my God, my water has broken.* Silence took over for a second before pandemonium erupted; chairs were pushed back and I was rushed to the hospital. I had an easy labor, and Donna Jean was born in the early evening of July 20, 1956. I started crying from sheer happiness. A baby girl! Susan had a sister. I admired my newborn's beautiful dark hair and dark eyes. She was smaller than Susan and had a slightly lighter complexion. Saeed and Susan soon came into the room and she ran with outstretched arms to my bed.

"My baby! I want my baby, Mama!" Susan said, as she tried to climb onto the bed. Saeed lifted her up and I hugged both my daughters.

"You can sit on Mama's bed and hold your new baby sister with me. She's too small for you to hold alone. When she gets stronger and you get older, then you will be able to hold her all by yourself."

Susan smiled happily as I placed Donna in her lap. She rubbed her sister's head while I looked down on my two girls. I knew my face must have been radiant.

****

I knew Yubba was going to be disappointed that Betty had given birth to another daughter. I knew he loved Susan, but he wanted boys. The first girl baby was welcomed because it meant the woman was fertile, but after that, boys were preferred. I really didn't care one way or another. If Betty never had another child I would be a contented man, but I knew better than to voice these feelings out loud. *I would really like a drink right now and I wish Betty didn't have such negative*

190

thoughts about drinking. I have always understood the need for moderation in everything; drinking was one of those things.

Betty's first days back in Irbid were a little hectic; she had Susan to take care of, Donna to nurse, and people dropping by to congratulate her on the new baby. She was exasperated and couldn't understand why they were congratulating her if they had wished for a boy.

I felt equally frustrated with the amount of company we received, and rubbed her shoulders for a minute before I tried to explain. "Yes, they would prefer a boy to a girl, but they are grateful the girl is healthy and the mother is well." I didn't want to tell her that some visitors told me that any woman who can give birth to a girl can give birth to a boy. It sounded so wrong and so unfair to Donna. I wanted to say something to them but thought it best not to. I watched Susan holding her sister on the bed, and my heart felt as though it would explode with love. She loved her little sister and would frequently sit on the bed, holding her in her lap, singing to her. I didn't know what she was singing, but it sounded beautiful and Donna loved it. Often they fell asleep in each other's arms. This was worthy of another picture. I snapped it and turned to see Betty watching before she said, "How can anyone not want a sister?" I agreed and said that we needed to show everyone how to love every child, no matter the sex.

The next day, Linda called Betty and told her she was pregnant. Betty was excited for her and said she hoped Linda would have another boy so Khalid could have a brother.

I said, "I'm sure that's what everyone is hoping." Later in the day, Yubba told me he wanted to rent a place in Irbid in order to oversee the building of his house. I encouraged him as I thought of Betty. I knew that school was going to start the next month and that way Noffa and Wadad would not have to live with us.

I was working with Mr. Gray to set up an extension service in Jordan to help with the United States agricultural aid program, and he asked me if I could move to Amman. I told him that I had to wait until Yubba moved into his new home in Irbid and that I needed to get the citrus farm started. I also realized that Yubba's house was massive and was going to take a couple of years to finish. I believed Yubba needed to live in Irbid and become more involved in the politics of all of

Jordan, not just the Valley. Moving would enable him to oversee his lands as well as mediate with the rest of the tribes who lived close by in the region.

The next morning I headed to the Valley to talk to Yubba about the citrus farm. "Yubba, the most important factor to consider when planting citrus is the ability of the soil to properly drain excess water. If water stays around the tree because we don't have good drainage, the tree will suffer. The same thing is true if water is unable to leave the roots.

"How are you going to know if the soil has the right drainage?"

"By digging a hole about three to four feet deep, filling it with water, and watching to see what happens The water should drain from the hole in about a day or a day and a half."

The experiment was a success and I felt that at last, I knew what we needed to plant. Yubba asked me why I had planted so many pine trees around the farm and wondered if they were worth the money and water. I explained that the Jordan Valley experiences some cold weather in the winter. Planting under large, overhanging trees will offer some protection from the cold.

Yubba wondered, "If cold kills the trees, why not plant in the desert?"

I explained that citrus is most productive when grown in the Mediterranean climates, which was our climate. "We have a distinct cold period that induces a dormant phase. Citrus trees are subject to damage from extremes of both heat and cold. The desert would kill the trees the first year."

"If this is a success son, it will make all the years of separation worth the sacrifice. Order the trees, and let us start our citrus growing."

Driving back to Irbid, I felt good about everything. I couldn't wait to get home and hug my three ladies. I was also excited about attending my friend, Dr. Barakat's, wedding in Beirut next week. I knew Betty was going to have a great time although she hated to leave Susan behind.

"I know that she'll be fine and everyone dotes on her. Oh Saeed, I hate to separate the girls, but I can't leave Donna when she's still breastfeeding."

192

"Honey, Susan will be fine, besides, we're only going for three nights."

"You're right; she would be miserable staying with strangers or going shopping."

"That's true, she would not be happy. As a consolation, I think we should go as a family to Beirut sometime next month." Her face lit up; I knew she would like that idea!

****

Dr. Barakat, a friend of Saeed's from school, was waiting for us at the Berliz hotel, where he had reserved a sea-front bedroom for us. I changed and nursed Donna while Saeed unpacked, showered, and dressed. I showered and put on my sleeveless black dress with the narrow collar. Pinned to the middle of the collar was a large magnolia blossom.

Saeed liked it and said, "My Southern Magnolia looks beautiful."

He watched as I lastly dabbed on my perfume and commented, "I can't help but contrast you to Yumma Arifa."

I laughed as I remembered seeing her putting on perfume. She literally sprayed every inch. She even sprinkled each ironed piece of clothing before she let the maids put them up in her closet. I had even written Mama about that.

"One thing for sure, you always know when Yumma Arifa is coming." Saeed joined me in laughter. What a woman. I always admired and loved her

We left Donna at a friend's house before heading to the pre-wedding party. I had a good time and thought the bride to be, Muna, very pretty.

The Barakats were a big family, and Saeed told me that it would be a large wedding. For that occasion I chose a red stretch, bengaline pencil dress with a curve-hugging silhouette and a beautiful, red embroidered bodice. Saeed said all eyes were going to be on me. How I love my husband.

My first big Middle Eastern wedding was held in one of the big hotels in Beirut and seemed to include everyone who was at all important. Beautifully dressed women on the arms of handsomely

193

attired men roamed the ballroom, which had been lavishly decorated with candles and flowers on every table. The tablecloths and chairs were adorned with matching lace. Most of the men and many of the women were drinking and seemed to be having a great time.

A band of ten men played an assortment of English and Arabic songs, which I enjoyed immensely. Saeed asked me to dance and we danced to song after song. The seemingly never-ending celebration must have lasted till dawn, but we left sometime after midnight.

"I can't believe a wedding can last this long," I said to Saeed as I yawned, and suddenly panicked. "How are we going to pick Donna up at this hour? We should have left earlier!"

"Don't worry, Honey, they know we are at a wedding and they're actually going to be surprised that we're here this early. You stay in the car. I'll go up and get Donna.

Although I was able to talk to Susan on the phone at least once every day, I still felt bad about leaving her. She sounded fine, but she asked when we were coming back, and I teared up when she asked about Donna. I vowed I would never separate the girls from one another again. It was not right, and in this instance, I felt it was just not fair to Susan.

When we returned, Susan ran to meet us but then stopped a few feet away. She looked directly at me, sucked her thumb, tilted her head, and, with her free hand, twirled her hair. I felt a jab in my heart as I handed Donna to Saeed and went down on my knees, opening my arms wide.

"Come to Mama, Honey, come." I smiled and my concern turned to laughter as soon as she ran and jumped up into my arms.

Saeed placed Donna in Noffa's arms and joined us with more hugs and kisses. He took his firstborn and threw her into the air over and over to her joyful shouts of "More Baba, More!"

When we got home, Susan would not sit down until I placed Donna in her lap. She kept saying,

"I want my baby, Mama. You took my baby."

I was nursing Donna when I heard Saeed on the phone. It was Ali letting him know that Linda was having the baby. I heard Saeed telling him that we would come by as soon as we could. We headed out the next day and after dropping the girls at the Gray's, headed to the hospital.

The moment I saw Ali's mother I knew that Linda had given birth to a daughter. Ayesha, his sister, smiled, but then threw a look at Linda, who sat on the bed, obviously afraid to show any happiness.

"Well, that's great news. You now have a boy and a girl!" I gave her a hug. "Don't let them make you feel bad. You're blessed that you have a healthy daughter. She will be your best friend, just like Mama and me."

"I know, and I'm really happy. She's so pretty. Wait till you see her!" Linda had started to feel better the minute I arrived.

****

A few months later, Saeed convinced Ali to take Linda and the kids with us for a two-day trip to Beirut. Once in Beirut, the subject of swimming at the hotel pool came up. I knew Ali was traditional, but I never expected he would object to her wearing a bathing suit. Linda was in tears and said she missed swimming but Ali was screaming and saying that he wished she would act more like his sisters did. Saeed finally convinced him to let her wear a bathing suit. A bit nervous about the whole incident, Linda even related it to Muna Barakat when we took them all out to lunch. Muna even said that one would think the man who belonged to a Bedouin tribe would be more strict with his wife than the one brought up in a big city.

That evening, Saeed and I went with Omar and Muna Barakat to the famed Casino du Liban. The whole bathing suit incident and being with Ali throughout the day had shaken me. I felt tense and melancholy. Saeed always told me that drinking calmed him and helped him to relax. I needed to relax and so when Saeed asked me what I would like to drink, I asked for a glass of whiskey. He raised his eyebrows and tilted his head in a questioning manner. I nodded; he got up, went to the bar and returned with two glasses of whiskey over ice.

I didn't like my first sip, and thought it awful! I wondered aloud why in the world people drink. I looked up into Saeed's grinning face. Omar Barakat laughed and said as he saluted me with his glass. "Just sip it slowly, and in about half an hour, you will know why people drink."

He was right, I thought the music sounded better and the dancing looked better. Everything seemed perfect and I no longer thought about Ali, Linda, or anything else. I had a blast. Later that night we made love the way we used to in our earlier days: the days before the girls, when I didn't care if I was loud or not. It was pure bliss. The next morning I told my love that he had been absolutely wonderful that night.

After breakfast, Linda and I tanned by the pool and watched the kids. I told her I had tried a drink last night and that I had enjoyed it. She looked astonished and said she hoped I was joking.

"No, I'm not Linda, and I don't feel that I did anything wrong."

Linda looked down and was silent for a moment. "Drinking is a sin. I would never let liquor touch my lips."

"You sound just like Ali when you talk that way."

"I do not!"

"Yes, you do. Most Christians I've met drink, and you and I both know Jesus turned water into wine and not vice versa." I felt myself getting angry, so I took a deep breath and went on in a gentler manner. "I know we were taught that drinking is a sin, and you know I've been thinking about this a lot. Getting drunk may be a sin, Linda, because you can do things you may regret, or worse than that, you may do things that hurt others."

I knew Linda didn't agree, but she was kind when she said, "I see what you mean, and you could be right. Drinking one drink is not like getting drunk. You drank with your husband, and that may be different."

****

I rushed home the minute I received Talal and Abid's acceptance letters into the University of Tennessee. I loved the moments when I brought good news that made Betty happy. I knew she didn't like living in Irbid, and that we were supposed to be living in Amman by now. I was proud of her and of her ability to assimilate to her new world.

196

I found her in the girls' room and I whistled softly to get her attention. She spun around giving me that wondering look in her eyes and flew into my arms the minute I waved the letter saying that my brothers were accepted at the University. I enjoyed her wrapping her arms around my neck as she showered me with kisses. "Oh this is so exciting! When are we going to go?"

I had promised that we all would go to the States with them; Betty, Susan, Donna, and me. I decided traveling in August would give my brothers plenty of time to settle in to start school in the fall; however, Betty didn't want to wait another three months. I didn't like the idea of her traveling alone with two little girls. I asked Ali to let Linda and the kids go with her, but he didn't agree because she had not been in Jordan long enough to go back. I was glad when Betty decided to wait until August. Then, out of the blue, she received a call from Mrs. Gray informing her of a couple who worked at the embassy who were planning to leave for the States in mid-June. She said that they would be more than happy to help Betty with the girls if they wanted to travel with them. Although I would have preferred she wait another month and a half, I had to agree when Betty said that it was meant to be. I knew she missed her family and I knew that it had been a long time.

Talal and Abid couldn't contain their excitement when they heard the news. They couldn't believe they were going to study at the same university I had attended. They both talked and laughed at the same time.

Donna in her mother's arms

Susan, Donna, and Betty

CHAPTER 13

KNOXVILLE

I couldn't sleep the week before my trip. My excitement made it impossible to even rest. I packed and repacked almost every bag and bought gifts for everyone. The girls were also becoming excited about going to America.

The big day finally came, and as I walked toward the plane, I turned to wave. My eyes rested on Saeed's face; everyone else at the airport disappeared. I waved bravely and fought back tears as I held onto my girls. My traveling companions Teresa and Eddy were from Missouri. Slender, of medium height, and very sweet, Teresa reminded me of a cousin. Eddy was a quiet man and said very little, but seemed nice.

The plane ride into London was smoother than expected, and Susan and Donna were good the entire way. They read books and colored before dozing off. I ordered a drink, and thought of Saeed. He was right, there is no harm in a drink and it surely did help me relax. I smoked cigarettes, and read a mystery novel. The flight to New York the next day was longer, but pretty much the same. On the third day, I was finally on a plane heading to Knoxville. My heart pounded as I stepped down from the plane. It had been four long years. I started to run the minute I saw Mama and Daddy. Hot tears ran down my face the instant their arms enfolded me and the girls. I turned around and saw my brothers and little Debbie. They had grown so much.

I couldn't believe how green and how beautiful my Tennessee was. It seemed even greener than I remembered. Driving over the bridge, I almost cried from the sheer beauty of the landscape. I inhaled the air and it even smelled beautiful. I was happy to see all the family members and friends waiting for us at the house. As I stepped into my childhood home, I felt a difference in its size. I walked into my bedroom and it seemed so small compared to my bedroom in Irbid. But I didn't care; I was exhilarated to be back home with Mama and my family. I basked in this glorious reunion, and the girls were a hit. Everyone thought they were adorable, and the women remarked about their gold earrings. Susan showed off her bracelet to Grandma Riley, proudly reading her name, which was engraved on it,

"You're right Sweetie, that's your name." Grandma Riley said as she hugged her great-granddaughter.

"They look so cute with their earrings. I've never seen anyone this young wearing them. At least none that I can recall," Aunt Skeet commented, as she played with the girls. Susan and Donna loved all the attention but were used to it from Saeed's family and friends.

"I want to pierce my ears, Mama, and I want a bracelet with my name on it." Debbie stomped her feet and crossed her arms.

I hugged Debbie. "I've got a pair for you, too, Sweetie, and we'll go get your ears pierced if it's okay with Mama."

Debbie threw her arms around me. "Thank you, Betty," she said, then quickly forgot about the earrings and ran to play with Donna, who was four years younger than she.

I said. "In Jordan, they pierce the ears of baby girls the first day they are born." This remark received a lot of attention, and I went on to say that I never mistook a baby boy for a baby girl.

"I guess that's one way of telling them apart," Grandma Clark said.

"Isn't that the truth. Lord knows how many times I've made that mistake, and mothers don't like that at all," Aunt Skeet said.

Mama made her famous hamburgers and potato salad, and relatives brought cakes and other delicious dishes. I ate until I couldn't eat another bite. At some point, Cousin Patsy turned around and said, "You know what? You lost your accent, Betty Jean."

"Well, I never realized how southern I must have sounded to most people in Amman until this moment. You all sound really southern!" I said as we all laughed, but then I added, "There are many British and most of the Americans I know are from up north, except for my best friend, Linda, who's from Alabama."

"Did you try to lose your accent? Did people dislike it?" Patsy asked.

I had to laugh. "Oh no, they actually loved it! I never intentionally changed the way I speak, but you're right. I do sound different. How do I sound?"

"Well, I wouldn't say you sound like one of them Yankees, but you just sound more polished," Aunt Skeet said as others nodded in agreement.

"Don't worry about that, Sweetie. Your accent will come back soon enough. Why I remember when your Pa went off to work in Cleveland. He came back and sounded different for a while, but after some time, he started sounding like the rest of us again," Grandma Riley added with a knowing look.

I finally had time alone with my immediate family. I gave everyone the gifts I had brought. There were gold loop earrings for Mama and Debbie, as well as beautiful lengths of silk that Mama held up to her chin.

"They feel so nice. I could make Debbie beautiful costumes that …"

"Mama, I want you to make a dress for *yourself*," I said, and hugged her close.

Daddy loved the two shirts and three ties I had chosen for him. "They're silk, Daddy. Don't they feel nice?"

"Lord, yes they do, but you didn't have to bring me anything."

I was satisfied with everyone's reactions and knew the rest of the family would love what I got them. I bathed the girls and put their

201

pajamas on. As I fixed the bedcovers the way they liked them, I heard Susan talking to Mama in the kitchen.

"No, no, Granny, I want *haleeb.*"

I smiled as I walked in on a somewhat flustered Mama. "*Haleeb* is milk in Arabic, Mama; Susan wants a glass of milk." I knelt and explained to Susan, "This is *haleeb,* Honey. In America, we call it milk."

"I know milk, Mama, but I thought it *Arabe,* not English."

It took me a minute to realize what Susan was trying to tell me. She didn't know for sure if a word was Arabic or English. *How confusing the different languages must sound to the girls! How will they ever know which word is which?* I realized I would need to be more patient with them. I hugged Susan and murmured, "Don't worry. You'll learn the difference all in good time, Honey, you're such a good girl!"

Not long after the girls drank their milk, they both fell asleep. I took my shower and went to bed. I lay awake staring at the ceiling. Just before I fell asleep, I thought of Saeed and my heart ached.

I woke up at dawn finding it hard to believe I was home. I lay in bed for a while before I glanced at the girls. Their breathing was deep and even, and I knew they would sleep a little while longer. I rose quietly from the bed, put on my robe, and went into the kitchen. Feeling a little disoriented, I made myself a cup of coffee and walked out onto the back porch and inhaled the familiar, pine-scented air.

"Why are you up so early, Sweetie? Couldn't you sleep?" Mama looked a little worried.

"No, Mama, I slept well, and I feel great!" I gave her a hug, noting how tired she looked and noticing that she had aged. "I can't imagine ever complaining about the sound of the cicadas. I never thought you could miss sounds and smells so much, but I have, Mama. I've missed people and places. I've missed seeing, smelling, hearing, tasting, and even feeling things."

We sat and talked until I saw Susan standing at the door.

"I'm hungry, Mama."

****

My first few days were a whirlwind of activities. So many people and places I had missed and wished to see. I enjoyed going shopping and showing off my two little girls. Talking with my parents, playing with my brothers, and getting to know Debbie provided delightful moments. I also looked forward to Sunday.

"I've missed going to church, Mama. I did go to a couple of churches, but it's so different over there, and they all cover their hair when they go into the church. They also sing in Latin. It's just not the same."

"I guess it's like going to different churches in the States. They aren't all alike here either."

"You're right, Mama, and that's what Saeed said, too." I sighed softly. "I miss him so much, Mama."

Sunday morning I dressed myself and the girls carefully. I was quiet on the way to the church, and as I stepped inside, I felt as though time had stopped. The pastor greeted me warmly and told me I looked wonderful. I gave him the mother-of-pearl Bible I had bought especially for him. It had been crafted in Bethlehem, the Jerusalem cross etched on the back and the Bethlehem star on the front. He mentioned it during the sermon, his voice faltering with emotion as he read from it and openly admired the gold-leaf finish at the edge of each page. Later I told him about my visit to Jerusalem. After I finished, he asked me to repeat this to the whole congregation. That evening, I talked it over with Mama and expressed my trepidation. She encouraged me saying, "Sweetie, Grandma Riley cried when I read your letters out loud to her. You just stand up there and tell everyone what you wrote. They'll love you, I know they will." Next Sunday I arrived with sweaty palms and a wildly beating heart. The congregation loved every minute I spoke, and I had to answer question after question. It went well and I was proud of myself.

The girls and I missed Saeed so much and they kept asking when their *Baba* was coming to see them. They got along well with Debbie since they were used to having cousins and family around, but I saw that Debbie wasn't used to sharing the spotlight, and she and Susan got into fights sometimes.

"Mama, Debbie keeps telling me what to do and what to wear and where to sit. She also tells Donna." Susan peered intently at me as she said the last words.

"I know, Honey. Debbie is older and is trying to take care of you," I said,

"She screams, Mama, and I don't like that!"

"You're right. Debbie shouldn't scream at you. I will talk to her and tell her she can't scream at you."

"Or at Donna!"

"Or at Donna," I said, and hugged Susan close and wished Saeed was with us.

Protective of Donna, Susan would often intervene when Donna tried to say something and the others laughed because they didn't understand her. "She wants to drink water. *Maya* is water. Right, Donna?" To which Donna happily agreed.

I wrote Saeed every day telling him what I did, who I saw, what we ate, and, most importantly, how much we missed and loved him.

"Oh, Mama," I said one day, "I sure forgot how much work it was keeping up with everything. You must be exhausted."

"I guess I'm used to it by now. When you got married, I had to count more on your brothers."

"They're good boys, and I know they help, but it's still a lot of work." I sat down at the kitchen table and looked at Mama, "I'm pooped. I must be getting old, Mama.

The next day I got a letter from Saeed. The pages shook in my trembling hands. When I finished reading it, I sighed, hugged the letter, and closed my eyes. I opened the letter and reread his words over and over, *I don't even like to go home at night, it's so lonely without you and the girls.*

Oh Lord, I hated to complain to Mama, but I sure missed having someone to help me with cooking, ironing, cleaning, and the girls. I got tired so easily and wished Saeed would hurry and come, I prayed as I rested one afternoon. Although napping was a habit I had thought I disliked, it was a custom almost all men and women in Jordan followed. Now, it was something that I craved daily.

A couple of months later, the awaited letter came saying that Saeed would be coming at the beginning of September, which was in another two weeks. I marked off each day, and when September finally came, my attention shifted from the calendar to the telephone. Every time the phone rang, I raced to answer it. When I finally heard his voice, I wanted to cry. He was in New York and the next day I would see him. I covered my face with my hands and cried the minute I hung up the phone.

I dressed with care the next day in a pink and blue Persian print in drip-dry cotton, with a full skirt, and then I dressed both girls. Daddy drove us to the airport as we sang, "Baba is coming, Baba is coming!"

At last, my eyes lit up at the sight of him. The girls raced toward him and soon engulfed him in a sea of kisses, hugs, and shouts before he ever reached me. I began to cry the minute I entered his arms.

"Good to have you home, Son." Daddy said after hugging Saeed, and shaking hands with his brothers.

There ensued quite a scene as I greeted Talal and Abid, who were glad to see me and the girls. Talal carried Susan and Abid carried Donna as we all crammed into the car for the ride home.

After everyone listened to Saeed's retelling of his travels, and after the girls had enough hugs and kisses from their daddy to settle down for the night, we retired to my childhood bedroom.

I lay awake wishing Saeed had come to stay for good. I finally dozed off, dreaming of a white house with a white fence all around it.

****

Betty was in my arms and I was in Knoxville again, It felt so good and so right. I wished we had never had to leave, I tightened my arms around my wife as she snuggled closer and told myself to enjoy this time as much as I could. I had missed this place more than I ever thought. I was up bright and early the next morning and went outside. I marveled at the beauty that surrounded this valley. I looked up and admired the majestic trees. I felt I was in a forest and hesitantly went inside to shower, shave and dress while my brothers, alternating turns in the shower, did the same. We all enjoyed Lolli's giant biscuits and gravy as well as the eggs and ham.

"I thought Betty best cook; now I think different," Abid said, and we all laughed except Betty, who feigned a hurt look that brought on more laughter.

I stayed busy the first few days taking care of my brothers. They registered for classes and settled into their dormitory rooms. I was glad that was done and that I could now enjoy my time with my wife and girls. Betty and I went out almost every night and we had a ball. We enjoyed a memorable visit to the Hadads; she began talking to them in Arabic, to everyone's delight. She also charmed them with her ability to help in the kitchen as well as her knowledge of all the names of the spices and foods. But the final shock came when Betty accepted a glass of wine at dinner. My maturing and changing Magnolia!

"This is truly a new Betty! Does your mother know you drink now?" Joe asked.

I waited for my wife's response, and she said, "Yes, I wrote her about it, and she wrote back that she didn't like it, but said I'm a grown woman and can make up my own mind."

I had missed going shopping and we went to our favorite stores. I loved watching her parade different clothes, but it worried me when she got tired so quickly. I worried that she was overworking herself trying to help Lolli, but I didn't want to say anything to her. I knew we would be going back in a short time and there was no need to upset her. She had the biggest heart of anyone. I of course knew she would want to help her mother.

Going to the movies was one thing we both had really missed and so we did a lot of that. I think we went to every new release. We also took the girls to the mountains for picnics, a favorite mutual pastime. A couple of weeks before we were to go back, Betty complained of morning sickness and said that she thought she might be pregnant. Her words were true. Now it made more sense that she tired so quickly. After a thorough check up, the doctor informed us that she had low blood pressure and that he didn't think it was a good idea for her to be traveling, especially overseas. On the way back to her parents, Betty was quiet and I asked what she was thinking about.

"I feel that the Lord knows I am not ready to go back. I really want to experience more of my world before I have to leave. These past

206

months were tiring, yet exhilarating in many other ways. I have so missed being home for four long years and I need to stay longer."

We talked and talked some more and at the end, decided that it would be best if she and the girls stayed in Knoxville till after the baby was born. The only major flaw in our plan lay in the fact that I would not be with her when she gave birth to our third child. I knew she had mixed feelings. One part of her was thrilled that she had a reason to stay longer, while another part of her wanted to be with me. I wished I could have stayed with her; I did notice that there was much to be done in my in-laws' house, and I saw her working hard to take care of Susan and Donna as well as help Lolli. I also noticed that Debbie wasn't always nice to Susan, which made my love nervous.

****

I held my tears until after I put the girls to sleep, and then I hugged the pillow that Saeed had slept on, breathing his scent into my aching heart, and sobbed it out. I prayed for his return and finally, before the tears had a chance to dry, fell into a dream where I was lost in some strange land and didn't know how to get back home.

Donna opened her eyes only seconds before Susan opened hers, and I marveled at their bond.

"Where's Baba?" Donna asked for her daddy as Susan tried to explain that he was up in an airplane. Donna looked sad but satisfied with her sister's words.

I hugged my girls. "We have a busy day today. I'm going to take you girls to your first ballet lesson, and then we're going to go downtown and have ice cream."

I tried to stay busy, but I couldn't shake my feelings of loneliness. After a week, I faced the person I had become as I smoked a cigarette with Patsy on the back porch.

"I don't feel this is my home anymore. I feel like a stranger here sometimes."

"You just miss Saeed, and I don't blame you. He's so sweet, and he's always helping you no matter what you're doing. I'm sure he'd be pregnant for you if he could have done that."

"Oh, Patsy," I said through my laughter, "you say the darnedest things, but you're right. Saeed is always helping me, and I do miss him." I closed my eyes and battled the tears.

"Plus, there's so much work to do at Aunt Lolli's. You've been gone four years and are used to having people help you."

"You know what's funny, Patsy? When I was there, they would get on my nerves. Now that I'm here, I can't imagine why. I haven't ironed in years, and I forgot how tiring it is. Not to mention all the washing that goes on, and that stupid machine breaks down every other day! I know that the boys try to help Mama, but they can't do the cooking, cleaning, or ironing."

I loved it when Talal and Abid came to visit, which was at least once a week. I would always cook an Arabic dish, to everyone's delight. Debbie, Susan and Donna loved it, too, because they got a lot of attention and candy.

Every evening, after the girls were bathed and in bed, I would pour out my feelings in letters to Saeed; I told him about my daily activities, the girls, and missing him. I expressed how I would love to have a car instead of having to count on Jimmy, Patsy, or others to take the girls to the various dance lessons I wanted them to experience. I wrote that Patsy said he was sweet and that she thought we complemented one another beautifully. I believed we were better people together than we were apart. *My love, you complete my very existence.*

****

I sat on the balcony reading Betty's words. I always waited until I got home and had a bite to eat. Then I would sit, have a drink, smoke, and savor her words. I missed her and wished I could see her, hear her, and be close to her. I would then start my letter to her. I explained the slow progress of the citrus farm, but conveyed my hopefulness. I wrote about my wish to have enough money so that one day, we might buy a vacation home in Knoxville ... and a car. I also wrote to her about my work and related my daily routine. I told her how much everyone missed her and the girls and wished for their speedy return. At the end of my letter, I told her that she would always be a complete woman, with or without me. A Magnolia that would always delight its viewers!

I worked hard on Yubba's house and spent my time between the Valley and Irbid. Yubba saw how lonely I was and asked me how I could bear for Betty to be away so long. He said that a woman should be with her husband. I wanted him to understand that she would have never wished to be without me if she had had a choice.

"Yubba, she couldn't travel because of her health. Betty is very delicate, and the doctor was worried. Talal and Abid are with her, and so is her family. She did the right thing, Yubba."

Yubba grunted and motioned to Ya'goob, who hurriedly brought a cup of *gahwa sada.*

I asked for Soda and took her for a long ride and thought of my wife.

****

"I hate to leave you with all this ironing, Mama, but I seem to tire so easily nowadays. I wonder if it's me, or if I just got used to having help."

"You know what they say; we are creatures of habit, and I sure am grateful that there is one good thing about you living in Jordan."

"You sure the girls are going to be okay?" I worried that Debbie would start fussing with Susan.

"They're fine. Stop worrying about every little thing."

"Debbie tries to tell Susan what to do, and Susan is used to being the eldest. No one is ever bossy to her in Jordan." I really wanted to say that I thought Mama needed to discipline Debbie when she got into one of her moods. Mama knew I was right, but didn't want to hear it. I was tired and had to rest. I wished Saeed was here. Then I could rest, knowing he was looking after the girls. I felt torn in two; I wanted the girls to experience this side of life because when we go back to Irbid, there was nothing like this for them. I wanted them to love dancing like I do. The lessons would teach them to listen and catch the beat when they danced.

The girls wouldn't go to sleep that evening and were up when their granddaddy came home from work at eleven. He ate and played with them for a while. He was reading his newspaper when Debbie and Susan got into a fight.

"Stop this!" Daddy shouted at them, and Susan came running to me.

"I want Baba, I want to go home! I don't like this place." She cried until she finally fell asleep.

That night, I cried myself to sleep, too.

I went for my monthly check-up and Dr. Jones said that I might have the baby in about three weeks. The next two weeks passed quickly, filled with daily activities and visitors. The nights were longer, though, and I missed Saeed more than ever. His letters sustained my strength. I felt really tired by the third week, but the daily activities didn't wane. I felt restless because I didn't get one letter from Saeed. I fixed my hospital bag, knowing that the baby might come any day now. I worried about Saeed and Mama tried to make me feel better.

"Sweetie, nothing bad is going to happen. You've got to trust in the Lord and know that he'll take care of you. Try to sleep, and if you need anything, you holler. Goodnight."

I woke up in the middle of the night feeling very tired. My body ached, and I felt something wet between my legs. I removed the covers and noticed blood on the sheets. I rose and walked into my parents' room and told them that I was bleeding.

Hours later, Dr. Jones congratulated me on my healthy baby. He held up my screaming, squirming little boy and asked me if I had already chosen a name.

"Clark Saleh Gazzawiya," I said firmly.

Although Saeed and I had discussed naming a boy *Saleh*, I didn't see any harm in making his first name Clark and his middle name Saleh.

****

I received the telegram while I was at Yubba's new house, thousands of miles away. I quickly tore the seal and read aloud, "Betty and the baby are fine."

Yubba's face showed his disappointment. He waved at me impatiently.

"Son, go and wire your in-laws a telegram and ask about the sex of your child."

I was overjoyed when the awaited telegram came two days later. I read, "You have a son, Saleh."

"Son, that name is bad luck. None of the Saleh's ever lived to be fathers. The soothsayer warned me long ago not to call the name Saleh again."

"I'm not you, Yubba. The bad luck is broken because you didn't name me that. I'm your son, and if I name my son Saleh, then he will live."

Yubba turned his face from me as he covered it with his palms and quietly said, "God willing, Son, that you never live the pain that I endured."

The next day, I started getting ready to go bring my family back. I wished I felt better, but I felt weak and my stomach hurt. I rubbed my temples and hoped the aspirins I had taken would start to work.

My excitement soon plummeted as fate interfered with my plans. The ill feelings had been a warning: I came down with typhoid fever and was dangerously sick for weeks. Yubba moved me into his home and kept a close watch over me. For three weeks, I lay in bed with a raging fever, unable to do much of anything. The doctor came daily to check on me, and a nurse stayed with me the whole time. I kept mumbling Betty's name, and in my feverish dreams, I often reunited with the ones I loved.

"Yubba, please write Talal and Abid and tell them not to mention my illness to Betty."

"She's your wife; she needs to be here with you!"

"I don't want her to worry about me, Yubba. Her load is heavy, and she can't take this kind of worry. Please, Yubba!"

At last, and to everyone's relief, especially Yubba's, the fever abated, and I slowly regained my health.

****

I was oblivious to the illness that was shaking my husband's body. All I knew and cared about was the fact that I had not received a letter from him for three weeks. Twenty-one days and I had gotten nothing, when I was used to getting a letter at least once a week and often two ... if not three. I wished I could call but knew that was impossible. The fastest thing would be to send a telegram. I discussed that with Talal and Abid who came by that afternoon.

The brothers came by the hospital and brought me flowers, chocolates, and candy, which cheered me up considerably. They were ecstatic that I had borne Saeed a son. They held him and cooed to him. When I mentioned that I hadn't heard from Saeed, Talal said,

"He is going to come any day. He is just very busy with the farm and building the house."

"I thought the house was finished!"

"The last touches are the most difficult," Abid added.

A welcome interlude came when the Grays drove from Nacogdoches, Texas to see me, the girls, and the baby. They decided to stop in Knoxville on their way to visit their daughter in Asheville, North Carolina. Mr. Gray had retired that year and the couple had returned to the States for good.

"Saeed is a lost puppy without you, my dear," Mrs. Gray said over and over in her gentle manner, which I admired and loved. The woman dripped with class, and I learned a lot from her.

"But he has not sent one letter in a little over three weeks. Do you think he has forgotten about us?"

"Now dear, don't you let that mind of yours go to the wrong place. You know how much Saeed loves you and his girls. You know how things can go wrong. He may be having problems with the farm or his father's house." Mrs. Gray patted my hand, "You know, my Dear, his father could be sick."

"You're right, but why wouldn't he write and tell me?"

"He may be worried and too busy himself."

"Oh Mrs. Gray, what am I going to do without you. Jordan was bad enough with you there." I tried not to sound down, but it was the truth. I knew I was going to miss them when we went back.

"The good Lord always sends us what we need. I know that you will soon move to Amman,"

I quickly sat up, "Did Saeed get a job?"

212

"Not yet dear, but I know that he will. All things come at the right time. Once you are in Amman, you will meet many new friends."

"I wish I didn't have to leave the states."

"Do you think I wanted to leave?" she looked at me with her head tilted and her eyebrows up and answered herself. "I didn't. I missed my grown children, home, and family. But with time, I appreciated my travels and all that I had learned and become. Think of the positive things, Betty; Susan, Donna, and Clark will grow up to be bilingual and will be able to belong to two continents."

"You're right Mrs. Gray. I can already see how they can interact with Debbie here, and their cousins back in Jordan."

"That's my girl. Meanwhile enjoy your stay and do the things you want to do here that you can't over there."

Her words comforted me and she gave me a big hug. At night, the Grays stayed at a hotel near the hospital and insisted on having Susan and Donna stay with them. The next day, much to my surprise, Susan wanted to leave with the Grays. I looked at her and asked, "You want to leave me, Donna, and the new baby?"

Susan thought for a minute and then ran back to hug me. Everyone laughed.

Before they left, Mr. Gray told me that he had urged Saeed to come and visit Texas. He said that he wanted to show him the citrus farms in the Lower Rio Grande Valley. He said Saeed really liked the idea and thought that I would love that too. That gave me great happiness and I knew that we would have a great time. Meanwhile, though, I just wanted Saeed to come.

Back at home, life resumed its pace except for having the new baby in the house. Nothing can compare with holding an infant. Clark brought me the peace which I sorely needed. I tried to heed Mrs. Gray's words, and continued writing to Saeed, but as the days drew close to another two weeks, I couldn't help but worry. I cried myself to sleep many nights and knew Mama and Daddy must have heard me.

****

Debbie, Susan and Donna were going to perform at the Tennessee Theater. That day I got all the girls ready in their beautiful long dresses

213

with matching flowers in their hair. I sat in the audience, watching them on stage, beaming with happiness and pride. Debbie sang, "Be Mine," Susan sang, "Pink Shoelaces," and Donna sang, "Sugar in the Morning, Sugar in the Evening." I glowed and thanked people who complimented me on how beautiful the girls looked. How I wished Saeed could have seen them, he would have been so proud. Back at the house, everyone was happy to hear how well the girls had performed. As I was helping the girls change back into their everyday clothes, the phone rang. It was Saeed!

"Honey, I'm in New York. I'll arrive at 4:30. I love you."

I couldn't move or say a word. I just stood by the phone and openly sobbed, scaring Mama and Daddy half to death. I later laughed as Mama kept mimicking the way I looked. I thanked the Good Lord over and over. *Everything will be just fine. Saeed is here!*

At the airport, we scanned the sky anxiously, but we heard the plane before we saw it. The girls and I ran toward it the minute we saw Saeed disembark. He looked different, I noticed he had lost a lot of weight and looked tired. Our faces touched, and tears gradually evaporated into smiles. We hung on to each other for moments, oblivious to our surroundings. Then Susan and Donna cried out for his hugs and kisses, jerking us back to the present.

"I sure am glad you're home, Son. Betty and the girls missed you something awful." Daddy said as he winked at me.

Back home, Mama opened the door holding Clark in her arms.

"You have a fine son, Sweetie, and I'm so glad you're here." She held Clark out to him and said, "Baba is here, Clark!"

"Clark? Honey, we talked this over. We decided to name him Saleh!"

"I know, but it's easier for my family to say Clark than Saleh," I said, as I saw his perplexed look. I wanted to change the subject and went on, "Is *your* Baba happy?" I nudged up closer to both my guys.

"Yes, he is. Although I have to admit, he didn't like us naming him Saleh."

I saw circles under his eyes and gently touched his face, "You look tired, Honey. Was the flight bad? You've lost a lot of weight and you didn't write for five weeks. Is everything okay?" I was asking a lot of questions and I knew he must be bone tired.

"I'll tell you all about it later on, Honey. The main thing is that I am here." He said as he kissed both my hands.

A few hours later, we were alone at last in the dark privacy of our bedroom. Our lovemaking was quick and strong. We held on to each other and to all the passion that had been building up for months. Afterwards, he held me and told me why he hadn't written. I clung closer to him and started to cry as I thanked God over and over for taking care of him. I couldn't imagine life without him. He talked softly and kept saying that he was here now and that everything was fine. We fell asleep in each other's arms.

The next week, Mama suggested that Saeed and I go to the mountains for the weekend. I didn't want to leave her with all the kids, but she insisted, and said Patsy would help her. In the end, I agreed and thank God I did, for we surely needed this mini vacation. We had a wonderful time, and our love only strengthened and reawakened even more within the atmosphere of privacy and romance. We talked and laughed as we enjoyed each other's company. Life had again become wonderful; this was the life I wished I could always have, but I resigned myself to loving a man who belonged to a different continent. There would always be problems because of this, and I accepted my fate.

Saeed told me that he had finished his father's house and had designed the first floor for us. It had its own entrance, its own garden, and a fireplace. I thought that sounded nice and said that it would keep us warm in winter, and the girls could roast hotdogs and marshmallows. I was beginning to think about going back, and although it did sadden me, I knew it had to be, and I would make it work. Mrs. Gray was right.

The next week, Saeed, Susan, Donna, Saleh, and I all headed to Texas. Excitement was high in the car and we all enjoyed our first road trip as a family. Two days later, we arrived at the Grays' and it was a joyful reunion. Susan, Donna, and Saleh got a lot of attention. The Grays had our rooms ready, toys for the girls, and spaghetti and meatballs for a late dinner. After dessert, Saeed went off with Mr. Gray to have a couple of drinks at the Country Club before it closed, while I rested with Saleh. Mrs. Gray played with the girls in the living room.

The second day Mr. Gray took Saeed to visit a few farms. He said that citrus was the ideal tree for the climate of the Jordan Valley because the weather there is similar to the weather in that part of Texas. He said the words that Saeed and I both wanted to hear. He believed our farm would be a great success. I prayed that his words would prove to be true.

The week went by quickly as we all had a great time. We shopped, visited friends, and went sightseeing. One day before we left, Saeed surprised me, telling me about his having been interviewed by the local newspaper. I was so proud of him as we reread the article together.

Prince of Jordan visits B. F. Gray

A prince from Jordan visited Wednesday in Nacogdoches with Mr. and Mrs. Benny Gray, who recently returned from five years in that Middle Eastern country. Although he is actually entitled to be called a prince, Saeed Gazzawiya of the Irbid district of Jordan says, "Three hundred years ago, yes, maybe; but now, no." In other words, his family, whose "tree" goes back much further than three hundred years, is a ruling Arab clan. However, Mr. Gazzawiya seems to feel that his princedom is out of place in our modern world. This democratic feeling of the dark, handsome young man may perhaps have come from his years spent at the University of Tennessee at Knoxville and his marriage to an American girl, a native of Tennessee. "I was up visiting Saeed once and went along with him among the villagers and farms on his people's land," Mr. Gray explained. "You know they don't have courts like we do. When there was an argument or dispute over possessions or some other such matter that we might take to court, those involved just came to Saeed, explained their difficulties, and accepted his decision." So, perhaps despite his American wife, American clothes, and Buick automobile, Mr. Gazzawiya is in reality a prince of Jordan ... not in the sense of prestige, but in the sense of his responsibilities to his people and the demands they make on him.

Nacogdoches Daily Sentinel, 1959

****

Back in Knoxville, we began preparing for our trip to Jordan.

"Honey, do you think I should type out the ballet and tap lessons and routines for the girls?"

"That's a good idea. That way, you'll have something to do with them in Jordan that's a change from the usual activities."

For several days, I had been busy typing a copy of Susan's tap lessons and routines. I also typed out the girls' ballet lessons and drew all the diagrams of dance patterns for the coming year. I didn't want them to miss any of the lessons, so that when they came back to Knoxville, they could be on track with the rest of the girls in the classes. I hoped that we could all come back next year. Saeed's enthusiasm equaled mine and he said that now that we had a son, our family was complete. Traveling with three kids was not bad at all and he asked me, more than once, to make sure to take a whole year's prescription of the birth control pills.

The day of our departure was a sad and hectic Friday. After hugging everyone else, I finally hugged Daddy and Mama, and that was when I broke down in tears. Mama tried to be strong, but when she saw me crying, she followed suit. She hugged me tightly, and we openly sobbed. Saeed touched my shoulders lightly and said that Susan and Donna would soon start crying too.

I turned around and, holding Saleh closer to me, squatted down to comfort them. "It's okay. Mama is sad about saying goodbye to everyone, but I'm okay."

Flying from Knoxville, Tennessee, to Amman, Jordan, did not make for an easy trip. We flew from Knoxville, into Ireland, Holland, Vienna, Istanbul, Ankara, Beirut, and finally Amman. I couldn't believe we had to stop in so many airports just because we missed our flight into Turkey.

The ride back to Irbid was smooth, and I finally got my first look at the new house. Huge and impressive, it was filled with people wishing to welcome us back and to congratulate us on our first son. In a way, I was glad we had missed our flight; otherwise many of these people would have been at the airport to welcome us back. It was noisy, but I was now more adept at dealing with my family, and, most importantly, I could communicate with them. Instead of being in a world of incomprehensible noise, I was in a noisy world that I understood. That didn't make it great; it made it reality, and, in a weird way, made it our home.

Saeed's father stood at the top of an expansive set of stairs waiting for us. He opened his arms, and I slid into them effortlessly, enjoying his scent. I had missed seeing many loved and familiar faces and happiness filled me to see all the attention Susan and Donna received. Their aunts doted on them and had bought them lots of candy. I laughed out loud when they spoke English to everyone. Yumma Arifa kissed me multiple times and gave me a gold necklace with a beautiful blue stone to protect me from evil eyes. She then showed me around the new nine bedroom house. There were three beautiful verandahs, one boasting a stained glassed dome that I absolutely loved. It reminded me of old English homes I'd seen in movies and magazines. Mamdouh and Seta had two bedrooms and a bathroom at the end of a long corridor on the main floor. Another two bedroom/bathroom suite was on the second floor. Saeed came looking for me and asked if I liked the house.

"Oh, it's beautiful!" I answered. "I'd love to see the pergola, but I'll wait until tomorrow."

"It'll look better in the daylight. Why don't you let Wadad and Noffa take you and the girls downstairs where you can rest? I hope you like what I did to the place," he added as he gave me a quick hug before he turned to go back to the *majless*, calling out to his sisters as he walked away. I knew he must be as tired as I was, but my love was always thinking of me.

We went down a flight of stairs leading into a big room; Noffa said that it was the laundry room. We walked across and through another door at the opposite end and entered a hallway. To the right was a large kitchen with a small back porch that led to the downstairs garden. Going back into the hallway and through a door to the left, we entered into an L-shaped living and dining area that had a beautiful fireplace, as well as another stained glassed-in balcony. "Oh, I love it," I said out loud to everyone's delight. Our living quarters had three large bedrooms, one bathroom tiled in blue, and a water heater. Susan and Donna ran into their new room and started to play with familiar old toys. I went into the kitchen and made myself a cup of coffee; I sat at the kitchen table and smoked a cigarette while conversing with Shamma and Fayga; Saleh nestled in Noffa's arms as we all talked. A couple of hours later, we ate and I gave everyone their gifts. Then I took a long, hot bath, and Wadad bathed the girls while I nursed Saleh and fell asleep. At some point, Saeed slid between the covers and hugged me.

I liked the fact that Saeed could visit his father simply by going up a flight of stairs. My girls often played in the upstairs gardens or with their aunts, uncles, and the family children. Another advantage was that I didn't have to cook because there was always food upstairs. Thrya and Fathma also moved with their husbands and children into quarters at the big house, nestled at the end of the upstairs back garden. I liked them and especially liked Thrya, who was the younger one. Her husband, Abadi helped take care of Susan and Donna. Having them near was convenient when I needed assistance with the children or when I needed babysitters or help with visitors. Still, a certain loss of privacy continued to nag at me, and Saeed encouraged me to be open about my feelings. He said I should explain that I have my own habits, and that I need privacy when I have visitors. I needed to be more assertive with what I liked and didn't like. I knew I was not going to change overnight and transform into another person. I said I would. I'll start with using *la'a* whenever I felt it was the right moment.

Saeed would tell me that we came from two different cultures and each one forces behavior that is deemed acceptable or not, and when there is a contradiction between one culture and the other, the only feasible solution is to explain how you feel. Either that, or be misunderstood and feel like an outsider. He was right, and for me to be happy I needed to voice my truth.

When I had held Susan's first birthday party, everyone had been awed and happy about this concept of being King or Queen for a day.

"Doesn't every year seem too much?" Noffa had asked me, as she asked about everything. I think she thought I knew everything.

"Once a year is *not* too much. How else will people know how old you are?"

"I think that's why people don't celebrate their birthdays," Wadad said, staring at me. "I don't know any woman that says her age. They're all 'in their twenties,' even when their daughters are getting married."

We all laughed though her words were true. I was ardent about throwing a great birthday party for Donna. I wished for all to see that having a son didn't diminish my little girl's standing. Saeed felt the same way. He lavished love and attention on Donna, and was filled with pride at everything she did or said. Susan taught Bedouins to love and spoil their firstborn child; Donna would teach them to love and spoil *all* their daughters."

Donna's birthday party ended up being a great success, and everyone thoroughly enjoyed it. What a strange mix of people! Christian Arabs like Tereza, Suhair, Mary and others. American friends such as Linda, her children, Mrs. Seals, and others attended the party, as well as the Bedouin relatives-Yumma Arifa, Shamma, Seta, and many others. I tried not to exclude people, but I had to be selective. The look on Shamma's face when I lit the candles on the cake was adorable. She looked more excited than her kids did. I was so glad Saeed took pictures of her. Giving out the party favors was a favorite moment of mine. It was wonderful, and everyone was so good at playing the games, especially, pin-the-tail-on-the-donkey. Oh, Lord, I didn't know who had more fun, the children or the adults.

Saleh was only three months old and I didn't like this new situation at all; I had missed another period. I dreaded telling Saeed but knew I had to.

"Are you sure?" His eyes searched my face, and I think he hoped I was joking.

"I've missed two months, and I haven't been feeling so good lately."

"Maybe we need to ride up to see Dr. Stevens. I'm sure the girls would enjoy the trip. What do you think?"

Dr. Stevens was happy to see us and, after a lengthy check, confirmed my suspicion.

"You are pregnant, Betty, but your blood pressure isn't good." His brow creased but he smiled kindly. "Your body hasn't yet recuperated from your last pregnancy, and I'm guessing you still feel weak."

"What do you think, Doctor?" Saeed asked, his voice heavy with concern.

"Let's do some blood work first, and then we'll talk later."

Dr. Stevens drew some blood and sent the tubes to the lab. "Let's go to the house," he suggested. "Miriam has baked a cake and is waiting to see you."

We had a lovely afternoon together, catching up on everything that had happened since we had last seen each other. Just as evening fell, a nurse came to the house with my results. Dr. Stevens read through the pages and then folded them in his lap.

"I don't like this, but as a doctor, I recommend that you terminate this pregnancy."

I couldn't believe what I was hearing, and my hands started to shake as I covered my stomach and said that I could never hurt my child, never. Tears welled up in my eyes, and I felt so tired, I wanted to go home. Silence reigned as both of us struggled with this situation. On our way back, the girls went to sleep the minute they got into the car. Finally Saeed asked if I was okay.

"I'm stunned that Doctor Stevens would say something like that!" My pulse raced, but my hands, busy comforting Saleh, had finally stopped shaking.

"Honey, he's a doctor and a good doctor, too. The first priority is the mother's health, and you have three other children to think about. Saleh is only four months old."

"You can't be serious, Saeed. I would rather die!"

"You would rather die and leave all of us? We're your family, and you're not thinking of any of us. Doctor Stevens must think you're in real danger or he would never have suggested this."

I sat in silence, my heart pounding and aching. He went on,

"I never wanted many children. I am very blessed to have you, Susan, Donna, and Saleh in my life. I want to make a good life for us."

"If God didn't wish for me to have a child, I wouldn't be pregnant. I have never missed one pill. You know that," I started to cry and cried all the way back.

I grew weaker by the month but feigned feeling better in front of Saeed. In spite of that, he could see I easily tired and shook for the slightest reason. The fireplace added an atmosphere of peace sorely needed in the winter household. During the long days, I often sat and read in front of its glowing embers, and my aching body relaxed, along with its tiny occupant. The evenings were also enjoyable. We entertained guests, but drinking alcohol had become a problem.

"If Yubba finds out that we drink, he will be very disappointed and angry, too."

"Isn't it funny? That's one thing we have in common. Your parents' reaction to alcohol is the same as my parents' reaction."

"I never thought about it that way, but you're right, Honey." Saeed rose from the sofa and walked across the room to make sure the connecting door to the upstairs was closed; he also checked the back entrance. He went into our bedroom, unlocked the closet, and got out a bottle of whiskey.

"If we were in Amman, this would not be happening. We're adults, and if we wish to drink, then we should be able to without having to hide it." I was feeling cranky.

"I don't like doing this either, and you know that. I'm working on our leaving, and hopefully before you give birth. The Barakats should be here any minute, and we're going to have a great time."

****

The girls loved the fireplace too and their biggest happiness came from the fact that Santa Claus now had the chimney he needed.

"I'm going to stay up all night on Christmas Eve and see Santa when he comes down," Susan said.

"Me, too! I won't even close my eyes for a second." Donna's eyes sparkled with excitement.

"Oh, you'll get tired and sleep. You always fall asleep before me."

"No, I'll keep my eyelids open with a clothespin," Donna protested as she held her eyelids open with her fingers.

"Don't do that, you'll hurt your eyes!" Susan ran over and pulled Donna's hands away from her face.

I laughed at their antics. "Okay, girls. Are you ready to decorate the tree?"

Shouts went up, and the excitement began. We loved this time of the year the most. We sang our favorite tunes as we decorated the tree: "Santa Claus is Coming to Town," "Jingle Bells," and "I Saw Mommy Kissing Santa Claus," which always made the girls giggle. I made hot chocolate with marshmallows for everyone. This was one time that I taxed my body to its limit, and Saeed didn't want me to have many people on Christmas.

"Oh, Saeed, Noffa, Thrya, and Abadi help with the cooking, and Wadad takes care of Saleh. Everyone in your family waits all year to get to have chocolate chip cookies, turkey and gravy, pies, and cakes. I want Christmas to be special for them, like it is for me." I loved the fact that many of Saeed's relatives were starting to cook my recipes and referred to them as "Betty's food." I saw their happiness when they gazed in awe at the sparkling tree. They had never seen anything like it, and they loved to sit and stare at the lights and decorations. Their amazement tickled me no end.

"It looks like the sky is close and all the stars are near," Shamma told me, as she stared and stared at the tree. She stayed many afternoons and hardly said a word. I felt a kinship to this woman; I didn't always like her demeanor, but realized that wasn't her fault.

When I later told Saeed about her reaction to the tree, he shook his head laughing and said, "This Bedouin tribe has been introduced to Santa Claus long before many Jordanians will ever hear of him."

A few days before Christmas, I overheard Susan talking to one of her cousins.

"You have to have a Christmas tree, and you have to have a chimney before Santa can come and visit you."

"*My* mother says that *your* mother puts the gifts under the tree," Na'ila responded.

"Amty Sita says that because she doesn't believe in Santa Claus," Susan said, her little face flushing with annoyance.

"You have to *believe* that he's real." Donna joined in the conversation, but they didn't seem to convince Na'ila.

I chuckled, but I felt a little sadness for Na'ila and the other cousins. I was glad Mama always sent extra candy. *I'll put something under the tree for the other small children in the family,* I decided.

Cries of "Mama, Baba, Santa came!" woke Saeed, me, and baby Saleh, and Christmas Day began for the whole family.

I had a full house that year, and we all exchanged gifts. The Amir and Yumma Arifa gave me a gold coin, Seta presented me with a gold ring, and Saeed bought me a gold bracelet. Other friends and family members came by to congratulate me on my feast. At the end of the day, I had a lot of boxes of candy and many beautiful flowers.

The following months took a toll on my body, and two months later, the doctor ordered me to stay in bed for the remainder of the pregnancy. Saeed tried to be home more and spend time with Susan, Donna, and Saleh. He worried endlessly about my health and was afraid something was going to happen to me.

"Tomorrow is Saleh's first birthday. I think I'll ask Noffa to bake him a cake. She's getting good at baking," I remarked as I lay in bed watching Saeed play with his son, who giggled out loud.

The next morning, I sang to Saleh as he opened his eyes. "Happy Birthday to you, Happy Birthday to you, Happy Birthday dear Saleh, Happy Birthday to you!" I swirled him around, planting a big kiss on his soft little cheek. I stopped suddenly as a pain shot up my back and into my belly. I let out a yelp that caught Saeed's attention.

"Are you okay?" He quickly took Saleh, who had begun to cry, out of my arms.

"I think I'm going to have the baby!"

The delivery was quick, and on April 16, 1960, Sami was born. He was so small that he almost slipped out, unnoticed, into the world of adults. I didn't hear him cry. I looked down on my little bundle of silence, and then I looked up into Dr. Stevens's eyes.

"I don't think the baby is going to make it through the night." He hung his head and added, "I can barely hear his heartbeat, I believe he has pneumonia. Let's pray for the mercy of God." Dr. Stevens held my hands as we prayed together for Sami's safety.

The minute Saeed came into the room, I burst out crying. He ran to my side, holding me as I cried. Sometime during the night, I woke up in pain and drowsy. I heard my baby crying, and almost fell out of bed as I reached for my robe. When I entered the nursery doors, I immediately noticed a nurse trying to comfort him. I carried him back to my room and felt his body shivering slightly. Soon his little body relaxed, and he calmed down when I started to nurse him. I wiped at the tears spilling down my face. I prayed, cried, nursed, and cuddled my son all night. I banished all negative thoughts and willed my brain to think happy ones. As the dawn welcomed a new day, I at last fell asleep, my baby safely nestled in my arms.

In the morning, Dr. Stevens checked Sami and said, "He is doing much better than I ever hoped. God is great in his love and mercy."

****

Sami's birth brought more responsibility into our lives, especially for Betty. She enjoyed the help she got from my sisters and everyone, but she really wanted to be in Amman. I noticed she spent more time on the phone with friends she made in Amman. She said it was easier for her to form close friendships with Jordanian Christians, and more of them lived in Amman. She added that many Moslem men drank but didn't want their wives to drink. On the other hand, Christian men didn't mind if their wives drank.

I began to put more effort into securing a job in Amman. The previous year I had refused an offer to become the Director of Agriculture because I felt the need to be close to Yubba. Yet I realized I had to be Betty's husband as well as Yubba's son. I had secretly hoped that she would get used to living in Irbid and give up her desire to move to Amman. The move to Yubba's house had proven that this was not to be the case, and moving to Amman was the only solution. I set out to convince Yubba.

"I can still do the same work for the tribe, and I will be able to assist more when I have a government position."

"You do what you have to do, and I will support you." He reluctantly gave in; he knew he wasn't going to win this one. "I, too, have eyes, and I see Betty is not happy. Amman is not far away, and I know your dedication to the tribe." He motioned for his gahwa sada and sipped it slowly until his next words came to him. "I'm proud of what you have accomplished in the Valley. I know the banana crop was not a success, but your citrus farm is looking good and is very promising."

"It has been five years since we planted it, Yubba, and it looks like we'll start making good money in the next couple of years."

"I like what I see, but how often do we have to replant?"

"The trees will live for a long time, Yubba,"

"God willing, they will. Nothing will prosper unless God wills it to."

"Yes, Yubba, you are right. God willing, the trees will live for many years."

Silently I hoped that the surviving Magnolia tree would also bloom one day. I knew that would make my love very happy.

Yubba wished to have citrus trees at his home in the Valley because he enjoyed their dark, evergreen foliage, their fragrant blossoms, and their delicious fruit. He loved the idea of his lands filled with trees that gave fruits in winter. The next month, I started the second citrus farm behind Yubba's Valley home.

226

****

I loved the school Susan and Donna attended. The Rosary College was a Catholic school down the road, and the nuns were terrific. The girls were getting an education in Arabic, English, and French, which pleased me. They may not know how to tap and do fancy ballet moves, but they'll be able to speak three languages. Although I still worked on their dancing lessons, I didn't have time to practice daily with them. They needed a class and a proper instructor. I tried to explain this to Saeed, but he always said that I was doing a great job, and that the girls danced beautifully. I tried to help the girls with their homework, but could only work on their English. I suggested to Saeed that we needed to learn how to speak French and he said that he had always wanted to speak French. He recalled that many of his classmates had gone to *Le Sorbonne* to study. I told him his accent was great as we both laughed.

We both took months of French lessons, and finally, after one of our grueling classes, I decided that it wasn't working. I believed that to master a language, one needed to start young, or live in a country where very few people speak your language. Exactly what happened to me. I learned to speak Arabic quickly because I had to, not because I had a knack for learning languages. I marveled at my daughters' ability to speak two languages simultaneously, albeit with some problems. The biggest was not being able to differentiate English from Arabic. I heard Susan telling Donna once that she needs to speak in English when she is speaking to me. Donna looked at her and asked,

"Are we speaking English now?"

"No, we're speaking Arabic."

"How do you know?" Donna looked confused.

I discussed this with Saeed, who reassured me that the girls would learn with practice, and that school would help because then they would know when they were in an English, Arabic, or French class.

****

I heard Saeed come in and went to greet him. The minute I saw his face I knew he had a surprise for me. I loved that mischievous look and the

227

grin that accompanies it. This surprise was the best I had had in a very long time. Saeed had just signed the papers for his new position in Amman. He proudly announced that he would be the Director of Agriculture in Jordan starting the next month.

I started to scream the moment "Amman" slipped from his lips. The children knew something exciting was happening, and they came running into the living room.

"Oh, next week will be Saleh and Sami's birthday! Their birthday will be the last birthday I'll celebrate in Irbid. The next birthday will be Donna's." Everyone looked at Donna. I tickled her and said, "Your next birthday will be in Amman! Yay!"

On April 16, 1961, I threw my last lavish birthday party in Irbid; Saleh turned two and Sami turned one. Feeling happy and hospitable, I invited more cousins than usual.

Saeed worried that I was overworking and wished I didn't invite so many people. I didn't mind, I just wished I felt stronger. The birthday party didn't disappoint anyone. Everyone had a fabulous time, and I walked on air. Linda and her kids came down to stay the night, and both of us were equally thrilled about the future. She told me that she couldn't believe I was finally moving.

"I know, Linda! The Amir truly is an amazing man," I agreed. "I thought Saeed was never going to leave his father. I'm awed by this man. He really is a great father and loves Saeed very much. Ali's father, on the other hand, always insisted that all his kids live close to him. I seriously never thought the Amir would give us the money to build a house, but he truly wants us to have our own home.

"Saeed mentioned renting for a year until we could build our house. We are actually going to go to Amman tomorrow to look at some houses. I do hope I find a nice one to rent." I closed my eyes, opened them and just grinned. "I can't believe that I will finally have my own home."

****

"Life is so different here. In the States, the Director of Agriculture could afford to build his own home." I was still a bit confused about exactly how

"That's true," Saeed agreed, but went on to explain that jobs in Jordan were more for prestige than money. You had to have family money if you wanted a big home or a fancy car.

My excitement mounted as the days flew by. I spent every free hour looking through *Better Homes and Gardens* and *Good Housekeeping* magazines, scouring the pages for floor plans. I must have shown Saeed a dozen and he liked every one. Finally, we had our future home sketched from the many different plans we liked. All we needed was an architect.

After showing us three homes, the rental agent found a nice, three-bedroom that I liked. Signing the contract didn't take more than an hour and then we had the keys.

As we headed back to Irbid, Saeed took me to see the piece of land our home was going to be built on. It lay on a hilltop on the outskirts of Amman; minutes away from the road leading to Irbid and the Jordan Valley. That way, it would be easier to get out of the city. I stepped out of the car and admired the view. I liked the fact that neighbors weren't too close; I saw only a few homes nearby. I loved that I could see trees in the distance as well as the downtown mountains, where I knew I would also be able to see city lights at night. It was perfect! I loved it!

I could not believe that I was not dreaming.

Ernest, Lolli, and Betty

Grandpa and Grandma Riley, Susan, Betty, Aunt Skeet, Saeed, and Donna

Susan

Donna

CHAPTER 14

AMMAN

Almost seven years and the time had finally come. The move to Amman wasn't easy, but with all the help we had, it was accomplished in one day. I hated to see Noffa and Wadad crying when they helped. I kept telling them that we were moving only to Amman and not to America. They laughed when I said that and it made me feel better. Everyone cried ... even Yumma Arifa. She held on to Saleh, kissing his face and neck as she told him how much she was going to miss him. Saeed's father stayed in his majless, he didn't want to see us leave.

Saeed looked at me and said "Yubba is heartbroken."

"Aww, I know this is hard on him but with time he'll see that you are not that far away, Honey. Go inside and tell him that we will come and spend the night once a week, I promise!"

By nightfall, everything was in place. I said a prayer and thanked the Lord for this blessing. I knew that my life would be so much better. I walked through the house and knowing that no one could just barge in on us made me feel like I finally had my home, even if we were only renting. We ate the sandwiches I had made earlier. I put the boys to sleep while Saeed put the girls to bed. I heard him still reading as I walked back to our room. My heart raced as I put on a sheer, marabou-feathered baby doll sleeping gown and high heels. I looked at myself in the mirror and smiled at my reflection. When he finally came to the living room, his happily surprised face lit up when he saw me with two glasses of scotch in my hands and seductively purring, "Would you care to join me for a drink, darrrling?"

We had been in Amman only a week and I had already met many new friends. Saeed looked up old friends from school and wanted me to meet one couple he thought I would really like. He was right; I liked Salah and Kadura the minute we met. Kadura was fair with big brown eyes, full lips, and a full head of light brown hair. She was dressed in a tight-fitting black dress with a red flower at her throat, and her coiffed hair added considerable height to her already tall figure. I was surprised when she drank a glass of wine. I learned that she was a Circassian: a Russian Muslim, member of a sect which made up about five percent of the population. They had come to Jordan around 1880; another history of persecution because of religious beliefs.

Saeed looked pleased to see me having a good time.

Kadura was excited that we would be moving to Shmessani, which is where our piece of land was located. She said that they too had bought land there and would probably build their home in the next couple of years. She said that she'd introduce me to many of her friends. I liked her open and cheerful personality. She was about to say something when the doorbell rang; she rose to greet her newly arrived guest, Nicola. He was the architect that Salah wanted us to meet and who would be building their home one day. A couple of years younger than Saeed, he was a Christian Jordanian educated in England and liked to build contemporary homes.

The next morning we accompanied him to look at two houses he had built. We loved his work and he was excited to start on his next challenge, our home. We met with Nicola regularly to discuss our home, and Saeed was happy to deal with a man willing to listen to what I said. He told him that this was my dream home. Nicola told us it would take a year to finish and that it was going to be one of the prettiest houses in Amman.

My wish of being close to the embassy had finally come true. I wished the Grays hadn't retired, for I missed them terribly, but they had introduced us to many wonderful people whom I now saw on Wednesdays - movie nights at the embassy. I also started to attend church on most Sundays, depending on the children. The very next Wednesday, as I sat next to Lilly, one of Mrs. Gray's old neighbors, I noticed a tall slim woman, dressed in a tight fitting blue dress, high heels, and an ornate hat. She was in her fifties and was talking to everyone and laughing all the time. I couldn't get my eyes off her and finally she said hello to Lilly, who introduced me to Louise Griffins. We started talking and she said she was very pleased to have another Southerner to talk to. She and her husband Jack were from Texas and at the end of the evening, she invited us to a party they were having the next night.

Everything at their party was great; the food, the music, the guests, and the dancing. I met another couple, April and Bo, who also were older, but so nice, and they were from Boston. I had a ball and my spontaneous laughter rang out intermittently throughout the evening.

Life in Amman provided me with the privacy I had lacked for years. Although relatives continued to visit, it wasn't as easy for them since Amman was double the distance that Irbid had been. I didn't mind Saeed's immediate family visiting, but I did feel annoyed when distant cousins popped in unexpectedly for no good reason.

Linda and her children came over almost daily, and sometimes we saw each other twice a day if we were entertaining. Saeed hooked up with Fou'ad, who was now married to a Jordanian girl, Hana. I liked her and we often saw one another. She was very nice, a petite brunette who was very quiet, and didn't drink or dance. I told Saeed I understood why they visited Linda and Ali more often than us. Since Saeed had Fridays off, we would often go to Irbid or the Valley on a Thursday and spend the night. I enjoyed those days when I talked and laughed with Yumma Arifa, Wadad, Noffa, Shamma, Thrya, Fathma, Abadi, and others.

****

234

One day, after we had been in Amman for about three months, Saeed arrived home earlier than usual. I wondered if anything was wrong, but he hugged me and said, "Honey, I'm traveling to Holland for three weeks on official business next month." He beamed proudly, "I was thinking it would be nice if you flew into Holland with me and then went on to visit your parents."

"What about the kids? I couldn't manage all four without you." I hated to leave them, but Saeed quickly assured me that Yumma Arifa, Wadad, and Noffa would come to stay with them in Amman.

When the day came to leave for Amsterdam, the Amir, Yumma Arifa, and Wadad went to the airport along with Susan, Donna, Saleh, and Sami. I kissed and hugged my children many times before giving the others a final hug. Yumma Arifa held a laughing Saleh, kissing his neck and rubbing her nose against his soft skin. She loved him above all. They had a connection similar to the bond between Susan and her grandfather, who now stood holding her hand. Donna was saying something to Sami, who seemed about to cry. I walked away, looked back, and saw Wadad running around, carrying Sami in her arms. Donna followed them, laughing.

The trip to Amsterdam proved pleasant. We had a nice supper at the hotel before we went to bed. We rose early, had breakfast, and headed off to the airport again. I felt a pang of despair when I kissed Saeed goodbye. I looked back and he blew me a kiss.

Back in Knoxville again, Mama and Daddy couldn't have been happier; although they wished I had brought the children with me. I felt weird being without my kids, but kept telling myself that it would only be for three weeks.

I lay down looking at the ceiling that by now I knew was lower than those in my homes in Jordan and thought that I really did belong to two worlds at the same time. Not fully here nor there. I chuckled to myself as I thought about eating dinner earlier. I had kept waiting for someone to ask me to take a second plate, or offer to get me something to drink. Sometimes I caught myself thinking like an Arab, too. I guess Saeed was right. He told me once that the culture we live in, even when it's not our own, would subtly become a part of who we were and how we thought. I closed my eyes to hold back the tears that suddenly welled up. I missed him so much. I missed my babies and wondered how they were doing without me.

I spent the first few days getting to know my brothers and young sister again. I wanted to be on the road, see the trees, watch the cars, and hear Americans speak. Most of all, I wanted to go shopping. There were so many things I wanted to get, and all the children were waiting for gifts from America. I also did a lot of visiting. One day I was at Cousin Patsy's house, visiting her and her three girls.

"Remember all the work we had to do back then, before we had washing machines and supermarkets?" Patsy asked.

"How about plucking the chickens?" I said, and we laughed.

"I never realized how much we had to do then, but all I see now is how hard Mama worked." I filled my glass with iced tea. "Debbie needs to help. I swear, I've never seen that girl lift a finger. The only thing she does is ask for a new outfit every day. I told Mama that the last time I was here, but Debbie's her baby, and I think she wants her to stay a baby."

"It's good for children to learn to take responsibility, just like we did. All my children have chores," Patsy said, as she lit a cigarette and took a puff.

I made a face!

"What does that look mean?" Patsy asked.

"I guess I was thinking that my children don't have any chores around the house." I grinned and shrugged. "It's a different world over there," I added. "Most homes have live-in help, and children aren't expected to help out. It would be different if the mothers were the ones working."

I related my conversation with Patsy to Mama. I said that although I gave birth to my children, where they grow up will affect who they are."

"Sweetie, a mother's influence on her children is strong, and your children will learn how to act by watching you," Mama said, a cigarette perched between her fingers.

"I know that, Mama, but they'll also watch their daddy, grandmother, friends, and aunts." I looked up at the sound of the front door closing. Daddy was back from work. He gave Mama and me each a kiss and asked us what were we up to.

"I was trying to explain to Mama that my children are different from me."

"Of course they are, Sweetie, they're fifty percent American and fifty percent Arab. This is a part of who they are; they belong here, too, and this is their country."

Later in the evening, we sat outside on the back porch for a while talking and listening to the evening sounds of birds and insects before settling down for the night.

"By the way, I'm going to visit the Hadads tomorrow evening. You want to come with me?" I asked Mama.

"No Sweetie, you go and enjoy yourself"

I wore a maroon dress that I had bought two days ago. I had missed the Hadads and also eagerly anticipated a glass of wine.

The evening would have been perfect if I hadn't missed Saeed so much. I talked about him the whole evening. When it was time to leave, Mary hugged me and said,

"I know you love your country, my dear, but I believe you love Saeed a lot more."

Everyone laughed, but I wanted to cry. "That's true, Mary. I would give up everything for Saeed." As I walked down the front steps, I remembered something and turned around. "I almost forgot, I'm going to throw a belly dancing party soon, and I thought you might enjoy it. Would you like to come?"

"A belly dancing party, why we have those every month, my dear, but I thought you would not enjoy them. I guess you are now a little more like us."

Seeing Talal and Abid once a week provided happy interludes for me. I always thought of Saeed as I watched his brothers kidding around. I hated to see them leave, and always thanked them for coming. Time seemed to fly.

"I have one more week before I go back, and we haven't been to the mountains yet. I also want to buy magnolia trees for my new home," I said, as I packed a few things.

"We could all go on a picnic this weekend, and you could go down and get those trees with Daddy tomorrow," Mama suggested.

Just then, Debbie came into the room. "We haven't been on a picnic since I don't know when!" Debbie said, and she hugged my neck.

"We used to go on picnics often, Mama. What happened?" I asked.

"It's not the same without you, Sweetie," Mama answered, as she eagerly began to plan for our outing.

Jimmy drove with Daddy and Debbie in front. Mama, Bobby, and I rode in the back. We drove for about an hour before finding the right spot. Right on the creek; it had picnic tables as well as grills to barbecue Mama's hamburgers. Everyone had a ball, and although it was too cold to swim this time of the year, we sure did enjoy the chicken, cole slaw, and potato salad. She also baked coconut cake, which she knew everyone liked.

I took a deep breath and continued in a slightly different direction. "I really feel sorry for the women over in Jordan. Most of them have to swim in their dresses while the men get to wear swimming trunks."

"I think they got it right over there," Jimmy teased. He bit into a piece of crispy chicken while waiting for the grilling hamburgers

"That's not funny, Jimmy. I'm serious. When I get back there, I'm going to start a support group for women."

As we were leaving, I said, "I still need to buy more candy and toys for Christmas. I also want to find something for Saeed." "You got him those pretty shirts, Sweetie," Mama noted.

"I want something else. We can go down to Watsons tomorrow; maybe I'll find something there."

I had no idea why, but Linda came to mind, and when Mama asked what I was thinking about, I said, "You know my friend Linda, back in Amman, Mama. I guess she came to mind when I thought about Christmas. When she first came to Amman, she always spent Christmas with me and we had such a good time. But after she gave birth to her second child, her husband said it was too much trouble coming to Irbid with two kids. But I'll be in Amman this year; maybe he'll change his mind." I smiled reassuringly at her.

"Is she the one who can't have a tree, on account of her husband?" Mama asked.

"Yes, but now he at least says she can put up a tree on Christmas Eve as long as she takes it down the next day."

"That's rubbish! That man has no sense." About to bust listening to this, Daddy had to say something.

The final day came. Tears were shed as I hugged Mama, Daddy, siblings, and other family members. A part of me felt sad about going back, but another huge part was excited.

After nine hours of flying, the plane finally landed at the airport in Amsterdam. I ran into Saeed's open arms as soon as I had gone through customs. I kissed him hard and long. Saeed got the luggage and was thrilled with the magnolia trees and promised that I would be the first woman in Amman to have a magnolia flower, just like I was the first in the Jordan Valley. He was staying at the Hotel NH Doelen these past three weeks, and he thought I would enjoy it. He said that it was in the heart of the city, right on the Amstel River surrounded by old buildings and interesting sights. He was right; I admired the exceptional architecture and interior design as we stepped into the hotel.

After unpacking, I told Saeed that I would like to take a long hot bath. He said to take my time and to join him in the bar when I finished. After he left the room, I quickly showered, changed into a new tight red dress, mascara, red lipstick, and the new platinum short wig I had bought the last day before I left Knoxville to play a trick on Saeed. I had told Mama ... who just shook her head.

Finally, I put on my fur-lined black coat.

My heart beat hard as I sashayed into the bar and spotted my husband sitting beside a window, admiring the view and sipping on his whiskey.

He glanced up casually as I entered the bar. As he took another sip from his drink, I approached his table.

"May I have a light?" I said as I hid my face with my coat collar.

He lit my cigarette and I slid into the chair beside him.

Quietly, but pleasantly, he said, "I'm waiting for my wife, and she should be coming any minute. Is there anything else you need?"

He looked uncomfortable and when I didn't move, he politely excused himself, took his whiskey, and sat at the bar facing the door. Seconds later, I followed and sat beside him. He turned and said irritably,

"I'm waiting for my wife!" He pointed to the ring on his finger. I thought that was so cute.

I took off my coat as I roared with laughter. He stared for a moment and when I turned my face toward him, he shouted, "Betty! What do you think you're doing?" He wasn't amused at first, but after a bit, he had to admit that it was funny. We ate, drank, and laughed before we went up to our room. We both were overcome with strong passion. Three weeks apart had seemed like an eternity.

The next morning we enjoyed a wonderful buffet of cheeses and meats, as well as a great assortment of sweet breads. Afterwards, we walked a little, did some shopping, and then returned to the hotel. Since we both were art lovers, the Rijk Museum, Stedelijk Museum, Van Gogh Museum, and Rembrandt's House were on our list of places to visit. We enjoyed our walks in this beautiful city, and I wondered aloud what it would be like if we'd been born here. Would we stop seeing the beauty after a while?

For our last evening, we had dinner in the nearby NH Schiller Hotel, located at the Rembrandtplein, a busy square in Amsterdam. When we boarded the plane for Amman the next morning, I felt relaxed and serene. "I had a wonderful vacation. I love you, now and always."

"Now and always, doesn't seem long enough."

****

My third arrival in Jordan began differently than the first two. Susan and Donna ran up shouting, "Mama! Baba!" and wouldn't stop until they were in our arms.

"Next time you go, we want to come with you," Susan said, as she hugged me.

"Yes, we want to go to 'merica too, Mama," Donna chimed in. She hugged her Baba, who stood up with her in his arms and went to see about our luggage.

As he walked away, I said, "America, Honey, not 'merica.'"

"Yes, Mama, America!" Donna answered happily over Saeed's shoulder.

When we arrived home, I pulled my boys close and inhaled their smells. I missed them very much and told them that they had grown. They laughed, and their excitement grew as they followed the suitcases into the house. They were soon rewarded with toys, candy, books, and clothes.

Saeed and I had decided to plant pine trees around the premises of our property just like we had done in the Valley. A few days after coming back, we decided to plant the three magnolia trees I had brought in the front garden. The kids were excited.

"We're going to plant the American trees," Donna explained to Saleh and Sami, who nodded as their eyes grew wide. She looked at me when she said "American."

"That's right, Honey, and when they grow, they'll have the biggest white flowers, called magnolias, you ever saw." I said as I hoped my words would become true.

"We will have magnolia flowers from the tree in the Valley before these, I hope," Saeed said as he hugged me and the children laughed as they called me, Mama Magnolia.

I had missed another period and didn't like it. I knew Saeed was going to be very worried and was going to get really angry with me. Doctor Stevens had wanted me to have a hysterectomy after Sami's birth. He didn't think that I could endure another pregnancy. I thought long and hard and decided to let God do his will. I decided not to have the surgery, much to Saeed's disappointment.

As I expected, when I told him, Saeed didn't like it and told me that this was not God's doing but my doing. His words hurt and I felt my legs trembling, and started to cry. I turned to leave the room, and he followed me saying,

241

"I'm worried. My words may have been harsh, but I'm scared." He held me close. "I'll take tomorrow off, and we'll go see Doctor Stevens."

The doctor confirmed our worst fears. "I don't think your health is strong enough to go through childbirth again. Remember the trouble you had with Sami? Why, if it hadn't been for the grace and love of God, he would have never made it through alive. This time, I'm afraid you're both in danger. I honestly think you need to consider an abortion, Betty." He held my hands and looked straight into my eyes, "For the sake of your other children, for Saeed, and for all who love you."

I shook my head as tears streamed down my cheeks. For the second time in my life, I didn't agree with this man whom I wholeheartedly trusted. I couldn't do it. I couldn't justify my health as a good enough reason. I wiped my eyes with Saeed's handkerchief, and sat until I composed myself.

"Things are different now that I'm living in Amman. My health will get better. I've just had so much on my mind, with the move from Irbid and the flying back to the States. I'm just tired. I'll rest and take better care of myself."

We were quiet on the ride back, and finally I said that I would have a hysterectomy after this birth.

Linda was the only one who thought I was doing the right thing. She said I needed to rest and take better care of myself. She also thought that I should stop drinking alcohol. I told her that drinking calmed me and it was better than taking medication.

Saeed had a government worker's schedule, 8:00 a.m. to 2:00 p.m. every day except Friday, his day off. He arrived home each day a little after 2:00 p.m., ate a bite with me and the boys, and talked about his day at work. He then went into the bedroom and played with the boys until the four of us took a siesta. The girls came in from school around 3:30 p.m. and woke everyone up. Susan and Donna then changed out of their uniforms and went into the kitchen to eat their second meal of the day. Meanwhile, Saeed got the boys ready, and then off we would all go to see our new house. I wanted to oversee every detail and had an opinion about every step in the building process. The

242

kids ran and played in the open space while the adults conferred about the house. It was a sprawling, two-level home, and I wished to have a large, open space where I could entertain and have dancing space.

Nicola's design included a large, square room divided into two living rooms, a sitting room, and a dining area, with only one column in the middle of the entire space. Sliding leather doors ordered from Italy separated the sitting and dining rooms. I also wanted large windows framed into as many walls as possible. I challenged Nicola in many ways, and every time, he rose to the task and excelled. I had floor-to-ceiling windows on three of the walls, and the front windows overlooked my beautiful magnolias.

Saeed had red rock imported from Cyprus, which was installed around the outside front of the house because I had admired their beauty on one of our trips to Beirut. It turned out exactly as I had imagined it would, and when the magnolias grew, they would be a lovely contrast to the stone. I clapped my hands and then moved them down to rest on my swelling belly. The custom-made, blue-and-white kitchen design brought me great pride. I found the plans in one of the home decorating magazines and showed them to Saeed, who also loved the layout and colors.

Nicola recommended Abu Khalil, who was a little man with an artist's heart; he loved working with wood and knew how to transform any picture into a beautiful piece of reality. He had brown eyes and black hair, which he wore longer than average. He listened to every word I said, looked closely at the picture of my dream kitchen, and made it his mission to accomplish it. He built the kitchen with its dividing island to accommodate a washing and ironing area. He worked his crew to create the recessed panels that hid the ironing board and laundry baskets. The men worked late into the night perfecting the chopping boards so they would slide in and out effortlessly. He also spent days trying to make the Lazy Susan faultless so I could spin my spices easily. I loved going and seeing the progress every day, but I had to admit it tired me. I tried not to show how tired I got because I knew Saeed would then want me to rest. I prayed that I would become stronger for the birth of my baby girl.

Many evenings were spent with our friends and we were so grateful to have Kadura and Salah, Louise and Jack, and April and Bo in our life. They added laughter and friendship that made my days wonderful. Linda and I didn't see each other as often. We still talked almost daily, but seemed to be drifting apart. She was becoming more Arabic in her behavior and, of course, with my new found friends, I was becoming more me. It seemed that she brought up my drinking more than I thought necessary, and I always made a point to speak with her kids in English. It irritated me no end when she spoke Arabic to them.

I picked beautiful Italian white marble, Arabescato Corchia, for the floors of all the living and dining room areas. Abu Khalil loved it.

"Madam, the wood look very good with the marble."

I tried to speak Arabic to him when we first met, but he was adamant about speaking English. I allowed him that victory after I complained to Saeed, who told me that he is proud of himself and thinks he speaks English like a native. He asked me to humor him and reminded me that the man was bending over backwards to please me. His final task had been building the dining room table, centered majestically within the wood-paneled area.

"I would really like you to use the same wood to cover the column and walls, but do you think that would be too much?"

"No, Madame, I think you idea great, like all idea before. Same wood very good. I can make beautiful table and chairs."

The table soon became another of his masterpieces. He constructed it in pedestal style from one thick slab of pinewood supported by two massive carved legs. He showed me more than one design before I picked the chair I liked. He worked on many projects, including all the built-in closets for the bedrooms as well as the vanities connected to them. For the master bedroom, he suggested we not use the same whitewashed wood he had used in the boys' and girls' rooms.

"Madam, use pinewood you love. I can make picture you show me with bed and drawers stuck to it, ezactly like picture. I can make beautiful, I know you love." He kissed his fingertips and smiled broadly.

"The pinewood would add a touch of pizzazz to the room," I agreed. "I also want a sitting area here." I pointed to the left corner of the bedroom, under one of the two huge windows in the room. "A couch against this wall, and I want this chair," I said, showing him another picture to duplicate.

"Ohhh, nice chair, Madam," he said, as he viewed the ultra-modern design.

"I'm glad you like it; it's a Swedish teak armchair lounge."

"*Sweedish teek.* Very nice." He looked puzzled, but nodded and smiled.

****

I felt great when Betty's first Christmas in Amman proved more joyous than she had expected. We all walked through our citrus farm in the Valley and picked a tree, which I hauled back to Amman. Susan, Donna, Saleh, and even Sami helped in decorating it with the help of many mugs of hot chocolate and Christmas carols filling the room. Finally, I lit the tree to screams of delight from everyone. We all were excited come Christmas Eve. The children couldn't wait till Santa Claus came, and we couldn't wait till the children slept so we could attend our first Christmas Eve party at the Griffins' home. Donna, who was five years old, fell asleep quickly. Finally, after reading book after book to her, Susan also closed her eyes. I kissed them, tiptoed out of the room, and went to get ready. I passed the boys' room and saw Betty asleep with Sami. I walked in, fondly watching her sleep for a few moments. I knew that she tired easily and I knew she was being brave for me. She looked so young and so fragile sleeping next to our baby and I worried about her each day. I prayed that God would take care of her, for all our sakes. I vowed that she would have a hysterectomy after this baby, boy or girl. How I wished I had been stronger with her back then, but this was going to be our last baby. I wanted her to live many happy years in the house I was building for her. Yubba had given me sixty thousand dollars, which was what it cost to build his massive house. But she wanted special materials that had to be imported. The house cost an extra thirty thousand which I borrowed because I couldn't ask Yubba for more. I didn't care what it cost; I wanted her to

245

have the house of her dreams and she deserved it. Of course, I was going to do all I could to have magnolia trees in our garden too. I listened to her steady breathing and hated to wake her, but we had a party to attend.

Betty began walking faster when she heard the music drifting from the Griffins' house. Jack opened the door, hugged us both, and ushered us in. She spotted Louise coming our way, and the two women hugged. Louise looked gorgeous in her tight-fitting, silver-embroidered dress and silver high heels. Betty danced and twirled in her red, ruffled dress as best as she could all night. I watched and marveled at her ability to dance, even when pregnant. I worried a little, too, but knew she would say she was fine if I fussed over her.

The next day, we were awakened at dawn by Susan and Donna staring at us. "He came, he came, Santa came!" Susan's voice brimmed with excitement, while Donna stood on her tiptoes, jiggling up and down. They dove into their gifts and the day began.

Linda, Ali, and the kids came later for Christmas dinner. Betty had something under the tree for each child. The kids opened their gifts and thanked Betty who told them that it was from Santa. Later that evening, as she lay in bed, I noticed how tired she looked and asked if she was okay. She said it was one of the best Christmases she ever had. I hoped that would always be the case.

I enjoyed my job in Amman and worked hard at improving the lives of farmers in Jordan. I was working on different projects that were possible through foreign aid. Many aimed to educate the farmers on what to grow and how to irrigate properly. Others were designed to improve the breeds of different livestock, especially sheep. I personally worked tirelessly to award as many scholarships as I could for agricultural engineers and studies in Public Veterinary Medicine. I believed education was the answer and the key to a more prosperous Jordan. I always enjoyed telling Betty how my day had gone and she was very excited and proud of my work.

When she was seven months pregnant, we went to Dr. Stevens for a check-up. He wanted her to consider staying with him and his wife for the last two crucial months, but she refused, saying that she would be miserable without her family. I felt the same and promised her I

246

would be close by all the time. I didn't stay one night in the Valley for fear of her going into labor; in fact, I only went when it was of the utmost importance. I could tell a difference in her; she no longer sang or played with the kids, not to mention dancing with Susan and Donna. I found myself thinking about her thirtieth birthday in two more days, and I had nothing planned. I called Louise Griffins and we talked.

"I see the worry in your eyes when you look at Betty, and I, too, have noticed how weak she looks. But don't you worry; she'll be fine once she delivers the baby. And about her birthday, I'll take care of everything."

The next morning, I bent to kiss Betty goodbye as usual. She let out a moan and opened her eyes. "Oh, Saeed, I don't feel good. I feel worse than ever." She raised herself up a little to return my kiss, and then cried out. "Oh, oh, my water just broke! I'm going to have the baby. Oh God, I'm going to have the baby!"

I knew we didn't have time to drive to Aj-loun. The baby would have to be delivered in Amman. I was thankful that I had taken her a couple of times to a local physician, Dr. Ma'ashir. He was an accomplished young man who had studied medicine in the United States. Her delivery was long, but I thanked God that no complications arose. I was also glad that Yubba and Yumma Arifa were with me. Ramzi, our new son, was welcomed into the world the day before Betty's thirtieth birthday. She called him her birthday present from God. I was thankful that the delivery went well, and felt very optimistic. Everything was going to be all right.

Betty, Donna, Saeed, and Susan

CHAPTER 15

HOME

We moved into our home in the fall of 1964, within weeks of the birth of Ramzi. Although it was not fully furnished, we decided to move in and not have to pay another year's rent. I couldn't believe only a year had passed. I felt my life had changed so much and I had changed with it. The first night in our new home was yet another celebration. After the kids were fed, bathed, and settled into their beds, Saeed came into the master bedroom with a bottle of champagne.

Saeed's father, Yumma Arifa, and other family members came the next day. I could tell they were not impressed with the open concept but they did admire the sliding doors that gave privacy to the big room. Although his father had seen the house many times, he must have expected an even bigger house. Saeed had installed the latest central heating system to ensure our warmth in the cold winter months of Amman. Every room had at least one radiator in it, and Abu Khalil was finishing the covers I wished to place over them for the final look. The landscaping still needed work, but the magnolia trees were thriving. Saeed had started two rose gardens, one on each side of the upper level garden. We both decided to keep the downstairs garden for the children with only grass and a couple of lemon and lime trees to go with our gin and tonics. The house had a covered patio that I knew would be the perfect place for our bridge games in the summer. Our stylish house needed furniture to portray that same feel.

The 60's was a lively decade with new trends in furniture design and decorations for the home. Many bright and exciting designs replaced the conventional florals of the fifties, and I couldn't wait to make use of them in our home. When I looked at magazines displaying all these new bold colors with their new bold designs, I wanted them. Thank God, Saeed and I had similar taste. We decided to shop in Beirut, and on our first trip for furniture, we found a dinette set perfect for our kitchen. It was made with the best quality chromium steel tubing in the latest design. It consisted of a kitchen table with eight matching chairs finished in bright blue and white leather. On our second trip, we discovered an upscale shop that carried beautiful Italian designs. After some deliberation, we decided to buy four different sets of chairs and two couches. Every set had a unique design with a splash of different color; lime green, bright orange, turquoise blue, and a light gray. The two couches were reddish orange with geometric splashes of gold throughout.

One main issue was how to have a bar that could be camouflaged in order not to offend the Amir. I believed that Abu Khalil could make something against the wall in the living room. After mulling over magazines, I came across a bookcase with a concealed bar in the middle section. Abu Khalil's finished product exceeded our expectations. He devised a retractable, mirrored shelf that slid out from the middle of the bookcase. This provided a surface where drinks could be mixed. He crafted a middle section with lights that came on to reveal a mirrored alcove with three shelves. I loved it!

The final project for the designer came when he finished the television room I requested. Situated in the back of the living room, it was to resemble the traditional presentation of the *majless*. Instead of mattresses, I wanted low, leather couches, and instead of the pillows that are traditionally used to support the elbows, I wanted circular leather pillows. I picked leaf-green leather and purchased beautiful carpets for the floor.

"This is the prettiest room in your house," Saeed's father said the first time he saw it. He loved it so much that he asked Abu Khalil to make him an identical one for one of the rooms in his Irbid house. That really made my day!

Saeed's father's laughter echoed throughout the house as he stepped into the brightly colored living room. Yumma Arifa shook her head and giggled loudly. He opened his arms to me, and I slid in, anticipating his scent, and I lingered for a moment before looking up into his gentle eyes.

"I am so glad you like the furniture and the house."

"I love your home, and I like what I smell cooking, too," he said, sniffing the air and tilting his head toward the kitchen.

After a delicious meal, Saeed went to the bedroom, and the Amir lay on the low leather couch in his favorite room. Yumma Arifa and I enjoyed coffee in the kitchen and talked until the kids came home from school.

"*Taeta!*" They shouted and ran to greet her; she kissed them and filled their hands with the candy they were expecting. The minute the Amir woke up, Susan ran into his open arms shouting, "*Jeddo!*" He flung her up in the air and caught her with his firm grip. They stayed the night, as they usually did, and Gazi, Saeed's second youngest brother, came over the next morning. I enjoyed their stay and made pancakes in the morning. I was becoming especially close to Gazi, who came to enlist Saeed's help in convincing their father to let him join the army instead of going to the States.

****

I didn't agree with Gazi, but in the end I gave in to his request and tried to help convince Yubba, who said, "Your brother is making a mistake, but if you think it's the right thing to do, then I'll agree." He inhaled deeply as I listened respectfully as he related the same story I heard so many times, "If destiny dealt me different cards, Mamdouh would have gone to the States while you stayed with the tribe. To truly lead, you have to be one of them. I had to give you up when you were young, so you couldn't grow up with your people and be one of them. Mamdouh had to stay, being the second eldest, and he will help you lead once I

251

am gone. But Gazi, I don't understand! Why would he give up the chance of getting an education in America, just like his brothers?"

The next week, Gazi endeared himself to Betty forever when he barged into our home, his eyes sparkling with excitement, and asked us to step outside. We went out, and were both speechless as we stared at a dead boar. He said, smiling at Betty, "You said you couldn't find pork at the supermarket last week. I knew hogs roamed the lower part of the valley, so last night, I went with a shotgun, waited until I heard one coming my way, and shot it for you. Are you happy?"

"You could have gotten seriously hurt, Gazi." I could hear the concern in her voice and she was right. I made him promise not to do that again.

Meanwhile, work was good, and the program for scholarships had grown tenfold. As for the citrus farm, it prospered and for the first time, we made more money than we spent on it. Yubba was so happy that we started two more citrus farms. The look of pride from the elders filled me with happiness. I was also happy to proudly announce the first agricultural lab in the Jordan Valley. Although they didn't understand what it meant, I explained that such labs test soils to determine what plants suit it best.

****

I met Barbara at a gathering in Fou'ad's house just before I moved to Amman. She was an American married to a Jordanian. She was tall, slim, and had large blue eyes that sparkled when she laughed. She had arrived in Amman about the same time I set foot in the Jordan Valley. She later introduced me to Elisabeth, a British doctor married to a friend of Saeed's, whose family was in politics. I admired her work at the government hospital and with time we became fast friends, too. The three of us were sitting in the kitchen talking about our families and plans for the first meeting for foreign women married to Jordanian men.

"You know, Betty," Elisabeth said in her serious tone, "Jordan is changing demographically. Many of the wealthy and good families are educating their sons abroad, especially in America and England. Because of the high expenses, most stay abroad until they graduate.

Many fall in love there and bring their wives back home with them, just like Saeed, Ali, and others did." She paused thoughtfully, and then continued. "The transition is not smooth for two reasons. The first is that many of them change when they come back to Jordan and transform back into an Arab man who watches and comments on his wife's dress or actions."

"You are right," I said as I thought of Ali.

"The second reason is that these men allow their families, in particular, mothers and sisters, to take over their lives and wives. These two reasons make the American women feel unhappy and alone."

"Oh, Elisabeth, your words are so true. These two reasons *do* make women feel alone. I mean, they see the men they left their own world for changing, and that's scary and sad."

"You're right, and the sooner we talk to these newcomers, the better off they will be in the long run." Elisabeth ate a bite of the lemon meringue pie. "I just love this pie. I have to have the recipe." She looked up and asked, "You must be excited about tomorrow, aren't you?"

She was talking about my hosting my first bridge gathering and I was excited. The next morning, the house grew quiet after the children were off to school. I hummed as I poured a cup of coffee and headed to the breakfast table to join Saeed. I sipped the delicious, dark coffee between bites of scrambled eggs, cheese, and honey. I watched him drive off before I fixed another cup of coffee for myself. I could hear the help cleaning in the living room. The phone began to ring just as I lifted the cup to my mouth. The cup jiggled momentarily and I straightened it before picking up the receiver. It was Barbara telling me that a new American woman, named Maryanne, had landed in Amman. She said she had called and welcomed her to Jordan and told her we would visit her the next day around noon. A couple of hours later the ladies began to arrive for the bridge games. I enjoyed playing bridge and loved the challenge of the game that Mrs. Gray had introduced me to. I still missed that lady whenever I thought of her.

"More Cinzano, ladies?" I asked, as I mixed the Italian vermouth with soda in tall glasses filled with ice.

The next morning we drove to Maryanne's in-laws' house and began our mission to try to make her experience in Jordan more positive. I explained that we, as wives, had an impact on our husbands and on our offspring; with time, this influence would play into the culture of the community. I also said that the best gift we gave was learning how to assimilate into this culture without changing who we were. I continued that in the Arabic culture, there is a definite difference between being nice and being gullible or downright stupid. You have to learn to say 'no' before you become angry; you have to learn to stand your ground before it is a fight. I took a breath as Barbara continued.

"Don't ever make it a fight, and, even above and beyond that, don't ever allow anyone to push you around. That is a definite sign of weakness in a culture that respects strength of mind and body."

Maryanne's mother-in-law came into the formal sitting room several times to serve juice, coffee, and water, and to stare openly at us.

"One more thing to learn, staring is normal," I said.

Barbara threw her head back and laughed, saying, "Ogling, my dear Betty, is more like it."

We stayed a couple of hours and Maryanne gave us both a grateful hug. She looked as though a spark of light had entered her strange, new world. My visit with Maryanne made me think of Linda and I asked Jean to drop me off at Linda's place. I told her Saeed would pick me up on his way home. When I got there, Linda threw herself at me as she bitterly sobbed.

"Oh Betty, I am so glad you came. I was about to call you. I don't know what to do." She continued to cry as I helped her and my shaking nerves to one of the couches. After a few moments, I asked her to tell me what was going on.

"Ali got mad at one of his sisters because someone saw her talking to a man in the street. Oh Betty, it was horrible, I thought he was going to kill her, I swear to God, I have never seen anything like it."

My hands flew to my mouth and she continued, "I tried to interfere and he turned his anger toward me. He punched me in the

254

chest and pushed me ..." she couldn't finish and started to sob again. Her next words froze my breathing, "I lost my baby ... I lost my baby!"

We cried together and I went into her kitchen and made a pot of coffee. As I gave her a cup she asked, "Betty, what can your women's group do to help me?"

"Only you can help you, Linda. We can advise and help you understand the country and its culture, but what you are going through is totally different."

"I do want to go home, Betty, but I can't leave my children."

After taking with Saeed, Barbara, and someone at the embassy, I asked Linda if her parents would be willing to send money to buy tickets for her and her children. She wrote to them and they agreed. I knew they loved her and wanted her home, but I also knew that it would be a lot of money for all three of them to travel.

The biggest hurdle we knew would be at the airport. The Jordanian government does not allow a woman to travel without her husband's consent. Barbara, myself, and a Jordanian male friend took her to the airport where he pretended to be her husband. By the time she was in the air, I felt that I was going to faint. I felt such relief that I cried.

That night as I related all these exciting events to Saeed, I told him that I was glad that her family would finally get to see her children. That brought a sad thought to mind and I told him that Mama and Daddy would never really know my children.

"Oh, Betty, don't say that. I know we all feel down sometimes, and I don't blame you. I feel the same way sometimes. But you know your mama and daddy will get to know our children."

"How, Saeed? I can't travel with five children and you are so busy."

"Well if we can't fly to them, why not have them come to us? That way they would get to see our children and our world, *and* they could go to Jerusalem!" He held both my hands and smiled into my staring eyes. "Write your mama and tell her about this tomorrow, and tell her that I will buy their tickets."

The next day Ali came to visit and he looked horrible. I wouldn't talk to him and he couldn't look me in the eye. After he left Saeed

255

related their conversation to me. He said that Ali felt such remorse at what he did that he planned to go and try to get Linda back. He reassured me that Ali told him that he could not live without Linda and their kids. I prayed for her safety and wished that all would go well. I prayed that she would be strong.

****

The next couple of weeks were all excitement. Finally, I couldn't believe it, but Mama, Daddy, and Debbie were coming the next day and they were going to stay six months.

Their awaited arrival caused great excitement in Amman, and when the day came, the airport was filled with people wanting to welcome them to Jordan. I could tell Mama and Daddy were overwhelmed and couldn't tell one face from the other, but they smiled, shook hands, and hugged. Finally, we headed toward home.

"Mama sounds so different from them; I don't understand a word they're saying," Donna told Susan.

"They speak Southern," Susan answered, as she eyed Debbie sideways.

"Don't they know how to speak English?" Donna looked surprised, and the other children stared at Susan, waiting for her answer.

"It is English, but it's another accent." Susan could see that Donna didn't understand, and she looked at me. I thought and said,

"Honey, do you notice how Jeddo and Baba say things differently? Baba says *Marhaba*, and Jeddo says *Hala*. Mama says things differently from your grandmother, too."

By then, we had reached the house. Mama's and Daddy's eyes lit up as they entered the house they had been reading about for the past year. Mama thought I had decorated it beautifully and said that it was like a house in a magazine.

"I reckon it's five times as big as our home," Daddy chuckled.

Mama loved the room they would be staying in and couldn't believe they had their own bathroom.

"Oh, Mama, sometimes I wake up and can't believe that this is my home," I said.

Mama gave me a long hug and said, "Lord knows how hard I prayed those first months you were gone, and I'm so proud of your new home, Sweetie."

Debbie quickly got used to the place and began to speak more slowly in order to be understood. Once enrolled in the school in Amman, she quickly adjusted and became known as the "Blonde American who danced like an angel." She gladly demonstrated her skill with a baton and her tap dancing finesse. I had tried unsuccessfully to keep the girls up to par with their dance lessons. I tried to explain to Mama that in Jordan they only taught ballet, and didn't know tap dancing. I told her that the girls didn't like to practice. She tried to comfort me by saying that not everyone loves ballet. That afternoon as we often did, Mama, Debbie, Susan, Donna, and I put on music and danced until we couldn't stand up. Saeed walked in from work and joined us, doing his best to follow.

Those six months enabled Mama and Daddy to live with us as well as enjoy our families. Mama and Daddy accompanied us to the cocktails and parties we were invited to. I cherished those moments when I could show off my world to them.

"Everyone is so beautiful, and their homes are just as pretty. The food and the dancing are like nothing I could have imagined, at least not in this part of the world. These people live in ballrooms. I feel like I'm in a movie!" Mama said after the first of many parties she attended. She bragged about these parties in letters she wrote to family members back home. The only thing I knew that they didn't like, was the fact that I drank one or two drinks in the evening. I hated to complain, but my body actually ached at different times in the day, and I could never guess why. It's like I would be fine one minute, and then the next, pain shot through me. After a drink, I always felt better. I tried to express my feelings to Mama and I think she understood. She would tell me that I was always strong, but then, at times, the slightest things would trouble me. I often wondered if something was really wrong with me, but I chased those thoughts away.

Doctor Stevens and Mariam came down to meet my parents and they got along famously. By then they had two little girls, Sarah who was five, and Sally, three. The girls played together. Susan and Donna were happy to see them, but Debbie didn't want to play with them because they were babies. We promised we would visit them next week as we said goodbye. The next morning Mama accompanied me to Jean's house for one of the meetings conducted by the American Women of Amman. She watched everything with interest. Mama turned to talk with Barbara and the other ladies. Later when we were on our way home, Mama patted my hand, saying that she thought what I was doing was great. I could hear the pride in her voice, and my heart soared.

One weekend, we took Mama and Daddy to the Jordan Valley. Yumma Arifa cooked mansaf and they enjoyed it. They even tried eating with their hands to the laughter of all who watched. After dinner, we drove down to the river. Mama walked to the riverbank and sat on a protruding rock. She trailed her fingers in the water and told me she couldn't believe that her daughter actually owned land on the Jordan River. Then we walked through the citrus grove, enjoying the fragrances and the sounds of birds lucky enough to live in such a paradise. I took Mama to show her the Magnolia tree and to everyone's delight, there was my first bud. I was so happy that I cried. All the children came to admire it. I felt such peace and that it was such a great omen for our farm.

When we had our second flower, I carefully cut it in the early morning hour, immediately put it into a bowl of warm water and took it to the big house. They loved the smell, especially Arifa, for she loved perfume. Saeed promised to bring a tree back the next time we went to the States, and to plant it at the house in Irbid.

Saeed explained the history of the Ghor and his experiment first with banana trees, and then finally citrus. While in the Valley, they had the opportunity to see firsthand how the villagers lived. They watched the coffee man pour the coffee and saw women squatting comfortably while they chatted.

One afternoon, I invited some of my friends to meet my parents. Before they came, I asked Mama for one of Debbie's dresses. Her puzzled look prompted me to say,

"I'm going to play a joke on my friends and pretend I'm Debbie!" I waved my wig in front of her.

Mama, Debbie, and the kids were in stitches as they watched me go back and forth, changing into the different outfits, wigs, and accents.

"See how Mama is speaking Southern when she is in the wig and has no lipstick?" Susan explained to Donna, who nodded and giggled out loud.

"Your sister looks so much like you, Betty, but of course her hair is different, and she sounds different too," Kadura said.

Finally, after almost an hour of fun and disguise, I came into the living room with the wig in my hand. Eyes opened wide, and roars of laughter rang through the house. I laughed just as hard when I related this to Saeed in the evening, and boy did he ever enjoy that.

One of the highlights of their visit was the day trip we took to Jerusalem. Mama's excitement mounted every minute as we neared the city. When we finally arrived, she jumped out of the car and immediately breathed in the scent of incense that wafted through the door of the Chapel of Ascension. I proudly retold many things I learned on my first visit as we headed to the Church of Our Lord and the Church of All Nations. After a lunch of grilled fish and rice, we finally visited the Church of the Holy Sepulcher, where Mama's eyes misted with strong emotion as she knelt, taking in every detail. She told me she wanted to memorize the scents and the scene so she could recall it for her pastor and family back home. I knelt beside her and thanked God for my blessings. Saeed took pictures for Mama to take home. She kept on saying she couldn't believe that she was walking the same streets that our Lord had walked, which reminded me of my first visit to the Holy City. I was so happy for her, so happy.

******

Four months had passed since Linda had gone to the States. I had gotten two letters from her: The first one said that she was home, safe and sound; the second was to say that Ali was there and they were trying to work things out. When the phone rang and I heard her voice, saying she had returned to Jordan with her husband, I had mixed feelings. I hoped that she had done the right thing and knew that only time would tell. Mama really liked her and had heard her story. She too hoped that my friend had done the right thing.

259

Mrs. Simmon, the French ballet teacher, made Debbie the star of the yearly exhibition, and Debbie shined. Mama showed off what she did best by designing and sewing dresses for Debbie, Susan, and Donna.

"This is a great farewell party!" Mama said. She enjoyed the show and all the recognition given to her baby.

"Yes, Mama, you're right, although the thought of you leaving next week just breaks my heart." I hugged her tightly.

Many hugs were exchanged and tears shed at the airport, and on the drive back home, I felt an emptiness creep into my heart. I knew I was going to miss them so much.

I returned to my daily life and wished my parents had stayed for my first Christmas in my new home, but I understood their need to be back in their own surroundings.

"This is your first Christmas, Baby; isn't it exciting?" I tickled Ramzi's belly as Saeed put on his pajamas. Susan and Donna ran into the room.

"We put the boys to sleep!" Susan said proudly.

Donna quickly added, "I told them a story about a bad witch and a good witch!"

"Ooooh, that sounds scary!" I said, and hid my face with my hands. Seconds later I removed them and screamed, *Boo!* to everyone's shrieks and laughter. After they quieted down, I told them they'd better go to bed, because we were going to the farm the next morning to pick our Christmas tree. The next morning, we all headed to the Valley after a hearty breakfast of bacon, eggs, biscuits, and gravy. The wonderful task of choosing the perfect tree occupied our minds as we walked around the perimeter of the farm and surveyed each tree. We all finally agreed on one, and everyone watched as the workmen cut it down and hauled it onto the pickup truck. After eating lunch with Saeed's family, we drove back to Amman. On the way, Saeed said that he thought his father didn't look good. He said not only did he look pale, but that he complained of numbness in his arms as well as extreme fatigue. He said he was going to go back tomorrow with the doctor. I prayed he would be fine.

"The tree is here!" Saleh shouted. He had been the first to spot the truck as it parked in front of our home. I put Christmas songs on the record player and went into the kitchen to make everyone hot chocolate and marshmallows. Susan and Donna took out the boxes and carefully sorted the balls to be hung on the tree. Saeed began to sort the lights and make sure they all worked, while the boys tried to help. Four little elves helped us as we busily hung one sparkling ball, light, or tassel after another until all the decorations were in place. The moment of awe came when Saeed turned off all the house lights, and the tree glittered with its own magic, spellbinding the whole family.

"What a great job!" I said, "Santa is watching, and he's proud of everyone!"

"Does that mean I'll get everything I asked for in my letter?" Donna asked.

Saleh chimed in, "Me, too?"

"I'm sure Santa's elves are busy trying to make everything you want," I said.

Saeed enjoyed all the festivities; he wanted his children to enjoy me and my traditions in a way that he had never had a chance to do with his own mother. The next day he took the doctor to the Valley to check his father. When he came back in the evening, he said that the doctor said that his father was diabetic and had high blood pressure. He put him on medication and told him not to eat sweets. I felt sorry for Saeed, for now he worried about my health and his father's. This put a damper on our Christmas spirit, and I prayed for him as I prayed for myself.

Saeed called with the good news that the boxes that Mama sent from the States arrived. I knew they guaranteed that Santa would be able to grant all the Christmas wishes.

I cooked up a storm in my new kitchen and enjoyed every minute of the days leading up to the holiday. Although I ached, I didn't care. I worked on cookies for one whole day, with both the girls and boys helping.

"We need to make more chocolate chip cookies, Mama," Susan said. She was in charge of counting the delicious treats. "All my friends like them the most."

"Yes, and my friends, too," Donna piped up as she helped spoon out the dough and place it carefully on the baking trays.

"All the dough we have left is for chocolate chip cookies, which means that we are going to have a lot more." I looked at the four faces peering intently at me. At the end of the day we had hundreds of sugar, chocolate chip, and raisin cookies, and they gave the kitchen a wonderful aroma. I baked pies the next day, and at the end of that day four pecan, four lemon meringue, two chocolate, and two coconut pies lined the countertops. Saeed walked into the kitchen and smiled broadly.

"Wow, look at all the yummy pies. Can I have a piece of the pecan one?" he asked, lowering his head and inhaling the smell of the nearest sweet dessert.

"Not until tomorrow, Honey, but you can have some cookies, like the kids did."

"Why don't you call it walnut pie instead of pecan pie?" Saeed wondered aloud. He knew I always used walnuts since there were no pecan trees in Jordan.

"I guess I should, but then no one would know what I'm talking about. The recipe is a pecan pie recipe. I'm just changing the nuts." We both laughed about that.

That evening, after weeks of waiting, Christmas Eve was upon us. We listened to and sang Christmas songs. I read aloud "A Christmas Carol" by Charles Dickens. The boys slept soon afterwards, but Susan and Donna were too excited to sleep. They kept coming back downstairs to ask us what time it was.

"It's been five minutes since you last asked," I giggled quietly.

"Only five minutes!" Disappointment tinged Susan's voice as she looked at Donna, who didn't look much happier.

"Why don't you girls count from one to one hundred? That always put me to sleep," Saeed offered.

"You mean counting sheep?" Betty asked.

"Why sheep?" Susan's face looked puzzled.

"I don't know," I answered truthfully, "Maybe because they're white and fluffy, like clouds."

"Okay, I'm going to count sheep." Susan trudged back to bed, followed by Donna, who had decided to count dogs instead.

After I made sure they were asleep, we went to the Griffins for the Christmas Eve party. We had a great time and returned home well after midnight. After checking on the children, we placed everything carefully under the tree and went to sleep.

"Mama, Baba, Santa came, Santa came!" The girls shouted as they ran through the hallway, waking up the entire household. I felt so tired, as if I only slept a couple of hours, but it was worth it.

"Oh, Mommy, Santa is *perfect*! He brought us everything we asked for!" Susan bubbled over with excitement, and all her siblings readily agreed.

"What's that look on your face?" I asked Saeed, and my heart beat faster. We had agreed not to exchange gifts this year due to all the expenses with the new house.

Susan was the first to notice this exchange, and she clapped her hands. "Baba has a surprise for Mama!"

They all participated in the hunt until we found a rug tucked in the heater room at the back of the downstairs garden.

"Oh, Saeed, you bought the carpet after all!"

My hands flew to my open mouth when I saw the beauty of the ten-by-twelve-foot carpet. It was light green with beautiful red, mauve, and gold floral patterns. I threw my arms around him and held him close. My kids always waited for this part of Christmas morning, watching to see what their Baba got me.

"Because Mama is old, Baba has to bring her something, so she doesn't feel bad," Susan explained to Donna, Saleh, and Sami.

"Doesn't he know that she is the one who cooks the cookies for him?"

"Santa is only for children," I explained gently, taking Susan aside for a moment and giving her an extra-long hug.

We all enjoyed the stuffed turkey, cornbread dressing, baked beans, mashed-potatoes, cranberry sauce, and gravy. We enjoyed desserts as family and guests dropped by with happy wishes and more gifts.

That Christmas Linda and her kids didn't come to our house and that delighted me. She had her own Christmas tree and made her first Christmas dinner. She later told me that even his parents and sisters enjoyed it.

****

"I can't believe it will be Easter tomorrow. How time flies!" I said one evening while I watched Saeed mix our drinks.

"I know. It seems only yesterday that we moved in here, and now here it is our second year." He handed me a drink, and we kissed before he settled down in the chair opposite mine. I was glad that it was warm enough to sit on the patio. Saeed said it reminded him of Knoxville weather and he loved it. He then asked me how many kids were coming over for Easter. I answered that I had told the girls that they could each invite two friends. Linda and the kids were coming, and the boys wanted our neighbors to come also. I thought we were going to have around fifteen kids.

Everyone had a great time coloring and searching for eggs until no stone remained unturned.

After the kids were in bed, we relaxed as usual with our evening drinks and our conversation together. Saeed was spending more time in Irbid since the Amir was spending more time there himself. I knew Saeed loved spending time with his father, and learned something new every time he was with him.

The following year brought more pleasure and friends into my life. I broadened my circle of American acquaintances married to Jordanians as I became more engrossed in my work with the American Women's Society of Jordan. Saeed and I also met many American and European couples who came to work in Amman and fell in love with the country and its inhabitants. Saeed's family came by about once a week. I always liked that; however, since the Amir had gotten sick, we enjoyed him and made over him even more. I tried to make sweets that didn't have too much sugar. I was glad when he liked Jello with fruits and it became the standard when he came. Yumma Arifa also loved it!

Our second Christmas was as joyful as the first and the children all joined in picking our tree and decorating it as they sang to the tunes they loved. Donna pleaded with me to let her kindergarten friend Elham come and spend Christmas day with us. I wasn't sure it was a good idea until Donna said that she wanted to taste turkey and gravy. I looked at her and sighed.

"I guess she can come to eat, but not too early, now. You know Santa won't have anything for her."

"I know, I already told her that Santa doesn't know her."

Christmas Day arrived, a wonderful time filled with fun and joy that everyone now took for granted. We saw many friends who wanted to wish us happiness on this special occasion.

We had been in our new home almost two years, and we were preparing for our first New Year's party. I had dreamed of having such a grand party every time I attended one. We invited sixty-one couples, and I worried that some of our Arabic friends would not bring their wives since liquor would be served. Saeed said that he believed most would show up with their wives. I loved my husband's constant optimism and to my delight, he was right.

The following day, Susan and Donna watched as I addressed the envelopes; their job was to recheck and make sure I spelled the names correctly. They also checked to make sure that the names written on the invitation cards matched the names written on the front of the envelopes.

"Could you please put them in a bag, Baby, so that the driver can deliver them?"

"Can we go with the driver, Mama?"

"I don't think he knows where everyone lives. He'll have to wait till Baba comes from Irbid. I'm sure you can go with him then," I said, as I headed to the kitchen to make macaroni and cheese. The kids loved it, but Saeed didn't think it was a meal, so I made it whenever he wasn't eating with us.

"Mama, Elham loves macaroni and cheese. Can I ask her to come and eat with us?" Donna ran after me, holding the bag with all the sealed envelopes in it.

"Of course you can ask Elham over, Honey," I answered. Something would seem amiss if Elham didn't come over whenever I made any of the American foods.

Three days before the party, my kitchen became a whirlwind of activities. Linda, Barbara, and others helped roll and stuff hundreds of grape leaves with meat, rice and spices. I surveyed Noffa and Wadad preparing the *fatayer*, the miniature meat, spinach, and cheese pies they were helping me make. I also had *kubba*, (homemade cracked-wheat balls stuffed with beef and roasted pine nuts), different varieties of hummus, some with roasted meat or pine nuts, *baba ghanouj* (roasted eggplant, garlic, lemon juice made into a pâté), *fatayer, warak dawali,* fried chicken, several dishes of curry, meat loaf, pork loin, potato salad, and three other kinds of green salads.

"What are you serving for desserts?" Barbara asked.

"I'm baking three pineapple upside-down cakes, three chocolate cakes, and three orange cakes."

"I think by the time the party starts, you should be ready to take a nap," Barbara said, shaking her head in disbelief.

"Two chefs will come here the day of the party, and they'll actually do most of the cooking. They'll also bake some sweets. I plan on sleeping late that day."

I slept as late as I could the day of the party and then the fun started. I enjoyed transforming my home into a nightclub. We set up two bars, and throughout the house tables covered with white tablecloths and decorated with vases of flowers created the perfect final touch. Saeed had to remind me to eat a couple of times during the day. I hoped I didn't look tired. I knew I shouldn't have done all that cooking, but I had enjoyed it so much. We scattered party hats, paper noisemakers, little horns, packs of cigarettes, and bowls of nuts on all the tables. Lastly, I sprinkled the corn flour and confetti on the dance floor, a trick I learned at one of the parties I attended at the Bowens' house, where April explained that it made the marble more slippery and easy to dance on.

I slid into my gold silk dress. Saeed had brought the silk fabric from India years ago, and I had it sewn into a dress for tonight. Gold beads sewn around the high, column neck and along the side-slit overskirt added the perfect trim.

"Oh, Mama, you're beautiful!" Susan exclaimed, admiring the beautiful dress.

266

"The gold looks good on you. Which necklace are you going to wear?" Donna asked, and she ran to the jewelry safe the minute I opened it.

"I don't think I can wear a necklace with this style neckline."

"Wear this ring, Mama!" Donna handed me a huge, twelve-karat, yellow topaz ring mounted on two prongs in an eighteen-karat gold setting.

Saeed came out of the bathroom, "That's a beautiful color on you, Honey. You should wear gold more often."

"Which tie do you girls like more?" Saeed asked, holding up two.

"I like the red one," Donna said.

"But I think the black and gold would match Mama's dress," Susan quickly added.

I smiled and watched Saeed put both of them on for a moment before all three females decided on the gold-and-black, Christian Dior tie.

Our first New Year's party proved a great success. The house filled with ambassadors, foreign dignitaries, and government officials. Fancy cars parked outside, delivering bejeweled women dressed in their finery and escorted by meticulously dressed spouses. Just before midnight, the waiters came in carrying trays loaded with champagne glasses as Saeed, our guests, and I counted down:

"Ten, nine, eight, seven, six, five, four, three, two … one!"

"HAPPY NEW YEAR!"

Betty's home

Betty holding Ramzi's hand

Betty in her kitchen

CHAPTER 16

THE AMIR'S DEPARTURE (1965)

Since we went down to the Valley almost every weekend, Betty and I thought it would be a great idea to build a small house on our citrus farm. It took less than a year to build and was finished that spring. I was happy because I could spend every Thursday night in the Valley and be with Yubba. That was one of the biggest reasons for this house and I knew my blessing was having a wife who loved Yubba very much. She understood that we needed to be close by and in many ways, we both had a special bond with the Valley. We stopped by the big house on our way to our place and everyone was excited for us. I couldn't believe we would sleep that night in our own home in the Valley. It was a two-bedroom house with one large, L-shaped room that served as the family and dining area. A large fireplace provided the central focus.

Susan excitedly told her mother that we now had a fireplace so Santa could use it on Christmas Eve, and Betty told her that Santa was the main reason we built the fireplace. Betty knew she was going to have a crowd that evening, and made extra hamburgers and, of course, a Pineapple upside-down cake with half the sugar the recipe asked for. My love for her couldn't get any larger. Our weekly stay at the farm was good for all of us, especially Betty. Although I spent most of the time in the big house, I knew that she would be fine there. She loved gardening and enjoyed the garden I had behind the house. She also never tired of looking at her magnolia tree and admiring the way it was growing. She often invited friends from Amman who enjoyed being out of the city and in nature so close to the Jordan River. I was glad to be spending more time with Yubba. His health seemed to have deteriorated since he had been diagnosed about a year ago. He no longer was able to ride Anter for more than an hour, but I still cherished the times we went riding together. Mamdouh often joined us and we would visit other tribes or members of our own tribe. I didn't know everyone's name as they did, but I was doing my job in Amman. I worked relentlessly on securing and creating agricultural government agencies to help Bedouins, especially in the Jordan Valley. I was now working on trying to secure electricity and running water, but Jordan was not a rich country and things moved slowly.

One weekend in autumn, Yubba had such a bad spell of coughing and shaking that I decided he needed to be in Irbid closer to the doctors. Betty, the kids, and I went along with everyone to Irbid. We had three of the best doctors there, two from Amman, and they agreed it didn't look good. They said that his days were numbered, but they couldn't give me a number. We stayed the night and Yumma Arifa made one of his favorite meals, chicken liver cooked in concentrated pomegranate juice. He looked frail and wouldn't eat. He finally ate a small amount from Susan, who fed him with her hands. I stayed by his side until I could hear his steady breathing. He looked a little better the next morning and managed to eat breakfast.

We left for Amman and I said I would be back on Thursday, four days later. I didn't feel good about leaving him, but I knew I was only an hour away and I had an important meeting with foreign delegates the next day.

The ringing of the phone in the middle of the night startled us. I jumped out of bed and picked up the receiver, my hand trembling.

I knew it was the dreaded call. Yubba was fighting for his life. The doctor told me I'd better hurry if I wanted to say goodbye. I hung up, shaking with Betty by my side. Our eyes met, and I answered before she asked.

"He's alive." Before I had a chance to say anything else she was getting ready. I told her she didn't have to come, but she dressed as I did. I felt in a daze and couldn't wait to get to him. The drive was quiet, and we saw hardly any other cars traveling so late into the night. My thoughts strayed to the night before when we had been with Yubba. Betty saw me rubbing my eyes and asked if I was okay. I knew she too loved him and was worried.

"Yes, I was just thinking about last night when Susan fed him," I heard myself choke and thought I was going to cry. I felt Betty stroking my arm.

When we reached Yubba's house, the whole place was ablaze with lights, and surrounded with cars, and people. I helped Betty push through the throng of relatives and tribesmen who wished to greet and hug me. I felt tense as we pushed through the stairs, the front door, the sitting rooms, and finally the long corridor leading to his bedroom. I stood at the door, and Yubba looked up and smiled faintly at me. I rushed to him and kissed his hands and head multiple times. He mumbled something that I couldn't understand and I squeezed his shoulders gently.

I saw Betty kissing him on both cheeks before she greeted Yumma Arifa, Noffa, Sita, Wadad, Mamdouh, Abid-Elgader, and others seated around the massive bed. I didn't want to leave his side and held him, thinking I could keep him safe. He began to shake as the doctor approached the bed. Emotion welled up in me as Yubba struggled to rise and then fell back again into my arms.

"Yubba, hang in there; don't leave now, Yubba. You have to see what I'm going to do in the Valley. There's so much I want to show you; don't go, Yubba." My eyes brimmed with tears, as I cradled him in my arms. He closed his eyes.

The doctor pushed me aside and tried to revive him. They had to be more forceful with Arifa, who clung desperately to Yubba and began to wail. Yubba was gone!

I saw Betty trying to reach me, with tears streaming down her cheeks, but she couldn't because too many relatives separated us.

271

Moments later, I heard wails slicing the night air. I saw the Sheikh from the Valley's mosque as well as the one from Irbid coming in, carrying holy water from Mecca to prepare Yubba for his burial. My mind churned, and I wished to run from the room. Just then, I felt a hand on my arm, and I looked up into Mamdouh's red, swollen eyes. His mouth moved, but I could not hear the words.

He leaned closer to me and whispered, "Be strong, Ya-khou, my brother. You cannot leave the room now. You are now the leader. All eyes are on you. You have to help with washing Yubba. Follow my lead."

I lowered my head when I touched Yubba's body and began to wash him with the help of the two Sheikhs, my uncles, and my brothers. Shortly after we began the ritual, the door sprang open, and, to everyone's astonishment, Arifa burst into the room and announced that she would wash her Amir. I knew women should not bathe men, but when they looked at me for guidance, I nodded and told them to leave her be. I knew her pain was equal to, if not more, than my own, and I didn't care what they thought. Yubba was washed three times, first with plain water, second with salted water, and lastly, with camphor added to the holy water. He was then wrapped with ten meters of white muslin before Yumma Arifa felt that the amount of wrapping was right for the love of her life to meet his maker.

"Is everything ready to transport our Amir to the Valley?" my uncle asked me.

"I'll go make sure of it," I said, but I left the room feeling unsure and shaken to the core. I soon felt Mamdouh's footsteps alongside my own.

"You did well, my brother. I'll go make sure all the cars are ready to take the women. We have everyone in the Valley ready. You go on and ride with Yubba, and I'll meet you there."

I held my head high and walked my destiny; this is what I was born to do. I could do this. I would act like Yubba wished me to. I began barking orders at everyone in my way. There was a great man to be buried, and that must be the only thing I concentrated on now.

272

******

I had never seen or heard the likes of the sobbing and ululating I witnessed in those early morning hours. I watched as hordes of women entered the room, replacing others who left. Each group came in howling in eerie shrieks, pulling their hair, ripping their veils, and squatting in front of Yumma Arifa and other close relatives. They rocked back and forth on their heels as they mourned the loss of this great man.

Shamma noticed that I was shaking, so she pulled me away, taking me to Seetah and Mamdouh's room, and told me to rest before she hugged me and closed the door. I stood shivering, trying to compose myself and slow my heartbeat. I understood that this was how they would act. Saeed's father was their leader. I guess I never knew I would be so shaken by his death. I missed him and wanted to scream, yet couldn't. I wished I could express myself in that fashion, yet was unable to do so. I changed into the black suit I'd been holding quite unconsciously all along, and then exited the room, head held high. I was the wife of the eldest son.

I saw that the big bed was now empty of its important occupant, and wished I understood what was happening. For the first time in years, I felt isolated and began to cry. I felt Wadad's hand slipping into mine, welcomed the touch, and squeezed her hand.

"They wouldn't let me in the room where they were washing him. I wanted to be with Yubba," Wadad said through her tears.

"Who was washing him?"

"Yumma, Ya-khou Saeed, Akhu Mamdouh, Akhu Talal, and Ami Abid El-Gadir." She stopped crying as she recalled aloud who was in the room with the Amir.

"What happened after they washed him?"

"They closed Yubba's eyes and wrapped his body with cloth shrouds." She noticed the puzzled look in my eyes, and it dawned on her that perhaps I had never witnessed this ritual. "You have never seen this?"

"No, I have never been to a burial," I said. I tried to imagine Saeed washing his father, and knew that it must have been incredibly hard on him. I said I wished I could comfort Saeed.

"No, no, the women never go to the burial ground. Only the men will bury Yubba. The women will stay home. We should be going to the Valley soon." Wadad covered her face with her hands, beginning to sob along with me and the many other women of the tribe.

The wailing rose to an unprecedented pitch the minute Yumma Arifa emerged from the room down the hall. All the other women stood up as she walked closer, a dazed look on her face. I had never seen this always well-manicured woman look so bedraggled.

"How can I face a life without him in it? How can I live my days and not hear his voice?" Yumma Arifa wailed and shouted these questions out while pulling her veil and uncovering her hair. She cried uncontrollably, and only now did I understand the depth of love that she had for her husband. I closed my eyes and prayed that the Lord would spare me the pain that she was feeling.

I squeezed between Noffa and Shamma in one of the many cars heading to the Valley. The scene was reminiscent of the first day I arrived, except for the stillness. Instead of gunshots, the riders rode with their heads bowed and many covered their faces, as they shed their tears. As we drove into the Valley and the clearing between the Amir's house and the village, I saw huge tents erected side by side. I knew there would be mattresses, as well as chairs, lining the insides of the tents. I welcomed the hot coffee offered and sipped it as I thought of Saeed. Minutes turned into hours, and the processions of weeping women never ceased. I shed my own tears at the thought of never being in the Amir's expansive embrace again. He had always made me feel safe and loved. I walked through the back door and stood, watching the cooking pots, smoking a cigarette, and sipping my coffee. I smelled the food and suddenly realized that I had not eaten all day. I walked around until I spotted Hamda and asked her for some food before they loaded it onto the waiting trays. Hamda's face drooped with fatigue and her eyes filled with tears as she nodded and gave me a long hug. I went into my old room and ate in silence as I thought about the proceedings. I could hear sermons coming from the men's tents through loudspeakers.

274

I couldn't understand the words, but knew they were about the life of the Amir. Every once in a while the speaker's voice faltered, as if fighting the urge to cry. When the sermons stopped, the Sheikhs recited verses of the Koran in shifts. I closed my eyes as I remembered Noffa's telling me that they would recite the Koran around the clock for seven days. The door opened and Shamma came in. I stood up, gave the weeping woman a hug, and listened as she talked about a father she hardly knew but loved and had wished to be loved by all her life. She said that she had always been the little girl who watched without being seen and listened without being heard.

I cried for that little girl and said a prayer for the mourning, grown woman. After Shamma left, I sat down, covered my face with trembling hands, and cried. Sometime later, the door burst open, and Thrya announced, "Your friends have come, *Ya'kte*, my sister"

I followed as I wondered who they might be. I saw Kadura, Muna, Layla, Doctor Elisabeth, Barbara, and others who kissed me and sat down with me. Later Kadura said,

"This must be difficult for you but you are doing great. By the way, Saeed asked me to take you back to Amman when we leave."

"You saw Saeed?"

"No, no, not me, Salah came and told me." She smiled kindly at me and continued, "Saeed will not be able to go back to Amman for at least three days. You know that the *aza* will go on for seven days."

I welcomed the arrival of these friends, as I welcomed Linda and her mother-in-law and sisters-in-law. Even Ali's aunts and other relatives came.

Finally it was time to leave, and I hugged and kissed Yumma Arifa and many other relatives who voiced their astonishment at my departure.

"Ya-khou Saeed wants her to leave and take care of the children. She will be back tomorrow," Fayga said as she suddenly appeared, ushering me through the questioning crowds and out to the car.

It was dark by the time I got home. The children were already asleep when I checked on them. I made myself a cheese sandwich and drank a gin and tonic. I cried again when I finally went to bed. I couldn't imagine living here without Yubba, I just couldn't!

275

I woke up early and was dressed and ready when the driver came to pick me up. It was still dark outside; none of the children were up yet. I thought of them as I slipped into the car. When I arrived in the Valley I noticed that the men's tents were already full. I walked into the house and saw a pale Yumma Arifa standing in the middle of the room. I moved quickly to her side. I hugged her and gently urged her to sit down. She looked confused at first, but then welcomed the hot coffee that I poured for her.

I knew that most men and women would come the first three days, and many would try to come all seven days, especially if they were family or very close to the family. I also knew that most would come every Thursday for forty days after an important man passed away. I welcomed the presence of my friends, but still felt such a loss and still cried that day. I asked Kadura what time they were leaving. I hoped they could leave early enough that I could see my children today and tell them the sad news.

"We will leave earlier than we did yesterday. Do you want to ride with us?"

I didn't expect the strange welcome I received the minute I walked through the door of my home.

"Why didn't you tell me, Mama? The nuns were talking about it. You should have told me!" An upset Susan confronted me, and I didn't know quite how to answer this. I felt that I had let her down.

"I'm so sorry, Honey. I didn't want to wake you up last night, and I left this morning before you were up."

"You should have told me, Mama. I called everyone a liar. *Jeddo* is alive. He can't die, Mama. He's the Amir, Mama. He can't die. No, Mama." Susan pressed tightly against me, crying and crying until there were no more tears.

I sat down on the couch and held my firstborn close. I hadn't thought about the probability of the nuns talking about this. I should have left Susan a note. I saw Donna standing nearby and called out to her, "Are you okay, Honey?"

"Yes, Mama. Susan cried all the way home. I'm sad, but I don't feel like crying."

"It's okay not to cry, but it's okay to cry too." I answered, rubbing Susan's back and pushing the hair from her wet cheeks.

The third day unfolded the same as the previous two, but the great blessing came when Saeed showed up after dark to drive us both back to Amman. We rode again in silence, and I leaned against him, offering comfort by being near. The kids were asleep when we got home. After taking a shower, Saeed mixed a gin and tonic for each of us, and I made grilled-cheese sandwiches, slicing some tomato and cucumber to go along with them.

"What time are we leaving tomorrow?" I asked.

"I'm going to go alone tomorrow, Honey. It's the fourth day, and everyone will understand that you need to spend time with the children."

"I hate for you to drive alone."

"I won't be alone. Talal came back to Amman today, too, and he'll pick me up in the morning."

I felt much better knowing that Talal would be with Saeed. I always liked all of his brothers, and I knew they meant a lot to him.

"How do you feel?" I ventured to ask

"I can't believe he's gone." He looked like a lost kid and his eyes brimmed with tears, "All my life, I've had him to depend on, to look up to. I keep thinking of him laughing, talking, and riding. Yubba was bigger than life. How can he be gone?"

"I don't think I can ever make another pineapple upside-down cake." I couldn't go on and started to cry. Saeed was holding me as we cried together. Our lives would never be the same without the Amir.

The next day, Saeed left with Talal. I felt relief at not having to go to the big house, but knew I would want to go tomorrow. I spent the day reading and talking on the phone with Barbara and Elisabeth, who both had come down the first and third days of the funeral to pay their respects to the family. I also cooked the kids one of their favorite meals, southern fried chicken with all the trimmings they loved. They enjoyed having me home, and loved the chocolate pies I made for them. Later in the evening, the girls and I sat and talked about their Jeddo as we remembered how he loved to come and stay with us. We named all the foods he loved and Susan cried again.

The Amir's mourning continued for seven days and nights. Governmental dignitaries and heads of Bedouin tribes in Jordan and neighboring countries came to pay their respects to the Al-Gazzawiya. They loved and respected him, and many had admired his strength and acute sense of fairness. He would be sorely missed.

Going to the Valley or Irbid was hard that first year. Everything seemed so different without Yubba. Even the coffee man seemed lost in the majless. Mamdouh was there every day, but since he wasn't the eldest, many decisions would have to wait until Saeed came on the weekend.

"I'm trying to take a more active role in the governing of the tribe, but in my heart, I feel inadequate without the strong presence of Yubba. I realize now more than ever before that I truly am not one hundred percent Bedouin." Saeed looked at me sadly.

"You've been here more than ten years, Saeed. I'm sure you're doing great!"

"How can ten years go so fast? I don't feel like he taught me all I need to know."

The next morning, Saeed came into the bedroom with excitement filling his face and said, "Come on, there's something I want you to see!'

I followed as I looked at him and shook my head. He led me outside and stopped in front of one of the magnolia trees and pointed. The prettiest flower was blooming on one of the upper branches. I almost cried with delight.

"Magnolias for my Magnolia," Saeed said as he hugged me. "I wish Yubba could have seen it! Remember how happy he was when you took that flower to them? Aww Betty, when will I stop hurting, when?"

Saeed at the Amir's Funeral

Manasif (plural of Mansaf)

CHAPTER 17

THE SETBACKS (1966-1970)

I was on my way to meet with Louise and April. They said they wanted to tell me something important. I felt a little nervous for I had a suspicion of what they were going to say. I looked out the window and admired the landscape. Amman was a pretty city with its hills and valleys and I had resolved myself to look at it as home. That never meant Knoxville would stop being home, I just had two homes and that was not a bad thing. I realized that there would always be things or incidences that upset me or that I couldn't understand. I resolved myself to focus on my happiness, my husband, my children, my wonderful family, and my great friends. I was determined to say something when I saw things I didn't approve of; that way I would continue to make a difference. My love for animals was tested more than once and I was heartbroken by it, but I taught my children and their friends to love animals. Again I was glad to belong to a nomadic tribe, for they valued their horses and appreciated their dogs.

It had been almost six years since we had moved into our home. Life was good and I was happy. I felt blessed except for my health; things weren't always good. Although I had undergone a hysterectomy after Ramzi's birth, at Saeed's insistence, I continued to feel tired many mornings for no apparent reason. My legs and arms would ache, as if I were bruised, but I wasn't. I continued to have problems when I used the toilet, although the doctor said I didn't have a urinary infection. So many questions and never an answer; I guess that could explain my nervousness, but it didn't explain my dizzy spells or pain.

Saeed took me to many doctors and one even said that having lived those first months hearing only Arabic had affected me and he recommended that I associate more with the English-speaking world. He wrote a prescription for vitamins and said that he hoped I would feel stronger soon. We thanked him, and Saeed took solace in the fact that the doctor said I was physically fine, brushing his worries aside just as I wanted to. I joked and said that I was going to stay around and drive Saeed nuts. I prayed I would be right.

We tried to take the doctor's advice, and immersed ourselves in making our home more of an American home in an Arabic world. I reassured him that the vitamins seemed to be working. I didn't get better, but I didn't get worse. I just rested more and usually slept ten hours a day. That always helped and made the day pass without jitters or great pain. We both loved going out and we also cherished the evenings when we had no company or invitations and could simply enjoy one another and our family. The kids liked the evenings when we went out; they turned the house upside down as they role played us and the parties. They also looked forward to the evenings when we stayed home, and we all ate dinner together accompanied by soft music and candlelight.

My thoughts went to the surprise birthday party that Louise had for me a couple of weeks ago. Everyone had a great time, especially the children. I turned thirty four and prayed that this would be the year I would either improve or the doctors would at least find something they could treat.

Minutes after I sat down, my suspicions were confirmed. April said that the United States Embassy had asked its personnel and all its citizens to leave Jordan because the raids on Israel had continued over the last year. As she explained, "Israel is convinced that the only way to stop the raids is to control the source. That would be the West Bank, Golan Heights in Syria, and Sinai in Egypt,"

"Are you sure we're going to war?" I asked, as I dreaded her answer.

"A war is inevitable Betty, but Jack and many others believe that war will not make the situation here any better or any safer. He fears a war between the Arabs and the Israelis will only ignite the ongoing raids."

Her next words twisted me in knots, "I'm afraid we're going to go back home for good."

"Oh no, what will I do without you!" I said as a sense of hopelessness descended upon me.

"Jack and Bo were going to retire at the end of the year anyway, and if we go now, there would be no sense in coming back." April's eyes focused sadly on me as she pursed her lips.

I hadn't known a lot about politics before I arrived in Jordan, but now I knew more than I'd ever wished.

When I reached home, heaviness settled into my heart. I was on the verge of crying but didn't want to upset the children, who were cheerfully playing cards and oblivious to the situation. I hugged and kissed them before going to my room and changing into a cotton housedress that Mama had made for me when she was in Jordan. I sat on the edge of the bed and remembered the last time I'd seen Daddy. Tears ran down my cheeks in spite of my earlier resolve not to cry. He had passed away almost a year after Saeed's father, and now my children had no grandfathers. I couldn't believe Daddy had been gone for almost three months now. My thoughts went to that awful Tuesday when I received the letter. I'd been stunned that Mama didn't call, but then she wrote that she feared that a trip under such circumstances would have been hard on me. Plus the political scene was not particularly comforting, and she knew that Saeed would not leave the children. By the time I read the sad news, my daddy had been buried for three weeks.

Susan walked into the room and saw me crying. She ran and hugged me, saying, "What's wrong, Mama? Are you still sad about Granddaddy?"

"Yes, Honey, but I'll feel better soon." I hugged my firstborn and cried in her arms. For a short while, we switched roles as Susan stroked my hair and cried with me.

When Saeed arrived from work, he found me in the kitchen. He could tell I had been crying, and held me longer than usual rubbing my back. Then he went to the bedroom to change, followed by Susan and Donna, who insisted on hugs and kisses every time he came home. After the kids were in bed, we relaxed in the living room with our drinks. Saeed leaned forward on the sofa and asked if I was crying because of Daddy. Susan had told him that I had been crying over my daddy.

"Aww, Saeed, I was, but that's not all that's weighing on me." I related the events and conversations of the day and asked, "Do you think we really are going to war, and do you think we're in danger?"

"I cannot answer that question, but I pray we don't." He added more gin to his glass and refilled mine.

"You know that the Griffins and the Bowens are leaving Jordan for good."

"I know and I hate to see them go." He pulled his hand through his hair, breathed deeply, and gazed into my concerned eyes. "Honey, you know how people exaggerate things. I don't think we will go to war, and if so, it will be over in no time. I definitely know that Amman is in no danger."

"You know that when the embassy asks its people to leave, it's serious." I watched him as he took a sip from his drink and proceeded to light cigarettes for us both.

I extended my hand and took the cigarette from him. We inhaled for a moment in silence, and then he tried to shift the conversation to talking about the kids.

Two days later, the American ambassador called me, telling me that all Americans have been asked to leave the country due to the danger that the U.S. recognized was coming. War is unavoidable," he said, "I sincerely wish you to comply. You need to leave, Betty; it is too dangerous to stay."

"I know you're thinking of what is best for me and my kids, but Saeed won't leave on account of his tribe and what they would say and I can't leave him."

"Then you need to convince him."

My hands shook as I put down the receiver. *Lord; give me strength to make Saeed see that we have to leave.* A couple of hours later, Elisabeth called and said that the British Embassy had contacted her about leaving. We talked for a long time and I asked her what Majid, her husband, thought of the situation. She said he was sure we would go to war. My shaking got worse as I prayed harder.

After the kids were asleep, I told Saeed about Elisabeth's phone call and the ambassador's words. He looked tired and closed his eyes for a second before he said,

"Why don't you go with the children, and when it's over, you can come back."

"I'll never go without you! My place is with you, and your place is with us."

One word led to another and before long we were in a heated argument. I felt he was putting us all in danger and that he was being stubborn. I stormed to the bedroom and pretended to be reading when he followed me a little while later. He sat on the bed and I felt his gaze on me. I waited for him to say something, but only silence ensued. I finally looked at him and he gave me that smile. I fell into his arms and cried.

The next months were hard on me as I said goodbye to many friends. I cried as I hugged April and Louise, who wished we were coming with them. They remained silent, however, out of their respect and love for Saeed. The country grew tense and everyone listened constantly to the news. Talk of war was everywhere and seemed inevitable.

On June 5, 1967, Israel launched an attack on all airbases in Egypt, Jordan, and Syria. Six days later, the geography of the region changed dramatically. Egypt lost the Sinai Peninsula up to the Suez Canal, Syria lost a great part of the Golan Heights, and Jordan lost the West Bank of the Jordan River. The biggest blow was losing the Old City of Jerusalem. Saeed was right; Amman wasn't affected by the war, and there was no bloodshed in the streets or bombing of the city. However, Jordan's demographics altered with the coming of the Palestinian refugees. The departure of most of the westerners changed my lifestyle forever, and I became even closer to my American and British friends who were married to Jordanian men. One day Barbara, Elisabeth, several other American ladies, and I were visiting, trying to comfort one another when I blurted out,

"When is this fighting going to stop? I don't feel Amman is safe anymore!"

"It's been almost a year since the war, and it hasn't gotten any better. Every other day there is another Fedayeen attack on Israel, and they respond by shelling the border!" Barbara wrung her hands and pursed her lips.

"What do you expect from the Palestinian people?" Sally asked. "They have no country, and they're living in camps all over the Arabic world. Does anyone know that Jordan is the only country giving them citizenship? Most of the Arabic countries are only giving them permits to live in their country. They want their country back, and this is the only way they'll get it. You can't expect them to give up! Would you all give up if someone took your country from you?"

"I just want the fighting to stop. Anyway, let's go back to our agenda and finish up these instructions for the American women." Maggie, a petite blonde with short, straight hair and clear blue eyes, said firmly. She did not wish to go into that discussion.

We all worked on highlighting the reasons for Americans to dress modestly and not draw attention to themselves. We also requested that the women not go anywhere unchaperoned or venture downtown alone.

"I guess we should just say that now we need to look like our sisters and mothers-in-law," I added. Everyone laughed, easing some of the tension.

After most of the women left, I asked why Sally was so angry. Barbara said, "Her husband is Palestinian and that is becoming more of a problem. The Palestinians don't think that King Hussein is doing enough to get their country back. Many think that the Palestine Liberation Organization (PLO) is trying harder than the King."

"If this continues, I'm afraid that we'll have a civil war soon," Elisabeth added. "Frankly, Majid believes that the Fedayeen seem to have shifted their fight from Israel to overthrowing King Hussein."

This silenced everyone, as we all knew that Elisabeth's husband's family was well connected politically to the Palace.

Later that afternoon, I discussed this with Saeed, who shrugged it off as nonsense. "No one is going to overthrow the king, Honey. And as far as a civil war, I can't see that happening. We're one people. Many families are intermarried, and when I was growing up, there was no difference. You know that our tribe extends on both sides of the river. Did you know that Jordan, Syria, Lebanon, and Palestine used to be referred to as the countries of Sham for centuries?"

"No I didn't know that and I hope you're right. You know it was Elisabeth who told me that." I bit my lip, deep in thought.

"I haven't seen Majid in some time. I need to give him a call."

That week, Saeed received news that Jordan would attend a three day agricultural conference in Rome. He had hoped it would be postponed; he didn't like the idea of leaving me.

"I'll only be gone four days, Honey. You know Talal is here, and all our friends. I will try to call you every day." He wanted me to go with him, but I couldn't leave my kids, not at a time like this. I cried the minute he left the house. All five kids were in school, and I felt alone and scared. I called Linda, and we talked for a long time before I hung up and went back to reading a new romance novel until the kids came home. I ate with them and then we did homework, watched some television, and then I read to the boys until they slept, and talked with the girls before they went to bed.

I went to sleep early after reading in bed. Sometime in the middle of the night, the phone rang, and I sprang to pick it up believing and hoping it was Saeed. Before I could say hello, a sinister voice said, "This is not your country. Leave or you will be killed!"

I dropped the receiver and it dangled by the cord, hitting against the bed. I looked up and saw Susan standing in the doorway.

"Who was it, Mama?"

"Mama, are you okay?" Donna ran past Susan and picked up the receiver, holding it against her ear. "Hello?"

Susan climbed on the bed with me and rubbed my cold hands. "Who was it, Mama?"

"I don't know; I couldn't understand him."

The next day, I told Barbara, Elisabeth, and Linda about the call. They looked aghast and stared at me. They couldn't imagine who would do such a horrible thing.

"Try not to worry, Betty. It's most likely a kid who knows Saeed isn't home and thought it would be funny to scare you," Elisabeth tried to comfort me. "But if it happens again, we need to tell our husbands. We have to be careful."

The next night, there was another call. I stared at the phone ringing, finally picking it up. I put the receiver to my ear. My temples throbbed and my heart raced. I said nothing as seconds passed before I heard the same dreaded voice.

"You go back to your country where you belong. If you stay, I'll kill you!"

My shaking hand released the receiver, and it thumped loudly against the floor. Susan and Donna came running in, and Donna bent over and picked up the receiver before I had a chance stop her.

"Hello?"

"If your mother stays in Amman, I'll kill her!"

"When Baba comes, he'll kill *you*. Don't you ever call here again!" She screamed into the phone, her eyes blazing.

They crawled next to my shaking body, and we all held each other until we fell into a fitful sleep. I thanked the Lord that the boys slept through all this.

Although Talal posted a guard at the house the next night, I still shook with fear when the phone rang that third night. No one picked up the receiver this time; no one wanted to hear the ugly words.

Saeed had the phone tapped the day he came back after hearing of the threatening calls that had come three nights in a row. The caller never called back, and was never caught. I mentioned these calls in my weekly American Women meetings and found out that a number of others had received similar calls. A long discussion ensued as many voiced their concern for their children, who had to go to school but were unaware of the danger.

288

"We have to let them know that they're in danger, too." Barbara said.

Marylou, who had been in Jordan for eight years and had two sons, ages seven and five, stood up rather nervously to say, "Mahmoud tells me that our children would never be harmed."

"Do you believe him?" another woman asked.

"Yes, our children are not Americans to them."

"We still have to be careful, Marylou. I think we need to tell our children to take care and be watchful." My hands shook as I wrote down notes from the meeting.

****

A couple of months later, with the number of raids mounting daily, an Israeli brigade entered Jordan. It was March of 1968, and they attacked Karamah, a village said to be the Fedayeen's capital. The army went through the Jordan Valley, and two of my cousins were killed. Yubba's house was destroyed along with most of the village. Our little house in the farm didn't escape that fate either. The outcome shocked the world as the brigade was driven back by PLO fighters who ultimately claimed victory. I felt the blow deeply as I witnessed the evacuation of the Jordan Valley, and I thanked God that Yubba was not alive to witness it. The tribe experienced a great setback because we couldn't raise our crops. Many walked for days to reach Irbid, herding as many sheep as they could take with them.

This changed the Al-Gazzawiya tribal life, and the closeness of living in one village disappeared. My brothers, uncles, and elders tried their best to help our people relocate. Most went to Irbid, with some to other villages, and a very few to Amman. We were still collecting money from the government in exchange for the land that we had allowed to be taken to better the lives of many. We now used the money to help our people live. I tried to find jobs for many as I worked with the government on allowing us to go back to the Valley.

Their victory in the battle of Karamah filled the Fedayeen with more confidence, leading to more raids, which in turn resulted in more Israeli reprisals. Every time an attack occurred, the war sirens echoed throughout the major cities. Shaking with fear, Betty checked on our children after every siren. She called me on one occasion, crying and talking; I could barely hear her over the sirens that echoed through my office. My heart raced as I told her to please calm down. Finally I was able to hear her saying that Donna was at Elham's. I told her I'd go get her. When we got home an hour later, Betty was in the living room on her knees praying. She looked up and Donna ran straight into her arms.

"I'm sorry, Mama, I know you told me not to go, but I'm tired of always having to stay home."

"I know Honey; it's okay. We're all together now."

"When is everything going to be normal again, Mama, when?" Donna asked, as Saleh came through the doorway.

"And when are we going to go to the farm? I miss Sultan!"

Betty and I exchanged glances, neither having the heart to tell him that all three horses had been killed during the raid.

****

The next two years consisted of worrying about my children, Saeed, and my declining health. Although the schools didn't close and life went on as though normal, people lived under circumstances that were far from it. The sirens went off at least once a week, and many people ran to shelters that had been built by the government in different parts of the city whenever one of the many violent clashes occurred between the Palestinian guerrillas and the Jordanian security forces. I read more novels wishing them to transport me to a calmer world, but that didn't work. On some days, my shaking was so bad that I could hardly drink a cup of coffee without spilling half of it. I also noticed a new sensation of heaviness in my left leg, especially in the mornings. I didn't mention this to Saeed; I just started to massage it daily, hoping that it would improve. I wished to brush it off and changed my thoughts to going out that evening to welcome a new English couple who had moved into a house two streets away from us. We hardly went out anymore. The previous world of frequent gatherings was gone. No one threw lavish, or even small, parties anymore. I missed that life, and wondered if I would ever be able to dance again.

We enjoyed the evening with the new couple, Margaret and Roger, and invited them over the next night to meet our kids, whom we no longer felt safe leaving for too long in the evenings. As we drove back home, I remained quieter than normal. My leg was getting heavy and hurting. I was praying that it would stop and that I would be able to walk when we got home. I winced and Saeed asked if I was okay.

"Oh, yes, I'm just wondering how long Margaret and Roger will last in Jordan." I was thankful that my leg was better when we got home and I was able to walk, although slowly. Saeed stopped and asked me why I was dragging my leg. I told him about the numbness and heaviness, but said I didn't sleep good last night. He carried me to the bedroom and helped me into my gown. I felt better the next day, but he would only go to work after I walked up and down our bedroom.

There had been several attempts to assassinate King Hussein, and only God knew what would happen to the country if they succeeded.

These events escalated my shaking, and the numbness in my left leg got so bad that I couldn't walk at times. I made another visit to the doctor, but he again couldn't find any reason for my pain or numbness. Saeed kept pushing for answers and the doctor finally recommended that we go to a neurological doctor in London. We talked about this but knew that we couldn't leave the kids in such uncertain times.

A week later, three planes were hijacked: a Swissair and a TWA that landed in the desert, and a Pan Am that landed in Cairo. After the hostages were removed from both planes in Jordan, the planes were blown up. This act angered the king and after ten days he declared martial law and ordered the PLO to leave Jordan.

The PLO refused to leave and the situation escalated which brought even more Fedayeen and government confrontations. Jordan seemed to have two states within its borders. The foreign embassies again asked all their citizens to leave the country and once again I tried to convince Saeed that we needed to go.

"Honey, it won't be as bad as they think. The Palestinians will integrate and, with time, will become Jordanians."

"How can you say that, Saeed? They're killing each other. I can't see this settling soon and I certainly can't see it settling without a civil war."

"Betty, I know that things are not good, and yes, you are right, many have died." He ran his fingers through his hair, looked at me and sighed, "Why don't you go and take the kids."

"I already told you that I will not leave you. What if something happened to you?"

"Nothing is going to happen to any of us. They will make peace and the PLO will do the king's bidding. I am the leader of the tribe and if I left, it would be a sign of weakness and would look like I was deserting them. They are already feeling the brunt of not being able to go back to the Valley. If things should get worse, I need to be close."

I was so angry with him, my hands started to shake and I hugged myself to ease the tremors. Saeed reached out and pulled me into his arms.

"I worry about all this shaking Betty. I don't like it. If things get a little bad, you will get a lot worse. Please take the children and go. Please."

"I am not leaving you!"

"Honey, we have not made a penny from the land for the last two years. Money is tight right now."

"Then how do you expect me and the children to leave?"

"I have enough for that, but I have to be here to secure money for you."

"Well, how are we supposed to get to London?"

"I decided to sell the other plot that Yubba bought me. I am just waiting for things to calm down so we can get a good price."

His eyes held mine and before I could say anything, he pleaded, "Betty, please for their sake, promise me you will think about going away with the kids."

I promised him I would and I did. I talked it over with Linda, Barbara, Elisabeth and others. They all said that their husbands refused to leave and they didn't think it would be that bad either. I later told Saeed that I would not leave. He said that when the land sold, we would all go to London and then to the States. That gave me hope and I prayed that it would be over soon.

****

I was seriously considering taking Betty to London when Majid called and advised against it. He said it would be best to wait a couple of months, just in case the worst happened. Although I worked in the government, I wasn't political and never wished to be in a powerful position. I worried too much about Betty and didn't want to be away more than I had to.

Less than a month after my conversation with Majid, Susan turned fifteen. Betty had always made a big deal out of their birthdays and invited all their friends. This year, it was only us. Three days later, a vicious, thirteen-day civil war broke out. I was stunned and couldn't believe that we were actually in a civil war. How had this happened to one people who had always been one people. I had friends and loved ones on both sides. Jordanians and Palestinians had lived together for thousands of years. It was like hurting your own body trying to protect it. Lives and homes were shattered as heavy artillery and tanks moved through the major cities of Jordan.

I was glad that I had prepared a bomb shelter. We had a boiler room downstairs, next to a bathroom, in the back of the basement that was large enough to be turned into a shelter. I had had shelves made in the front and filled them with different food items and two large water jugs. Mattresses were laid to accommodate Betty and me on one side, Susan and Donna on the other, and the three boys and our two help in the back corner. I had hoped that it would never be used except for the occasional half hour or so when the siren went off.

Those fifteen days were the longest of my life. Although Betty tried her best to hide her shaking, I could see it just as I could see her dragging her left leg and grimacing with pain. It was hard on her to go up and down the steps whenever we went to check on the house or get things. I carried her a few times and encouraged her to stay downstairs. She busied herself with comforting our children. She read and sang with the boys and talked with the girls. We all played games and had all our meals together. We had plenty of food and Talal even managed to come in a tank to our house after the first week to bring us food. That brought a glimmer of hope and genuine laughter to all of us. Although we had no ice since we didn't have electricity, we still had our drinks. I knew they calmed Betty down. Some nights when the bombing was intense, she would start to laugh uncontrollably. The boys would sleep through it, but the girls worried and would come and ask what was funny.

We were blessed that the fighting never came to our neighborhood, but the noises at night filled the air with an ominous cloud. As the days went on, I could see Betty getting worse and that at times she couldn't move either of her legs. I had to help her go to the bathroom and I knew that hurt her deeply. The girls helped to feed her and drink coffee many times. I knew for sure that something bad was wrong. For the umpteenth time I regretted my decision not to leave Jordan. I berated myself over and over until I thought I was going to scream out loud. *Why God, why didn't you make me leave? Why did I feel such certainty that it was all going to be okay?* More and more self-doubt tortured me through the two week nightmare. I felt that I had let her and my children down. I held her night after night as she laughed or cried. I silently cried many nights.

Susan and Donna lay on the other side of the boiler room and I heard Donna asking Susan, "Why is Mama laughing so loud? They will hear her and come and shoot us all." I heard the fear in her voice and then heard Susan say, "They can't hear her, don't worry." I knew Susan would be patting Donna's hand.

"But why is she laughing that way? It doesn't even sound like Mama."

"Baba said Mama's not well, and he's going to take us all to London the minute he can. She will be fine. Now, try to sleep," Susan said.

They looked up and saw me. Donna jumped up, ran and hugged me, and Susan followed. I held my girls and wanted to say comforting words, but I had none. I simply tightened my grip on them.

Betty and Ramzi

Betty, Donna Saeed, Sami, Ramzi, and Saleh

Betty, April, Seeta, and Arifa

CHAPTER 18

FATE AND FAITH

Finally we all were on a plane headed to London; optimism was high and we enjoyed the flight. The airport was a little hectic with five kids, but we managed and finally were in our three bedroom furnished apartment. It had a door man and a concierge as well as room service, but the best surprise was the pool. The kids were very excited. Susan and Donna helped me unpack and get settled in, while Saeed took the boys for a walk in the park. When they came back flushed and happy, we headed out to get dinner. We all savored the fish and chips and the kids said it was the best they ever tasted. Sami said he wanted to eat it every day. I laughed and tried to enjoy the walk back but my legs hurt so much that the girls and I had to take a cab back to our place. After the kids were in bed, Saeed and I sat on the balcony sipping our drinks. I loved the view and breathed in deeply of the night scents. We went to bed early for we had a nine o'clock appointment with a neurologist.

After the initial test, the doctor told us that I had suffered a nervous breakdown. He took more blood for lab work and said that he would like to see me the next week. He gave me some tablets to take and said he hoped they would make me feel better.

Meanwhile, we all acted like we were on vacation and tried to have a good time.

"You girls want to go shopping this afternoon?" I asked the next morning. Both girls' eyes lit up at the prospect.

"Oh, Mama, I can't wait to go to Selfridge. I need to buy so many things," Susan said. She ran to the bedroom to change into her favorite jeans and multicolored shirt.

Saeed wasn't sure this was a good idea, but I insisted that I felt better. "Many people have nervous breakdowns and get better. That fact already makes me feel better. You take the boys swimming and I'll take the girls shopping." I gave him a kiss as I went to get the boys ready.

We shopped for several hours that afternoon, and I felt lucky to be with them, but I felt tired, and had to push myself to take every step. Finally, the girls had had enough; they proudly carried their bags as I hailed a cab. The driver swiftly came to a stop near us.

Donna ran on and opened the cab door, and Susan was about to follow when she heard my desperate voice.

"I can't move my leg, Honey. I can't take another step!"

Tears streamed down Susan's face. She let go of her bags and ran to hug me. Donna saw this, apologized to the cab driver, closed the door, and ran throwing her arms around my neck. We stood embracing for several moments, no one speaking. I felt terrible and wanted to cry, but I held on to my girls and said,

"It's okay. I think I can get into a cab if you girls will help me." I dragged my numbed leg with both hands, inching my way toward the next cab Donna waved down.

That night I sobbed in Saeed's arms. "You should have seen the look on the girls' faces. They were so scared and didn't know what to do."

"Nothing bad happened, Honey. They know you're sick, but you'll get better and this will soon be just a bad dream."

"God is mad at me and is punishing me for loving you." I regretted the words the minute I saw the pained look on Saeed's face, but I couldn't help thinking that. *Why was this happening to me, why?*

"Why would God punish you for loving me? You know that's not true. You always stayed faithful in your worship, and God would never do that to you, or to me, or to our children."

"I should have never started drinking; maybe that's …" Saeed squeezed my shoulders as he cut me off. "No, Betty, don't do this. You know God would not do this because you drink. Honey, what would God do to killers, thieves, and liars then? Our God is a loving, merciful God. You and I both know that, and we love him. Remember what you said just this morning, people have nervous breakdowns and get better."

We both looked up and into Donna's face as she stared at us while tears ran down her cheeks, "I hate *both* your gods. They are both bad gods." She turned and ran out of the room. I stared at Saeed before I asked him to help me up because my daughter needed me. He kissed my forehead and said that he'd go speak with her.

Saeed went after our girl as I did my best to follow. She was sobbing on the bed as Susan rubbed her back. Saeed sat down and she looked up and fell into his arms sobbing. He held her for a minute before he said,

"Honey, why did you say you hated God?"

"How can I love your god, when he's punishing Mama for not becoming a Muslim, and I can't love her god when he's going to put you in hell because you're not a Christian?"

"Where did you hear this? Who told you such nonsense?" It was my turn to be stunned.

"Kids tell us this all the time, don't they Susan?" She looked at her sister who nodded and looked away.

"Honey, that's not true. There's only one God. If there were more than one, we would not all look alike. Every God would have created his own humans, and Muslim and Christians would look different. Right?" Donna stopped crying as she looked at both of us.

"There is only one God and he'll put us in heaven or hell on our own deeds: what we do, what we say, how we treat others. He will judge us by our hearts and our love for him."

"Then why is Mama sick?" Susan asked.

"Good people and bad people get sick and get hurt, and we all will die one day."

"Why can't you both belong to one religion? All our friends' parents belong to one faith. Can't you both agree on one?" Susan asked.

"It's not right to change those you love. You love them as they are."

"So what are we?"

"You're half and half. Half Jordanian and half American; half Muslim and half Christian" I said as everyone looked at me. I felt drained and weak to my core.

"We can't be half and half in religion Mama," Susan said and I could see a confused look on Saeed's face.

"Then when you're eighteen, you'll read the Bible and the Koran and choose the religion you want."

"The main thing is to know that there's only one God and he loves us all." Saeed said, not knowing what else to say.

After settling the girls in, Saeed and I discussed what had just happened. He thought that I was confusing them when I asked them to belong to one religion. I disagreed and said that there was nothing wrong with that. They needed to pick. I saw the look on his face and although I knew he didn't agree with me, he didn't voice it. He pursed his lips and lit a cigarette. I felt completely exhausted.

We took it easier from then on and I lounged by the pool more and read while the kids shopped or went to the park with Saeed. A week later, I was diagnosed with multiple sclerosis.

I didn't understand and sat dazed as the doctor continued, "Multiple sclerosis is a disease that affects the central nervous system. Our nerve cells have a protective covering called myelin, and this allows for successful communication with the nerves in the rest of the body. MS gradually destroys myelin, causing muscle weakness and some of the other symptoms that you are experiencing, like the heaviness in your legs, and, of course, the shaking and the pain."

"Is there a cure, Doctor?" Saeed shifted himself and clasped his hands as he fixed his gaze on me.

300

"I'm afraid there is no cure. That is, as of today. Medicine has discoveries each and every day that could make a difference in your health and life." He tried to sound cheerful as he took my hands and explained that MS was different for each person. "You may go through life with only minor problems. On the other hand, you may become seriously disabled. Most people are somewhere in between. Meanwhile, we'll begin therapy that will ease the pain in your legs and hopefully stop the progression of weakness in them."

"Therapy? How long will that take?" I was thinking of the children.

"I understand you live in Jordan, but you can stay here a couple of months to learn some exercises that you may then continue at home."

We were quiet as we headed back to the kids; but in some strange way, we felt hopeful. At least we knew what was wrong with me, and that there was something that was going to be done.

That evening Saeed and I had a lot to discuss. He couldn't stay here for two months, neither could the kids. I knew I couldn't take care of them and of course school would be starting before that. We decided that I should start taking my medication and therapy and in about a month, decide on what to do. "Take it day by day," was what Saeed kept saying. I only wished I could stop worrying about tomorrow and could take it day by day.

I liked the physical therapist; he was young with blue eyes and blond hair. He showed me better ways to move when I did different tasks around the house. He worked with me on stretching, flexing, and strengthening exercises for my muscles. I enjoyed the gait training that would eventually make it easier to walk. I worked for an hour three times a week, and felt stronger, but still had pain. The kids were great and Susan and Donna were doing a super job with the younger ones.

Although I spent most days in the apartment, I managed to go to movies and restaurants from time to time. I wanted to create happy memories, and didn't know how many years or months I had left with my children. I enjoyed seeing old friends, like Margaret and Roger, but as the end of the month neared, I had to confess to Saeed that I really was not feeling that much better. I doubted that another month would make the difference I needed.

"Do you want to go back to Amman, Honey?"

"Oh no, Saeed, I don't want to go back to Amman. I mean, they didn't even know what was wrong with me. They wouldn't know how to help me." I wrung my hands and shook my head.

"What is it that you want, Betty?"

"I want us all to go to the States; I want to be with Mama. Maybe when I'm home, I could go to church and … " I didn't know what else to say. I didn't know how I even felt. Saeed came and held my hands and looked into my almost tearing eyes.

"Betty, the kids will be starting school in another three weeks. Going to the States now is not a good idea, and …"

I started crying before he could finish, "But I don't want to go back to Amman, I don't."

"Honey, please don't cry. I didn't say that you couldn't go."

I looked up at him through my tears as he continued, "Maybe I can go back with the boys to Amman and the girls can go with you to the States."

"But I want you with me. I want us all together!"

"I want that too, but life does not always work that way."

The next day I told Saeed that I had decided to go back to Amman with them. He insisted that I finish my second month and that the girls would stay with me. I didn't want to be without him but he finally convinced me when he told me that since I couldn't go to the States, Mama would be coming to Amman. I was speechless.

"What do you mean? How did you do this?"

"I called her and told her what was going on and she said that she could come when Debbie started school."

"Who's going to take care of Debbie? I know that Jimmy's living in Nashville now."

"She said that Debbie can stay with Sarah and Junior; you know how much they love her."

"Oh Saeed, how can I thank you. I've thought about having Mama come and stay with me, but didn't know how to ask." I got up and he stayed there holding me as I thanked him over and over.

Saying goodbye to Saeed and the boys was harder than I thought, and if not for Susan's help, I could not have stood to wave.

The three weeks went by quickly and in many ways it was a blessing. The girls and I were able to talk about a lot of things. I told them of my wishes and hopes for them. I talked about my life when I was young. For the first time in years, I talked about Pearl and my friend Betty and those days in school. They enjoyed listening and asked a lot of questions, especially Susan. She wanted to know about boys and if I had boyfriends when I was young. I knew this was a touchy subject because in Jordan, there was no dating. Boys and girls met in groups, usually with family and close friends. They were not allowed to go out separately, so I had to choose my words carefully.

"Yes, Honey, I did date."

"Will I be able to date Mama?"

"I hope that you will go to study at the University of Tennessee. I wanted to go and would have been the first in my family to graduate from a university. You'll be the first to do that, Susan, unless Debbie does. Although I doubt that, since she wants to be a dance instructor and open up a dance studio. When you go to Knoxville, you'll be able to date and meet the man of your dreams."

Susan's eyes lit up and she promised that she would graduate from the University of Tennessee. I hugged my eldest and prayed that I would see that day, too.

Mama arrived in London a few days before we left for Amman. It was so good to see her, talk to her, and most importantly, pray with her. I had started reading the bible regularly and it filled me with hope. I knew I had a battle in front of me. We had gone to the library where I read everything I could find on multiple sclerosis. At times I could not stop the tears from flowing down my cheeks, but I would always ask the Lord why he chose me to walk this difficult road. The girls enjoyed having Mama and she went sightseeing with them. She had never been to London and enjoyed it tremendously, although she had a hard time conversing with British people. She said that she'd swear they were not speaking English.

****

303

Back in Amman it was good to see everyone. Arifa cried when she saw me and held on to me for a long time. She gave me water from Mecca called *zamzam*, and said that it had healing properties and made me promise to drink some each morning. I was touched by all the love and by everyone's coming to see me. Now my Bedouin family understood me and they all left when I yawned. I had missed Saeed and the boys so much. I had missed my home. The next morning Susan came into my bedroom carrying a bowl with the most beautiful Magnolia flower nestled in it. She laid it on the table and proudly told me that she cut it and immersed it in warm water, just like I had taught her.

Days after we arrived back in Amman, Yumma Om Easa passed away in her sleep. I wanted to go, but Saeed insisted that I stay home. Mama had heard about Saeed's earlier years and wished to go with him. She said that she felt the need to go since I couldn't. A week later, Easa and Omar came and spent the day with us. They had appreciated Mama's going to pay her respects and wanted to see me since Saeed had told them that I was not doing well. It was good to see them. We talked about their mother whom we had loved and who would be missed. I cried that night and wondered if I would be next.

I marveled at how quickly Mama adapted to Jordan and its people. She got along by talking sign language and laughing a lot. Everyone loved her and I was blessed to have her, but after six months, she started to worry about leaving Debbie so long. Debbie was at Junior's home and he and Sarah were having some trouble about Debbie staying out late with her boyfriend. I knew Mama wanted to go back and although I was doing my exercises, I didn't feel any better. In fact, some days I felt worse. A new symptom that I really didn't like was sleepwalking. I would hear tales of my going into the boys' room to read a book, or going into the girls' room and sitting and talking to them. Saeed made light of it and the children thought it was funny, but I didn't like it and started to dread going to bed. Mama of course said it was because I was drinking every night. She wanted me to stop drinking for a week and said she was sure that I would not sleep walk anymore. I tried to explain that I need to drink in order to sleep. It helped with the pain and my thoughts. The worst thought was that of leaving my children.

Mama wanted me to go back to the states with her, but I didn't think it a good idea. I knew what was wrong with me and I was doing my exercises and trying to be a mother as best as I could. I promised Mama that if I got any worse, Saeed would bring me to the States. I felt really bad for her; I knew she was torn between leaving me and going back to Debbie. Mama cried at the airport and said that she hated to leave. I willed myself not to cry, for her sake.

Barbara, Elisabeth and their husbands came over that evening. They knew Mama was leaving that day and wished to cheer me up. We talked about different things and played a couple of games of cards. I had a good night, but when I lay in bed those horrible thoughts would come. I had a gut feeling that I was not going to live long and that weighed heavily on my soul. I often questioned why I was destined to have my children in a land so far away from my own. I feared they would forget me and all that I had tried so hard to teach them.

"Will they forget all about Christmas, Easter, and dancing?" I wondered out loud to Saeed, who reassured me that they would not.

"Will you still celebrate Christmas when I am gone, Saeed?"

"Betty, please don't talk that way."

"Please promise me to always have Christmas … Please!"

"I promise you that I will always celebrate Christmas and Easter. Honey, your children are a part of you, and they'll always remember who you brought them up to be."

"When we were in London, Susan asked me about dating." I saw Saeed's jaw tighten and I knew he didn't like what I was saying, but I had to continue. "I told her that she would be able to date when she went to the University of Tennessee." He nodded his head and turned away from me. I asked him to look at me and when he did I asked him if he was going to let the girls go to the States to get their degrees. He held both my hands and looked me in the eyes and his words made me realize why I loved him so.

"I turned my face away because I wanted to cry. I don't want to think of life without you." Tears ran down his face and trickled down his neck. I held his face and he held my hands, "I promise you that all your children will go to the University of Tennessee, but I wish I could ask you to promise me to be with us on the day they graduate."

A few weeks later, Barbara, our children, and I went to attend a baseball game at the American School in Amman. We used to go to almost all the games, but with my illness and all, we hadn't gone as much lately. It was a good week and I thought it would be fun. I saw friends whom I had missed and I had a great time. Ann, an American whose husband worked at the embassy, told me that they were having a weekly matinee dance at the Villa Rosa, an upscale dancing club that Saeed and I used to go to. She said they had started it when the high schoolers came from Lebanon for the summer. The American School in Amman did not have a high school. The closest one was in Beirut. Barbara and I exchanged glances and she shook her head and said, "No way will my husband let our daughters attend."

The look on Susan's excited face made me adamant about giving my girls a chance to go to a dance with boys and girls their age. Both girls were in an all-girl school, but because they were young, there was no other choice.

When I approached the subject with Saeed, he told me that there was no way he was going to let Susan or Donna attend a dance.

"Why not?"

"Betty, we are not going to discuss this. I said *No* and that is the end of it." His voice rose as he got up, "And if you have put any such notions into the girls' heads, you have made a big mistake."

I felt my heart hurting before I sensed my body shaking. How could Saeed talk to me like that? His tone was cold and he looked like someone I didn't know, and that made me angry.

"I don't know who you think you are, but they are my daughters too, and I have the right to make my own decisions."

Hurtful words were said before he stormed out of the living room and into the bedroom. I covered my face with my trembling hands and sobbed. I felt a presence and I thought that it must be Saeed coming to apologize, but it was the girls. They both just stood there looking scared and sad. They had never seen their Baba so angry.

"Mama, come and sleep with us." Susan said as she helped me from my chair and into their room.

"Are we going to go to America, Mama?" Donna asked. At first I didn't understand why she was asking, but then I remembered that my last words to Saeed had been that I was taking my children to America.

Later I listened to my girls breathing and wanted to cry but was afraid I'd wake them up. I still couldn't believe that Saeed could be so mean. I heard his footsteps before I saw his silhouette at the door. I closed my eyes and feigned sleep. He came and knelt beside the bed and whispered my name twice before I opened my eyes.

"I'm sorry, Honey, please come to bed."

I wanted to say no but one look at his face changed everything. He carried me into our room, laid me down and we talked.

"I told you once that your children are a part of you, and I need you to heed the words I say. As much as I don't want the girls to go dancing with boys, if you want me to, I will drive them to the Villa Rosa and pick them up myself."

I prayed and thanked God for Saeed. I also was grateful for his health. I knew he was a great daddy and would always be a great daddy, and I wondered at fate. He never wanted many children, and had begged me to stop after Saleh. Now he'd have to take care of five children alone. I kept thinking of different ways to prepare the girls for my leaving them. One day as we were sitting in my bedroom talking, I said, "You'd better pray that I die before your daddy does. I would die without him, and then you would be left without a mommy *or* a daddy."

"Why are you talking like this?" Donna asked, glancing at Susan, who was equally unhappy.

"I just want you to know that God always does the best thing for us." I was preparing them for a reality that I felt in my heart. I taught my children to trust in God, while Saeed taught them to love their creator.

I tried to stay active in the American Women's Association, but my health became progressively worse. Although we tried to live as normally as possible, we started to spend more time together. The frequency of our lovemaking increased, and we clung to one another afterwards in an attempt to hold onto every precious moment for as long as possible. I often went to the bathroom, letting the water run in the sink as I cried. Sometimes we cried together, holding each other and praying for a miracle from the one God who created both of us.

"I hate to leave you." I would tell my love, and I really did.

"You're not going anywhere. I will not let you! I love you too much."

That Christmas I sat in the kitchen as I taught my children how to bake and cook all the things they loved to eat at Christmas. They enjoyed it and were little angels. The girls helped with buying and putting the toys under the tree for the boys and we had a great Christmas.

Another year passed, but just before Christmas I couldn't walk or even stand. I panicked, and so did Saeed. The doctor recommended I stay in the hospital for further tests, but after a week of nothing new, I asked Saeed to take me home. Donna pushed the wheelchair back to show me that the magnolia tree had many flowers on it. I said they were lovely, but I really wanted to cry. I felt I would never walk again.

Mama had been begging me to come to the States. I decided this was the time to give it a try and Saeed and I traveled to the States. The girls said they would look after their brothers, but Arifa would not leave them alone. She always was there for me and for them. I knew they would be fine, I just prayed that I would see them again.

I began therapy in the States and after a month was able to stand and take a few steps on my own. Saeed felt very positive, but the doctor recommended that I stay at least a year. We talked and thought it best that he return to the children and bring them all to me in the summer, which would be in another four months.

When I said goodbye to Saeed, I had the strangest sensation of wishing to go back with him. I had the worst feeling inside my heart. Two weeks after he left, I contracted pneumonia.

First Magnolia Tree in Amman

CHAPTER 19

REST IN PEACE, BETTY

Bringing Betty home was one of the saddest days in my and my children's lives. A sick mother had left them in hopes of coming back healthy. Instead, they were met by an ambulance that carried a woman who no longer recognized any of them. Susan, Donna, Saleh, Sami, and Ramzi were openly crying as she looked blankly at them. She no longer knew anyone or anything except me. I was the only person who elicited the attempt of a smile on a face that had once smiled all the time. My dear Southern Magnolia was gone, and with her my heart. A dark curtain covered our once happy home, and life from then on was never the same.

We turned the girls' room into a hospital room with nurses and help twenty four/seven. Susan spent the most time with her mother; she would talk to her, read to her and tell her how much she missed her. Donna did too, but spent a lot of time outside with her brothers or at Elham's house. I would often find Saleh sitting with her and talking about random things. He would tell her about his horse. Sami and Ramzi, too, visited and gave her kisses. The saddest thing was how hard they all tried for her to remember who they were. I, for one, was glad she never regained her memories.

Almost two years passed and Yumma Arifa and my family came often to visit and see how the children were doing. Betty's friends still came to see her from time to time. They still missed her. Of course Elisabeth never stopped her daily check on Betty on the way home from her government clinic in downtown Amman. She remained a staunch friend who never forgot the laughing, vibrant woman she loved.

I usually ran into Elisabeth when she was leaving or when I went in to see Betty, but on this particular day, as I was parking my car, she rushed out of the back door calling my name. I quickly got out of the car to hear.

"Saeed, Betty is acting very strange. In a way, she seems alert, yet very agitated. When I came here she asked me why you were late. She was right. You are a few minutes late."

I looked at her worried face as we both hurried to Betty's room. She was right, I had come from a meeting that had taken longer than expected, but how did Betty know that?

Elisabeth continued, "She somehow knew you were here seconds before you showed up and she asked me to go get you."

Just as she was talking, we heard Betty shouting out my name. Something she had never done since that fateful day we came back from the States.

"Saeed! ... Saeed! ... Saeed! ... "

I ran as she continued calling my name. I brushed past Elisabeth who turned and ran with me. I was by her side in seconds and leaned over and kissed her cheeks as I said, "I'm here, Honey!" I held her hand and noticed that it shook very badly.

I looked into the eyes of the woman I had loved for twenty four years, and she said, "Saeed, I love you." Her voice came shaky and very low. Before I could answer, I felt her shaking stop, and I knew she was gone. Elisabeth quickly stepped up, but I held my love close in my arms and would not let her go as the tears streamed down my cheeks.

I thought of our girls Susan and Donna in the States, going to the University of Tennessee. Betty had never graduated from UT, but her children would; that was a promise I had made and would keep. The

311

boys were at school. I covered my eyes with my already wet hands and wept openly, oblivious to who was around.

Barbara and Linda arrived at the same time. I saw them hug briefly before they went inside. Cars were already lined up in the street and many family members were already here. They saw Elisabeth as she entered the room where Betty lay. Other family members stood by, crying. I heard Linda say that they would like to have a minute alone with Betty. She gave me a long hug as soon as she saw me, her eyes closed. I knew she wanted to cry and I couldn't say a word. After she composed herself, she said that she wished to read the Bible and I told her that Betty would appreciate that very much. Just when I was about to turn around, she held my arm and related one of the last conversation she had, before Betty forgot everything and everyone except for me.

She remembered asking her friend, "Betty, if you could, would you have done things differently?" She closed her eyes again as she recalled Betty's words.

"No, Linda, I would do it all over again. I would never trade the years I had with Saeed. Never!"

I had promised Betty a Christian burial, and that meant a priest and a coffin. Although I knew that the elders in the tribe would fight it, I didn't really give them much thought. I had never wanted to think of burying her, and now I had to. Mamdouh came and hugged me before he gently said, "Ya-khou, we all know that Betty was a Christian, so there is no need to get a priest to bury her. We have no Christians buried in our tribal grounds. It will cause talk and unrest with the elders. They will not like it."

I listened and really felt his concern, but a promise is a promise and so I said, "Bedouins always keep their promises; I was taught that by Yubba."

Mamdouh patted my back, I looked into his face. He nodded his head and said, "You're right , my brother. Yubba taught us that!"

My brothers, Yumma Arifa, and some cousins supported me in my decision, but many others tried to dissuade me from doing what they saw no need for. I, forever one who tried to please, was now unyielding. I had promised Betty a Christian burial, and that was what she would get.

That afternoon, as the coffin left the house with the woman who dreamed it, I looked up at the remaining Magnolia tree and saw one huge flower drooping. I wanted to cry but checked my tears and climbed into the car heading toward the Jordan Valley.

A delegation from the United Nations came to pay their respects and thus witnessed the first and only Christian burial in the Jordan Valley. Because of the many objections, I worried that some tribesmen would try to move Betty's body. I posted guards for many nights at her burial site. That was the last act of love I would be able to perform for her, and I took the task deeply to heart.

Betty was my Southern Magnolia who turned into my Desert Magnolia and although she no longer lived, she had forever changed the terrain of the mighty desert.

Betty Jean Clark El Gazzawi will always be remembered by the many magnolia trees living in a country that, before she arrived, did not know of their existence. Southern Magnolias became Desert Magnolias and lived on through their beauty and gorgeous scent.

I thought of my girls and wondered who they would grow up to be, but I knew in my heart that Betty Jean would be a very big part of who they would become.

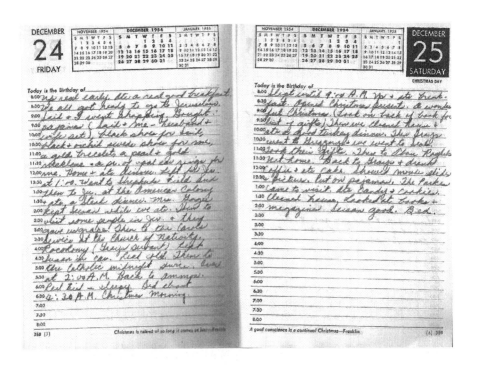

Diary

314

EPILOGUE

For the first time in my life, I am attempting to do something that I only fantasized about for many years. Until this moment, I had to face the fact that fantasies can only become realities when we are willing to work hard, and even then there are no guarantees. My parents were examples of acceptance, tolerance, and devotion. I would like my readers to know the great love that I witnessed and the terrible loss that I endured through their life together, their deep love for each other, and their final passing. I would also like my readers to know that this book is my labor of love for the parents whom I will always cherish. I relived their lives through my memories and my mother's diaries, and I wrote their world in my words.

This true story is my gift to my mother, my siblings, my children, and to all readers who are curious about the unique and genuine love between a Southern belle and a Jordanian tribal prince; a love that spanned the Atlantic Ocean and changed their own lives and the lives of so many others touched by their happiness.

Saleh passed away in 1981, leaving a void and shock in our lives. He will always be remembered for his enigmatic smile, big heart, and funny pranks. Susan, Donna, Sami, and Ramzi continue to be everything they can be as a result of belonging to a Desert Magnolia who taught them to love, honor, and value who they are as much as they love, honor, and value everyone else.

Donna El Gazzawi Habib

Made in the USA
Middletown, DE
29 February 2020